Tricks of the Trade for Divers

TRICKS of the TRADE
for
DIVERS

BY JOHN M. MALATICH

AND

WAYNE C. TUCKER

Cornell Maritime Press

CENTREVILLE, MARYLAND

The drawings are by John M. Malatich.

Library of Congress Cataloging in Publication Data

Malatich, John M., 1915-
    Tricks of the trade for divers.

    Bibliography: p.
    Includes index.
    1. Diving, Submarine. I. Tucker, Wayne C.,
1947-   II. Title.
VM981.M284   1986   627'.72   85-47839
ISBN 0-87033-342-9

Manufactured in the United States of America
First edition

*To my wife Elva who sat at home worrying
while I went away on many diving jobs*
—JOHN M. MALATICH

To my son Luke
—WAYNE C. TUCKER

With best wishes
John M. Malatich 6/24/86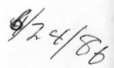

Contents

1. Coast Guard Provisions for Commercial Diving Operations; 2. Coast Guard Diving Regulations—Variance Procedures; 3. Marine Safety Manual

Preface

THIS is a commercial diver's book—for and by commercial divers—which assumes a basic background and at least some experience. This book is *not* intended to instruct the sport diver or novice on how to become a commercial diver. The authors assume that anyone using the information in this book is already a certified commercial diver recognized by the Association of Diving Contractors (1799 Stumpf Blvd., Building 7, Suite 4, Gretna, Louisiana 70053).

The book provides current and sound information about equipment and tools, ways of conducting successful search and recovery, making ship repairs, conducting salvage operations, pile driving, welding and burning underwater, employing explosives, and laying concrete, pipes, and cables. In it you will find the kind of advice which just might save you substantial sums of money. For example, you will get the kind of advice that would prevent you from pouring faulty concrete underwater, which could involve you in a costly lawsuit. There are also invaluable tips on how to succeed in the business end of commercial diving. In this context, you will find ways to avoid certain financial pitfalls, how to bid for the jobs you can do, and make a profit, how to handle the important aspects of safety, and how to deal in a positive way with labor unions, among other things.

The authors wish to thank the Naval Coastal Systems Center in Panama City, Florida, for providing many of the photographs in this text, and the Union Carbide Company for permission to use portions of *The Oxy-Acetylene Handbook*.

Tricks of the Trade for Divers

CHAPTER ONE

The Diver as a Businessman

MOST SUCCESSFUL commercial divers are independent and adaptable, and they are also opportunists of the highest degree. These are essential qualities of basic survival, and in order to become successful as a commercial diver, you must know how to survive; not only in a physical sense, but financially as well. Perhaps no other profession requires such a variety of skills and knowledge of equipment coupled with, at times, raw physical courage. These are the qualities for which a professional diver is paid. You alone must assess the difficulty and risks involved in your job in order to decide what it is worth. You must also remember that your youth is limited and that you must plan for the time when you will no longer be physically qualified to dive. You must, therefore, always charge for your expertise, because even when you are no longer able to dive, your advice will still be worth money.

Any seasoned commercial diver is familiar with the misconception that divers charge outrageous prices for the work they do. I have often been accused of being a pirate. "You were only in the water for ten minutes, how can you charge me a hundred bucks for that!" During the summer months, every kid with a scuba tank is a "commercial diver" and will try anything for a ten dollar bill. It is unfortunate that a real professional must sometimes contend with that kind of competition. A man who truly earns his living from commercial diving will be the last one called to do a job where all the amateurs have tried and failed.

The truth is, independent commercial divers often do not charge enough to stay in business for themselves. Trying to compete with people working as part-time commercial divers is the fastest way to go out of business. Part-time divers will not charge enough money to maintain their equipment, much less buy new gear. They are usually covered for their health and welfare by another job. They seldom carry any kind of liability insurance, and since they are essentially doing the "gravy jobs," they run little risk of running into the situations which make commercial diving so difficult and dangerous. In most cases, diving as a sideline does not expose the occupation to the scrutiny of such organizations as OSHA (the Occupational Safety and Health Administration) and the Coast Guard. However, the true professional must not only be equipped to meet proper safety requirements, but must also keep and maintain proper records. None of these factors are usually considered by the part-time diver, to say nothing indeed of the fact that part-timers seldom are trained properly or experienced enough to do jobs as safely, competently, and economically as a real professional.

With all that in mind, the first chapter of this book may be the most important "trick of the trade"—how to stay in business. No matter how good a diver and no matter how competent a worker you are, the trick is to stay in business; and that means looking at all of the costs of doing business and making sure that the fee you charge will pay all the costs, net you or your diver a good wage, pay employee benefits, and make a profit. Profit is essential to staying in business: it is not a dirty word. Profit is necessary so that you have reserves for those jobs where the unforeseen circumstances (which inevitably arise) will cost. In other words, there are times when you will lose money on a job. A true professional finishes the job even if he has to pay for it out of his own pocket. That is only one of the costs of doing business that divers often do not consider. Profit is essential in order to buy new equipment or to expand a business in any number of ways. A good businessman has money beyond his immediate needs in order to avoid borrowing. Borrowing money is expensive and one of the costs of doing business that can be held down by making a profit. Diving is not usually steady work, and a profit will smooth out the lean times when work is scarce. Just because you make five hundred dollars a day for two weeks doesn't mean you can live as if you make a hundred thousand dollars a year. Out of your five hundred dollars a day should come direct and indirect costs, wages, benefits, and profit.

To keep in business for yourself, then, you need to look at developing a comprehensive business plan specifically for the commercial diver.

Safety First

Before considering any of the other aspects of running a business, you should take a hard look at the hazards of your job and decide on your own plan for safety. Minimizing risks and taking the proper time to plan a job for safety is the most important investment a commercial diver can make. Diving is often a hazardous occupation. Every serious commercial diver accepts the risks as part of his job, or he gets out. You need not be foolhardy, however, in order to be a good diver. As an example, Hollywood stunt men of today are extremely diligent about safety. Although they seem to take some incredible risks, they are very scientific about planning a stunt to be performed. Computers often will help plan a stunt, and dummies may be used to test ideas. Before a stunt man actually jumps from an airplane into a moving automobile, the stunt is carefully planned and tested. Paramedics are always on location in case of an accident.

An intelligent approach to a difficult or dangerous situation can set a real professional apart from his competition. Although luck may play a part in doing a job with no hitches, the real professional will have a good approach to the problem and be consistent, whereas the diver relying on luck will eventually run into a situation where luck will not pull him through. If you are a seasoned professional you will earn a reputation for consistently getting the job done safely. As it turns out, that kind of reputation gets more work than the foolhardy one, because no one wants to hire a diver who is going to kill himself. Delaying a job for a short time to insure diver safety costs less than killing or injuring a diver. If as a professional you find yourself being pressed, remind your client that you intend to complete the job as rapidly as possible without jeopardizing diver safety; and that a few minutes spent to insure diver safety can avoid long job delays and the bad reputation associated with an accident. Since OSHA will investigate an accident and cite everyone involved with violations, the job may be shut down as a result.

The logical approach to safety is to investigate first what the law requires. The law works for the professional in a number of ways. Compliance with the Coast Guard and OSHA regulations makes a commercial diver competitive. It is also a good advertising point. The diver familiar with the law can avoid taking unnecessary risks or being pushed beyond reasonable limits, because the law clearly sets forth conditions the diver is *not* to be subjected to. Legal records must be kept on any diving job by the company and by the diver. These records help protect the diver and are a necessity in the event of a diving accident. (These matters will be discussed in greater detail later in this chapter.) But the law is not always enough. It does not cover every situation, it only offers general guidelines for widely accepted safe practice. Each job the professional diver does must be analyzed for its own risks. Each diver must honestly gauge his own limitations as well. You will be more highly thought of if you bring in another professional to work with you on a job you may not be able to do by yourself. Don't try to bluff your way through. Working with explosives is a good example (Chapter 8). Unless you work with explosives a lot, it is better to bring in an experienced blaster to work with you, rather than risk making a mistake that could be costly to everyone.

What the Law Requires

OSHA has jurisdiction over most commercial diving operations. The Coast Guard will also act to uphold marine safety especially where operations take place at sea. The law is quite specific about several aspects of commercial diving operations including:

1. Personnel requirements: qualifications of dive team, medical requirements

2. General operations: safe practices manual, predive procedures, procedures during dive, postdive procedures

3. Specific operations procedures: scuba diving, surface-supplied air diving, mixed gas diving, live boating

4. Equipment procedures and requirements

5. Record keeping

Federal publications which cover the law in detail are included in Appendix A. Without simply repeating the law, let's examine legal requirements with an eye toward the diver as a businessman. Keep in mind that the legal requirements are designed to cover all aspects of commercial diving including the huge offshore teams. Although it is necessary to comply with the law, it is also prudent to examine what aspects of the law may not be applicable to your operation. For example, it is not necessary to operate and maintain a recompression chamber on the site if the job entails diving within no decompression limits at depths less than 100 fsw (feet of seawater). An assessment of the capital outlay required to finance an operation where decompression dives are to be undertaken reveals extremely high costs in equipment, insurance, and personnel. If a job can be performed within no decompression limits in less than 100 fsw, it can be undertaken by a small commercial diving operation.

After you prove your capability to undertake and execute small commercial diving operations successfully while making a profit, you may be able to find backers for larger, more lucrative operations. In this chapter, we will examine the requirements for safety which deal with personnel, first aid, emergency procedures, and record keeping. Be advised; this discourse is not intended to interpret the law, only to clarify its intent to the small commercial operator. In Chapter 2, we will examine equipment requirements. In later chapters, we will deal with specific tasks you as a commercial diver may undertake and how to plan and execute them safely.

It is also worth mentioning that under some circumstances OSHA standards do not apply to commercial diving operations. They are:

1. Dives performed solely for instructional purposes using scuba and conducted within the no decompression limits

2. Dives for search, rescue, or related public safety purposes by or under the control of a government agency

3. Emergencies (An employer may deviate from the requirements to the extent necessary to minimize a situation which is likely to cause death, serious physical harm, or major environmental damage, provided that the employer notifies OSHA within forty-eight hours of the onset of the emergency.)

4. Dives performed for certain research activities within the no decompression limits (Anyone engaged in research involving diving should contact OSHA for clarification.)

The personnel requirements are twofold: first, you must have the training and experience required to perform the task. Second, you must be medically qualified. These requirements can be met by service in the military as a diver, or by attending a recognized commercial diving school, and by examination of a physician qualified to examine and certify a diver as fit for diving. (The physician should have appropriate understanding of hyperbaric medicine.) For futher information, contact the Undersea Medical Society, Inc., 9650 Rockville Pike, Bethesda, Maryland 20814, or Diver Accident Network (DAN), Duke University Medical Center, Durham, North Carolina 27710. To rent or lease appropriate equipment, you can contact Div-Med International, 1101 N. Calvert St., Baltimore, Maryland 21202. Everyone involved in diving or working around divers is further required to maintain current certification in cardiopulmonary resuscitation and standard first aid (American National Red Cross or its equivalent).

The Safe Practices Manual

To comply with OSHA general operations procedures, you should develop and maintain a safe practices manual. A copy must be at the dive location and available to each dive team member. The manual must contain a copy of OSHA standards (see Appendix A) and a statement of the company policy for implementing the standards. Also, the manual must include:

1. Safety procedures and checklists for diving operations

2. Assignments and responsibilities of the dive team members

3. Equipment procedures and checklists

4. Emergency procedures for fire, equipment failure, adverse environmental conditions, and medical illness and injury

Obviously, the larger the operation becomes, the more complex the safe practices manual will have to become, and it may require a special consultant to assure compliance with OSHA. However, for the small commercial diving operation not engaged in decompression dives, compliance with OSHA becomes a relatively simple matter. Most of what is required is common sense, and although it may seem like a lot of unnecessary paperwork to the individual interested in getting into the water, the amount of forethought necessary to develop this document can avoid unnecessary confusion during an emergency. Paperwork, in any case, is an awful lot of what being in business for yourself is all about; so get used to it! (For assistance in developing record keeping for commercial diving operations contact Diving Consultants Co., 42 River Street, Wakefield, Rhode Island.)

Before diving operations can commence, there are a few more requirements to meet. A list must be kept at the dive location of the telephone numbers of:

1. An operational decompression chamber

2. Accessible hospitals

3. Available physicians

4. Available transportation

5. The nearest U. S. Coast Guard rescue center

(Here again, contact Diver Accident Network, Duke University Medical Center, Durham, North Carolina.)

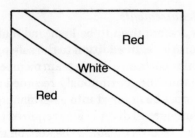

Fig. 1.1. Diver down flag.

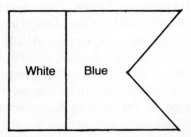

Fig. 1.2. International Code of Signals flag Alpha means diver down: keep clear.

First Aid Requirement

First aid supplies put together into a kit must be on every job site. The kit must be approved by a physician, and if it is to be used in the recompression chamber or a diving bell, the kit must be suitable for use under hyperbaric conditions. In other words, any of the supplies which could be destroyed or rendered useless under pressure must be replaced with supplies that can be used under pressure. A thorough analysis of the kit by someone familiar with hyperbaric medicine is recommended. In addition to the first aid kit, an American Red Cross standard first aid handbook, or equivalent, and a bag-type (sometimes called an ambu-bag) manual resuscitator with transparent mask and tubing must be available at the dive location.

In addition to first aid supplies, an appropriate warning signal must be displayed. The standard diver's flag (Fig. 1.1) should always be displayed, but in addition, the International Code of Signals flag A should be displayed (Fig. 1.2) to comply with OSHA.

Record-Keeping Requirements

Certain records are required to be kept and maintained on all commercial diving operations. In addition to the safe practices manual, the physician's medical reports on all dive team members must be kept. The depth-time profile must be continuously recorded on every dive, and a record of the dive must be entered into a permanent company log book. Each individual commercial diver is also required to keep and maintain a personal log book. Records must also be kept on the equipment. It is a good idea to have a separate log book on every major piece of equipment you own. The log should indicate when and how each piece of equipment is tested and how it is maintained. A record should also be kept on maintenance work performed.

Perhaps the most important document to the individual diver is his personal log book. It is required by law. The personal log book must meet certain criteria established by the Coast Guard and OSHA. (To obtain a legal professional diver's log book, write to ACDE (Association of Commercial Diving Educators), P.O. Box 36, Summerland, CA 93067. All entries must be made in ink. Identification of the person to whom the log book refers must be by photograph in the appropriate place. The photograph is overstamped by the issuing diving school or company. The diver's signature is then affixed on or near the photograph. The front of the log book contains appropriate personal information, medical information, and the diver's training record. There are forms for records of medical examinations periodically conducted throughout the diver's career as well as the diver's employment record. Finally, there should be a record of each dive, including a depth-time profile, any unusual conditions, and the diver's personal comments. The log book is complete when it is signed by the diver, the company supervisor, and stamped with the company's official seal for each dive. In this way, you, the diver, not only maintain official records for personal reference and evidence of your experience, but also protect yourself from any dispute with the company. You should be aware that you have the right to obtain copies of the records the company keeps on your dive. This helps eliminate the possibility of falsification of records, since two separate official records exist and both are accessible to the diver. If a dispute should arise involving the diver and the company, the diver has his own legal records, and may obtain copies of the company's records to resolve the matter. If you are injured or need to be treated in a decompression facility, records of injury and treatment are also required documentation by the company. If negligence is involved, as in improper decompression, the records will often indicate who is at fault.

During dive operations, copies of the U. S. Navy standard decompression tables or their equivalent must be on location and continuous depth-time profiles must be maintained on each diver. These profiles become part of the permanent records of both the diver and the company. Needless to say, it is of paramount importance that a competent person be placed in charge of keeping these records.

Insurance

The Longshoreman's and Harbor Worker's Compensation Act of 1927 and the Merchant Marine Act of 1920 are federal laws which provide benefits for workers disabled during marine operations. The Longshoreman's Act covers workers disabled by injuries suffered on the navigable waters or adjacent areas used for loading, unloading, repairing, or building vessels in the United States. The Merchant Marine Act covers operations on the high seas. Commercial divers and members of the dive team are covered by both laws. Every employer is liable for, and shall

Fig. 1.3   Mark XII Diver (left) meets Mark V diver (right). Photo courtesy of Naval Coastal Systems Center, U. S. Navy.

secure payment to his employees for the following due to injuries suffered on the job:

1. Medical services and supplies

2. Compensation for disability

3. Compensation for death

If the employer is a subcontractor, the contractor is liable and must secure payment of compensation to employees of the subcontractor unless the subcontractor has secured such payment. Compensation is payable irrespective of fault as a cause for the injury except if the injury was due solely to the intoxication of the employee or because the employee intentionally injured or killed himself or another.

If the employer is sued for damages by an employee for injuries, the employer may not claim as a defense that the injury was caused by the negligence of a fellow servant, or that the employee assumed the risk of his employment or that the injury was due to the contributory negligence of the employee. The liability of an employer for medical treatment of an injured employee is not affected by the fact that his employee was injured through the fault or negligence of a third party not in the same employ, but the employer may sue the third party for damages. No agreement by an employee to waive his right to compensation is valid.

The benefits to be paid are extensive and without exclusion. The employer is liable for payment of benefits without limitation, in other words, he may lose everything unless he is adequately insured. Indeed, according to the law, any employer *must* have adequate insurance in order to work. State laws also are in force with regard to workmen's compensation, so it is wise to check your own state laws as well.

Company Insurance

For obvious reasons, then, it is necessary to investigate what insurance, if any, you may need to conduct business without risking literally everything that you own. If you work as a diver employed by a company, the company will be liable for accidents and you, as an individual, are not required to carry insurance. If you work as a subcontractor for another contractor, the prime contractor will be liable for you and your employees; but he may require you to carry your own liability and workmen's compensation insurance so that he may sue you in case you are negligent. In some cases, it is possible to work under the prime contractor's insurance, but that kind of agreement must be clearly understood by both parties involved and should be formally stated in writing, signed by both parties, and notarized. You may need an attorney to help you do this if you have any questions or doubts.

Of course, if you are the prime contractor, you are liable for everyone on the job. Even if you are not negligent and comply with all the safety standards and someone gets hurt by his own stupidity, you still pay.

State Requirements

Some state laws and certain contracts will require you to carry specific insurance policies other than basic liability and workmen's compensation. You may be required to post a performance bond which you will forfeit if you do not complete the job, or if you fail to complete the job on time. Or, you may be required to post a bond for other reasons. Bonding is available through a number of sources, one of which is the insurance company. Insurance and bonding are incredibly expensive for marine operations. They may sometimes preclude the small contractor from being able to conduct business at a reasonable price. Here again, profit can help reduce the cost of doing business if you can afford to post your own bond. Liability insurance including completed operations scares the hell out of insurance agents, and for good reason. If you perform construction or make repairs underwater, you are liable for accidents during the time you are on the job. Completed operations liability covers accidents which may occur after you are off the job which are due to faulty workmanship on your part. For example, suppose you build a dock and someone knocks it down with a boat three years later. He claims that it was not built properly in the first place and sues you for damages. Now you go to court, and it could be anybody's guess who is really at fault, because the evidence all floated away. Nevertheless, it is going to cost you for a legal defense just the same.

Insurance is sometimes hard to get, especially if you have not documented your ability to do the job for which you need insurance. This is another reason for keeping an accurate log book on all jobs you do. For some types of diving work, however, insurance is neither difficult nor prohibitively expensive. For example, I performed a state contract for a bridge inspection on the Newport Bridge, in Newport, Rhode Island, when I first began contracting. The contract required that I carry a one-million-dollar liability insurance policy for the duration of the job. I was able to convince my insurance agent at the time, that there was little risk of damages involved in my looking at the structure underwater. He agreed and charged me a small fee to write the policy to the satisfaction of the state agency. Once you have established your credibility, it is usually a simple matter to get similar or more extensive policies written. Of course, once you have been in business for a long time with a good safety record, you won't have trouble getting insurance, and will find the rates become more reasonable.

When starting out, it is wise to shop around for insurance. If you know some good businessmen in the marine construction business for whom you have worked, or who know you by your reputation as a good diver, ask them to refer you to a good agent. If you anticipate a subcontract with a larger organization, ask about insurance requirements and use the opportunity to establish your reputation with their insurance company. Remember, when dealing with insurance agents and bankers, that they are in business too. You are the customer, and they want your business if you are successful at what you do. The trick is to establish yourself, and put them in the position of competing for your business. Don't assume they will all give you the same rate. Check out all of them, make yourself known to each, and establish relations which will benefit you in the future. You may have to take what you can get to start out, but if you are successful, you will find they will all want to do business with you.

Dealing with the Union

Commercial divers come under the United Brotherhood of Carpenters and Joiners. I have great respect for the union, and have had favorable dealings with it as a commercial diver. Regardless of how you feel about unions in general, it is wise to establish relations with this union, because sooner or later, you will have to deal with it. You should be aware of what the union pays for prevailing wages and what benefits are paid to its members. You should check the union contract to find out what is required of an employer who hires union divers. The contract the union has with a union company is designed to protect the workers. Without a contract, and without the union, you will find it hard to bargain with the management of a large organization. Of course, if you are in business for yourself, you may be the entire organization. However, you will still want to charge enough money to pay yourself the prevailing wage, benefits, and make a profit. Here is where many divers starting out will make a grave error. In their zeal to get started, many will often cut prices just to get a job. This is a mistake for two reasons: first, you establish a reputation for being inexpensive or "working cheap" and second, you fail to charge enough money to pay someone else to do the work for you. So you say, "I want to do the work myself anyway so I can afford to work cheaper." This is wrong. If you get hurt, and if you are under contract, you will have to pay someone else to finish the job at the prevailing union wage. If you get two or more jobs which have to run simultaneously, you will have to hire more people to work for you or give up the extra work (something you should avoid doing). Finally, if you think ahead far enough, you should realize, you will eventually want to be in the position of taking in all the work you can get. If you are in charge of an organization that can run itself, you are free to select the jobs you personally want to do, while making money on all of them.

The union can help you find work. One of the greatest difficulties in running a small diving business is keeping a steady flow of work. If you are working on a job, there is no time to be scouting for more work, and more often than not, when you finish a job, you are temporarily out of work while you look for the next job. Here is one place where the union can be helpful. The business agent for the union receives calls for divers; if you are a member as a diver, he can put you on a job as a diver. If you sign a contract with the union as a union company, the union can keep you informed of upcoming jobs you can bid on, or negotiate for.

If you are on good terms with the union, you may be advised of small jobs the union is not interested in. This is not a very likely possibility, and the jobs may not be of interest to you either, for example, someone who can't pay. However, there are some jobs the union is not generally interested in, simply because the client would have to pay too much for the union to be able to do the job. Commercial fishing vessels often foul their propellors with stray pieces of line. To clean a fouled propellor of line rarely takes more than an hour's time and to have a union diver do the job under union contract would cost the owner an eight-hour minimum plus benefits. Under most circumstances, no one is willing to pay more than one hundred dollars for that job, and in the summertime, the kids usually get the job for a lot less.

Diving jobs which last less than a day are usually of little concern to the union, and you can often get these without involving the union. I usually call the business agent of my local union anytime I get a small job to see if he is interested and get his okay to do the job without the union. Keep in mind, if you are going to become a union member, that you have certain obligations to the union, which means you should always give it the first refusal on any job you get.

The union is a brotherhood, and you will find, if you become a member, that most of the brothers will be eager to help you succeed. It is a good place to learn how to conduct business by observing how others who are successful do it. Establishing the attitudes of doing a job right and getting the job done will give you a good foundation for marine work. The attitude you bring to a job will have a strong bearing on how successful you will be on the job. It is my belief that the Carpenter's Union cultivates a proper attitude among its workers.

Advertising and Reputation

Advertising can be expensive, but it can pay off its expense by netting one good job. To start out with, the best place to advertise is in the yellow pages of the phone book. The listing will cost you a monthly fee which is added to your telephone bill. Of course, if you have a residential telephone, you will have to switch to a business phone line and you automatically receive one free listing in the yellow pages.

As you explore the market for divers, you may also wish to advertise in trade journals and periodicals which reach the people who may want your service. Marinas, state-operated piers, commercial fishermen, marine construction companies, power companies, the U. S. Army Corps of Engineers, environmental protection agencies (state and federal), engineering firms engaged in marine design, marine biological laboratories, in addition to any industry located on and using water as part of its operation such as coal power plants, oil refineries, nuclear power plants, U. S. Navy bases, all use divers from time to time.

Write, call, and send your business card to the engineering departments of water companies, electric companies, and industrial plants. All of them have intakes along rivers and lakes which need cleaning and inspection.

Periodically contact marine contractors who use divers. Keep letting them know you are in business and don't give up if they don't use you right away. They may have a reliable diver they use, but they may need more than one diver on a job. Their diver may get sick, or he may be on another job sometime when they need a diver. If you are persistent, you will get your chance.

There is a contractors' register used by contractors to locate materials and subcontractors. These books come out once a year and cover a region of several states. The telephone directory can help you locate the contractors' register in your area. The harbor news is also a good place to advertise. Ships' captains needing divers will see the ad as will longshoremen (They occasionally drop cargo overboard).

If you can afford it, purchase the *Dodge Bulletin* (to inquire about subscribing, write: F. W. Dodge, 858 Park Square, Building 31, James

Ave., Boston, MA 02116 or call: 617-956-4901) which comes out daily and will keep you in touch with any jobs needing diving contractors. The Army Corps of Engineers, water works, Environmental Protection Agency, public utilities, Navy, Coast Guard, and a long list of large private industries advertise jobs to be bid for river crossings, intake structures, outfall pipes, submarine cables, etc.

Contracting

Making a contract requires a great deal of forethought. More than any other aspect of doing business, a contract tests how well you know your business. A contract, in one sense, establishes the outcome of the job before it begins. A contract made in haste, without the proper consideration on your part, can commit you to performing work for which you will not be paid, and in some cases, you will pay to work. Nothing will make you more wary of contracts than paying to do a job. However, making a contract, with the proper considerations, will cement the foundation of your business, and establish your credibility in a permanent record. When you can commit yourself to an agreement, and consistently keep your word, your reputation will spread like wildfire.

Contracts, whether verbal or written, are legally binding, any book on business law will tell you that. Informal agreements made verbally are fine for simple tasks with trustworthy people, but as a practical matter, verbal contracts are not legally enforceable. People often forget exactly what they say, and as a job progresses, they often have different opinions of what was meant by what was said.

Beware of making a verbal contract for a job which is going to involve a lot of money. If the money is to be paid in advance of the work, then a verbal contract is not to your disadvantage. However, if you perform the work first, which is customary, and you have only a verbal agreement as a contract for payment, you are in a vulnerable position. All your client has to say in court is that he was not satisfied with the job you did, or that he only agreed to pay you half of what you claim; then it is his word against yours. Make no mistake about it, there are plenty of unsavory characters in the marine business who would be delighted to get you to work for them free. They will promise anything to get you to do a job, but when it is time to get paid, they will "not remember saying that" and you will have lost.

Make Important Agreements in Writing

Any job which is going to require you to spend money for materials, equipment rental, etc., and is going to take some time to complete, you must get money in advance for, and if the job is going to last for a long time (more than a week, say) get progress payments also. Advance money should cover whatever you have to lay out as working capital to do the job and then some. (When contracting with the government, you do not determine the conditions of the contract, they do. However, other contracts are generally more negotiable.) The red light should start to flash when you try to commit a contract in writing and the other party says: "Don't you trust me?"

Some contracts are difficult to make, and require you to have substantial security to perform a job. Typically, contracts with any government agency or local authority will be written by them, completely to their advantage, and they will allow no alteration of the contract without their consent. Contractors usually will be required to submit a competitive bid in order to get the job. A bid bond is often required and is usually a percentage of the contractor's bid price. The bid bond is refunded to the unsuccessful bidder. The successful bidder will have his bond retained and must usually post an additional amount up to one hundred percent of the bid as a performance bond. The bid bond will be forfeited if the bidder is selected and fails to sign the contract within a specified amount of time. The performance bond will be forfeited if the successful bidder does not satisfactorily complete the job or if he does not complete the job within a specified amount of time. On some contracts there will be a 10 percent holding figure. The agency will withhold 10 percent of the final payment for a specified amount of time after the job is complete. The money is used in the event that something goes wrong after the job is completed and the contractor is unavailable to effect repairs. This holding figure is sometimes required in addition to completed operations liability insurance. It is advisable when making a contract which requires this withholding figure to add another 10 percent to the bid price to assure that you still will make a profit.

These contracts are also generally worded so that if *anything* goes wrong during the job, the contractor is responsible for it regardless of fault. Needless to say, you had better have substantial resources and ability to contract under those conditions. However, government contracts have one positive feature; once they are completed properly, you will get paid.

Bidding a Job

There are two types of bids you will generally be asked to submit, competitive and noncompetitive. The competitive bid is generally solicited by governments and large organizations, and they have the option of selecting the lowest qualified bidder to do the job. The other type of bid generally bypasses the competitive procedure, and you will simply be asked for a price to do a job. Because of your reputation, or because the client does not wish to waste time going through the competitive process, he may simply select you to do a job. If you have dealt with a client fairly in the past, you will often be called to do a job, especially an emergency or rush job, without being asked for a price. You are pretty much free in these situations to charge what the market will bear.

Before bidding a job, or deciding on a price to do a job, all costs of doing business must be figured. There are many things to consider, and it may take some time for you to get your costs wired. For this reason, it is imperative that you keep accurate records of every job you do. Every cent you spend to do a job should be recorded. The IRS will want a complete accounting of your finances also, so you must keep records for tax purposes anyway. The records will help you refine your costs, to see where you lost money, or where you might cut some of your costs. They will also help you to bid jobs in the future, thereby becoming some of the most valuable information you will have. No matter how many books you read, you cannot get a handle on bidding a job until you have done it over and over enough to get your costs wired. Some of the things you will want to consider are: the overhead costs, equipment cost, labor costs, setup and breakdown costs, materials, and profit.

Estimating Overhead

Overhead involves the costs of doing business which are not directly involved with doing the job such as the cost of maintaining and running an office, cost of a shop, maintenance of equipment, advertising, insurance, attorney's fees, and the cost of bidding a job (your time is worth money). Office costs include secretarial services, supplies such as stamps, envelopes, etc., fixtures and furniture, rental and utilities, etc. Shop costs will include rental of space, utilities, supplies, and maintenance service.

Also included in overhead is the time you spend doing the books, writing letters, bidding jobs, promoting sales, overseeing or performing maintenance on your equipment and personal gear. Often overlooked by many critics of divers is how much time and money are spent on keeping the equipment in good operating condition. The time in the water is not a true indication of how much is involved in running the diving business. By my best estimation, every hour spent underwater by a diver is matched by at least an hour of maintenance and repair on his personal equipment to keep it operational. Company equipment maintenance requires even more time than that. The other option is to have money to buy new gear all the time. That is even more expensive than the time spent for maintenance and repair.

One of the advantages of running a small business is overhead costs can be kept to a minimum thereby making it possible to be more competitive in price. However, a common error in starting out as a small diving business is to cut the price to the bare bones. In other words, not charging anything for overhead costs. You say, I can run the business out of my house and store and maintain my equipment in my basement and garage. My wife can do the books, so I don't need to charge anything for these expenses. Think again. Even if it does not cost you directly for these expenses, you should still charge for them. After all, you may not be able to operate out of your house forever, and you probably will not want to. If you charge for the use of your house as an office, you can save the money as a down payment on a building for the business. Or, if your house becomes too small, you can rent a place for the business without having to drastically alter your price structure. Don't cheat yourself or your family by not charging for what the business uses out of your personal assets. You will simply deplete your own resources and your customer will get free service.

Costs for Equipment

Any equipment you use on a job, whether you own it, rent it, borrow it, or steal it, should be charged to the customer in the form of a rental fee for its use. If you own your equipment, you will want to replace it when it wears out. If you buy it on time payments, you will want to charge enough to make the payments and have money enough besides to buy another at the end of its useful life. If you borrow or rent the equipment, you will want to charge enough to pay your rental cost and have some left toward buying that equipment for your business later on.

Sometimes a special piece of equipment is required to do a job. It may be something that you cannot rent, and therefore must purchase for the job. It may also be something you will never be able to use again. In this case, the customer must assume the cost of the item, and it is arguable that he should be able to keep the item since he bought it. However, he probably has no use for it, so unless it becomes a real issue, you should get to keep the item.

I was doing some underwater inspection in Virginia on the new James River bridge during its construction. The client needed some very special underwater closeup photographs. I did not own a lens which would focus down to six inches, so I had to purchase one to get the photographs. The client refused to assume the entire cost of the lens; but I knew I would be able to use the lens again. I agreed to pay for half of the lens if the client paid the other half and I got to keep the lens. I should have written into the contract that specialty items were extras and cost was to be assumed by the contractee, but since I had not covered myself by the contract, I was able to negotiate an agreement which was satisfactory to both parties. As it turned out, the client was pleased with the results I obtained with the new lens, and I made a good profit on the job which dwarfed my cost for the lens.

How do you figure equipment costs? I had some difficulty deciding how to charge for equipment, so I had a chat with the owner of a local rental store, with whom I had had considerable dealings, and I asked him. He was not interested in renting diving equipment, but he often rented construction equipment to me. So I asked him how he figured his rental fees. He told me that items to be rented which are virtually indestructible bring the lowest fee. For example, he had a tow chain which he only charged two dollars a day to rent. He said there was little chance someone was going to break the chain, and it would probably never wear out. On the other hand, an item which might cost the same as the chain to buy, but was delicate or required some skill to operate without damage, he would charge a high rate for. As an example, a camera comparable in price to the chain would bring more like ten dollars a day. Another consideration in renting is how common the item is that you are renting. In other words, is it available in local stores, or is it something that is difficult to find? A lot of diving equipment is not easy to get. For example, how many places can you walk into and buy a two-diver radio? Another consideration is how fast an item will wear out and if and how often it needs replacement parts. Many tools for use underwater will wear out rapidly. For example, underwater burning torches don't last forever, and they need replacement collets for the rods quite often. The torch itself is not available in any hardware store, so you would be justified in charging a higher than normal rate of rental for the torch.

Bearing all these considerations in mind, a fair rate of rental for marine construction equipment which is used by you or under your supervision and which is not an unusual, delicate, or rapidly expendable item, is around one percent per day (somewhat less for indestructible items).

Any materials you use on a job should be charged on a cost plus basis unless the contract you bid on is for a lump sum price in which case you have already figured the cost of materials into the price of the job. You cannot simply charge the customer the price you pay for materials, because it costs you more than that to get them and handle them.

Burning rods for the underwater cutting torch may cost you two dollars apiece. But you can't go downtown and buy them one at a time, you have to buy them by the box, and it takes a long distance phone call to order them, a week to get them, plus shipping costs. This type of item you have to buy ahead of the job so you are ready to work on time. You can't hold up a job while you wait for rods. So they must be on hand all the time, especially for emergency jobs. The cost of having them on your shelf is in capital which is not available for other things.

The amount you charge for materials that you supply should cover all the factors mentioned and a little more. How much you charge for rods, to complete the example, will further be determined by how many rods you use on the job. If you use a thousand rods, you can get by charging $2.25 per rod. But if you only use a few rods, you would have to charge more, maybe $3.00 per rod. You may have to set a minimum charge for burning which will cover this and other factors to be considered later on.

Setup and Breakdown Costs

No matter what size job you do, there will be some expense involved in setting up and breaking down the job. A very big job with a lot of heavy equipment to set up will involve considerable expense in setting up and breaking down. Even a relatively small job requiring a lot of equipment will be expensive to set up and break down. For example, suppose you get a call to burn a cable out of the propellor of a tugboat. The job will probably require less than an hour of time in the water; but the amount of equipment involved to do the job will take two men most of the day to set up and break down if they know what they are doing.

The amount of labor involved in setting up a job can be deceiving, especially if the job is going to be conducted at sea. I did some repairs to a marine outfall pipe one summer. The end of the pipe was fifteen hundred feet offshore, in the open sea, so it required a sixty-foot tugboat to stage the operation. The work I did took two divers in band masks sixty minutes bottom time to complete. Most of the work involved placing sandbags around the end of the pipe as a protective measure. However, the amount of time to set up the job and break it down was considerable, and if I had not charged the client to set and break, I would have lost money on the job. Here is why; the sandbags used for underwater construction had to be burlap bags filled with a mixture of sand and cement. Prior to conducting the operation at sea, those sandbags had to be made up. The right size burlap sacks had to be found, the sand and cement had to be mixed (dry), then put into the bags, and the bags had to be tie-wrapped. After being filled, the bags had to be stacked on pallets and transported to the tug, then lifted aboard. The labor, transportation, crane time, and tug time were a considerable expense when compared with the total cost of the rest of the job. Added to that was the expense involved with setting up a dive station to run two surface-supplied divers on a tugboat (with all the safety considerations we have just mentioned); then consider that after the job was completed, everything had to be broken down and put away. All for sixty minutes diving time!

Labor

Labor costs are figured either by the hour or by the day per man according to the type of labor being performed. Obviously, the wage a diver makes will be higher than the wage a tender or other worker makes. Wage is not all that is figured into labor costs, however. The benefits for the worker's health and welfare must also be charged to labor costs. A good way to figure these costs is to ask the union for the prevailing wage and benefits for each type of labor you anticipate using. Social security payments, unemployment compensation, and insurance payments are contributed to by the employer and must be figured in the cost of labor. Workmen's compensation insurance is generally charged by the payroll according to the type of labor. Workmen's compensation is astronomical for diving time, considerably less for other types of marine construction labor and comparatively miniscule for other types of work. Therefore, labor expense should be carefully identified according to type of labor and time spent. The expense for workmen's compensation insurance is then added to the labor as an expense. When all labor costs are figured, a percentage is generally added to that for profit.

Considering a Profit

The profit you make on a job can be figured a number of ways. A percentage of your labor costs can be used to figure a profit for the job, or the total expense of the job can be figured and a percentage of that can be used to figure the profit. Either way is acceptable, but I always like to figure a job so I make money on everything. By making a profit on everything, it is possible to evaluate every aspect of doing the job for what it is really worth for you to do it including, perhaps, some of the labor. I filled the sandbags for the outfall job myself. It was a day of labor and a waste of time for me because I could have hired a laborer to do it, made money on him, and done something else myself to make more money at the same time.

The amount of profit you make on a job is nobody's business but yours and the IRS; so keep it to yourself. There is no shame in making a substantial profit on a job, because you're going to lose money on some other job. You should try to make an overall profit, but that does not mean if you lose money on your first job, that you try to make it all up on the very next job (sometimes you can). It means your business plan should be to make a certain profit as consistently as possible.

Profit on a job will be naturally figured at a higher rate as the risks of the job get higher. By risks, I mean not only risk of physical danger to the diver, but risks of financial loss due to factors such as the weather. If your contract requires you to finish a job in thirty days at sea in the wintertime, you have to figure what your chances are for the weather to allow you to do the job in that amount of time, at that time of the year. Being an intelligent sort, check the National Weather Service records for the last ten years to get an idea of how many working days you might expect to get. Suppose you find your chances are two in three. That means you are running better than a thirty percent chance of failure to complete the job on time. Not completing the job on time will cost you one thousand dollars per day for every day over thirty days according to the contract. But you figure that you have a ninety percent probability of finishing the job within forty-five days. That is fifteen days over the allowed time and fifteen thousand dollars extra for the job. Unless you are an estimator, figuring probability is a complex procedure. So add fifteen thousand to the price of the job and figure a profit besides. Odds are in your favor that you will complete the job in forty-five days or less and still make a profit. There is still a chance that you won't, however, and you still run a risk of losing money on the job. The risk here is worth taking since you run a better than even chance of completing the job on time and making an extra fifteen thousand dollars. If you stay in business long enough, you will find that you need that extra money for the job where you don't beat the odds. In marine construction, the surviving businessmen figure to make enough extra money to cover themselves for the jobs where unpredictable circumstances will arise and cause the job to lose money.

I was on a construction crew working as a diver laying a plastic marine outfall pipeline. The prime contractor ran into difficulty digging the trench underwater. The engineering firm that designed the job had hired some scuba divers to do a bottom survey and determine the bottom composition where the pipe was to be laid. The scuba divers surveyed two thousand feet of bottom ten feet wide in one day and concluded that the bottom was all sand. The contractor bid the job on the basis of that report. The contractor should have conducted his own underwater survey before bidding, or at least, have had a clause in his contract that specified that if unknown obstructions were encountered, removal would be at an additional cost. As it turned out, the bottom was all ledge rock, and we had to blast through a good portion of it, and drill rock anchors into the rest. The job should have been done over one summer, but it took the better part of a year to complete. The contractor lost well over a million dollars on that job. He is still in business today, however, and I suspect he will be for a good long time. He obviously makes enough to cover himself for those situations, and you should too!

CHAPTER TWO

Equipment, Tools, and Methods

THERE ARE MANY different helmets, masks, wet suits, and dry suits on the market today. Although most divers today prefer the more modern equipment, I have always found the old hard hat and a good dry suit to be superb equipment for harbors and rivers where the water is relatively shallow, but often polluted and muddy. The risks of skin and ear infections as well as injury from being unable to see are minimized by the protection a hard hat and dry suit can provide (See Fig 2.1).

Commercial Diving Equipment

The oil field diver makes his living in the ocean and naturally prefers modern equipment which is more suitable for that type of work than the old hard hat. The band mask is probably the most versatile piece of equipment available today. It can be used for almost any type of commercial diving work with a wet suit or a dry suit. It can be worn with boots on the bottom, or with flippers for mobility and midwater work. The main drawback of the band mask is the lack of head and ear protection. However, the head can be protected with a fiberglass shell which fits onto the mask. The band mask is ideal for many jobs where phones are required or the head will be out of the water frequently. Pier repairs often require the diver to be in and out of the water a lot. The band mask can be used on demand air with an oral nasal mask, thereby improving communications and reducing the air supply requirements. If the diver works hard enough, he can switch from demand to free-flow and get all the air he needs to work hard. The band mask has the added advantage of being easier to dress and undress in a short time and imposes the lightest weight on the diver's head. Furthermore, the band mask has bail out capability, which affords the diver the ability to carry

Fig. 2.1. Hard hat and dry suit. Photo courtesy of Naval Coastal Systems Center, U. S. Navy.

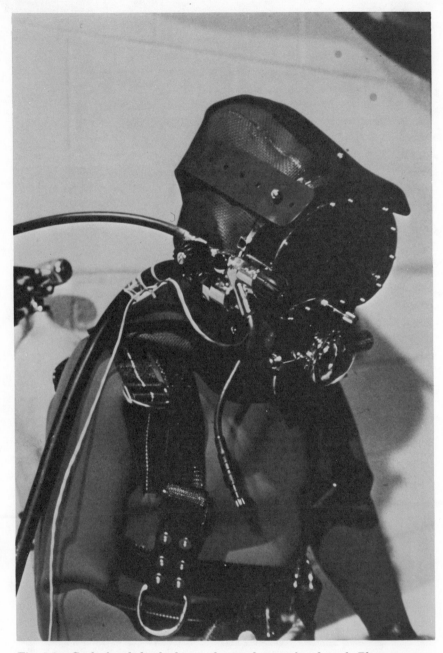

Fig. 2.2.   Scuba bottle hooked up to the regulator on band mask. Photo courtesy of Naval Coastal Systems Center, U. S. Navy.

Fig. 2.3. Scuba diver on downed aircraft. Photo courtesy of Naval Coastal Systems Center, U. S. Navy.

an emergency supply of breathing gas on his back in a scuba bottle hooked up to the regulator on his band mask (Fig. 2.2).

Where head protection is a factor, or when working in very polluted water, a helmet is the wise choice in diving equipment. Modern helmets offer the advantage of demand, free-flow, and bail out systems giving them the same versatility as a band mask for air supply requirements. The old hard hat and some of the new hard hats with the breastplate assembly offer the maximum protection to the head and neck by a rigid head and neck type assembly. The helmet and breastplate effectively distribute the forces over a larger and more rigid exterior. The helmet mounted on a breastplate does not turn with the diver's head and must have side and top viewing ports, or the diver must turn his body to see side to side. Helmets are expensive, running into several thousand dollars for a good one.

Scuba gear is excellent for inspection work, jobs of short duration, or where mobility is a factor. Scuba can be used without phones for short jobs by using a lifeline and hand signals. Working in scuba all day, however, is not recommended. The diver fatigues more rapidly due to increased breathing resistance.

Equipment used by the commercial diver can therefore be classified as either scuba or surface supplied diving equipment. Surface supplied diving gear falls more specifically into three categories for nonsaturation type diving:

1. The old hard hat or deep sea diving gear

2. Helmets

3. Masks

Modern helmets and masks are further delineated into either free-flow or demand type air supply. The safety requirements for operation of scuba and surface supplied commercial diving gear will be discussed below, and we will look at the proper methods of setting up the diver's equipment.

Scuba

According to safety standards, each diver using scuba must have:

1. Self-contained underwater breathing equipment including a primary breathing gas supply with a cylinder pressure gauge readable by the diver during the dive

2. A diver carried reserve breathing gas supply provided by a manual reserve (J valve) or an independent reserve cylinder connected and ready for use

3. A face mask

4. A buoyancy compensator or other inflatable flotation device

5. A weight belt capable of quick release

6. A knife

7. Swim fins or shoes

8. A diving wristwatch

9. A depth gauge

Furthermore, scuba diving is not to be conducted:

1. Outside the no decompression limits

2. At depths greater than 130 fsw

3. Against currents greater than one knot unless line tended

4. If a diver cannot ascend directly to the surface unless line tended

5. Unless a standby diver is available while the diver is in the water

6. Unless the diver is line tended from the surface or accompanied by another diver in the water in continuous visual contact during the diving operation

7. Unless a boat is available for diver pickup when the divers are not line tended from the surface

8. Unless another diver is stationed at the underwater point of entry and is line tending the diver when the latter is in a physically confining space

Scuba divers maintain their own depth-time profiles, according to the safety standards, but it is advisable to have a man topside keeping track of the scuba divers' time and depth (if possible) especially wherever these may approach the limits of no decompression.

Scuba divers generally use a flutter kick when diving. The constant movement of the legs on a long swim is tiring. I use another method called the frog kick and have found that I can avoid fatigue this way. To execute the frog kick (Fig 2.4), simply draw both legs up, then give a sudden thrust. This propels you forward and you can relax completely for a couple of seconds as you glide through the water. On long pier inspections where you must swim up and down each piling to inspect it, the frog kick will allow you to perform without exhaustion.

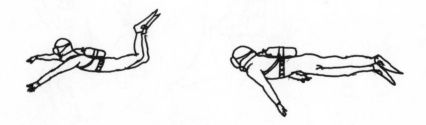

Fig. 2.4.   Divers executing the frog kick.

The buddy system is an accepted safe practice when scuba diving. Figure 2.5 illustrates an excellent buddy system for scuba diving, commercially or for sport. The diver always knows where his buddy is and the line to the surface provides safety when diving in murky waters. Under certain circumstances already described, commercial divers may dive in scuba without a buddy. In these situations, the inner tube method is a much better line tender than just a line to the diver.

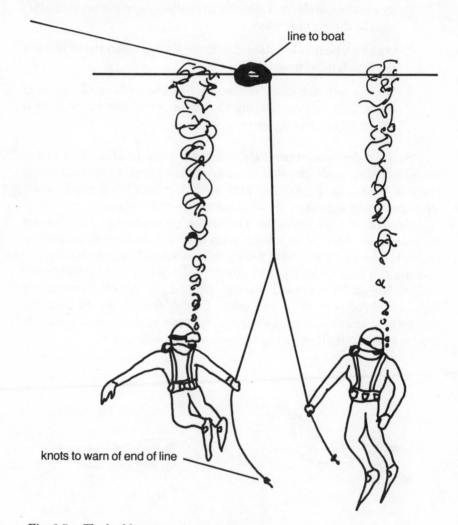

Fig. 2.5.   The buddy system in operation.

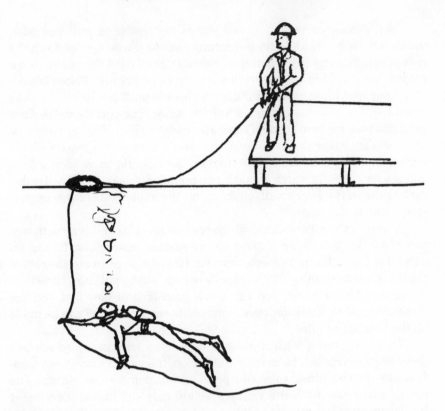

Fig. 2.6.   Diver searching the bottom with an inner tube on the surface.

For example, you get a call to examine a sunken barge fifty feet deep in a river. The muddy water created by the strong and treacherous currents affords you little visibility. Swimming against a current can wear your strength down rapidly and swimming with the current can slam you into stationary objects. By having a line to the inner tube tended by a man on deck (see Fig. 2.6), you can slide down on a descending line (see Tools for Commercial Diving Jobs below) dropped with a weight to the wreck. With the line from the inner tube in one hand, you can then swim around to make the examination. At any point, you can tie off the line and follow it to the surface for consultation, then return where you left off.

In a strong current, you can signal the tender to pull you back upstream, rather than to try swimming against the stream and run the risk of being dragged downstream. For example, I used this method on a very difficult bridge inspection in a river in Central Falls, Rhode Island. The river was lined with old mills which were built on the river banks with their foundations extended into the water. The outside walls of the factories rose vertically out of the water on both sides offering no escape route via the river bank. Downstream was a dam with a waterfall. If I were swept downstream by the current, there would be no escape from going over the falls which would mean certain disaster. The line tended inner tube worked very well, enabling me to complete the bridge inspection without incident.

Buoyancy compensators, which require practice and instruction to use properly, can carry a diver to the surface faster than he should ascend to avoid decompression sickness. It is hard to estimate the rate of ascent when swimming free in murky waters, but by pulling yourself up a line hand over hand, you can get a good idea of how fast you are ascending. Also, if decompression stops are required, they can be made on the line to the tube.

If, when diving with a buddy, there is an emergency where one diver requires mouth-to-mouth ventilation, the victim's buoyancy compensator or the inner tube can provide flotation for the victim. The rescue diver can ditch the victim's weight belt and tanks, then insert him horizontally through the inner tube in a face up position. Mouth-to-mouth ventilation can be performed in this position. Remember that pinching the nose of the victim and making a seal over his mouth with your mouth means that both heads can be underwater while you are inflating his lungs. But, the victim's head must be out of the water when you break the seal. While you are performing mouth-to-mouth ventilation, you can swim toward shore and call for help while beginning CPR (cardiopulmonary resuscitation) on land if necessary. As of this time, no effective method of CPR has been proven for use where victim and rescuer are in the water. Whenever the diver's flag cannot be displayed otherwise, or where there is a lot of boat traffic, the flag can be mounted on the inner tube marking the diver's location directly below.

Surface-Supplied Diving

Surface-supplied divers must have masks or helmets meeting the following requirements: each helmet or mask must have a nonreturn valve at the attachment point between the helmet or mask and the umbilical. These valves should be checked before every dive by removing them from the helmet or mask and blowing smoke against the flow direction to see if smoke can pass through the check valve in the reverse direction (Fig. 2.7). If it can, the valve is no good and must be replaced with a good valve before dive operations can commence. Also required is an exhaust valve and a two-way voice communication system between the diver and the surface. The mask or helmet must ventilate at least 4.5 ACFM (actual cubic feet per minute) at any depth or be able to maintain the partial pressure of carbon dioxide below 0.02 ata (atmospheres of absolute pressure) inside the helmet. (For further discussion refer to Wayne C. Tucker's *Diver's Handbook of Underwater Calculations* in Useful References).

Fig. 2.7. Mask or helmet with all requirements fulfilled. Photo courtesy of Naval Coastal Systems Center, U. S. Navy.

Surface-supplied divers must wear a safety harness with a positive buckling device. The safety harness must have an attachment point for the umbilical lifeline that distributes the pulling force of the umbilical over the diver's body and prevents strain on the mask or helmet. To fasten the umbilical to the safety harness, most commercial divers use a stainless steel snap shackle with a lanyard for a quick release in case it is necessary to ditch the gear (Fig. 2.8).

Diver's Umbilical. This device consists of a breathing gas supply hose, a lifeline, communications wire, and pneumohose. The breathing gas supply hose must have a working pressure at least equal to the working pressure of the breathing gas system. The rated bursting pressure must be at least 4 times the working pressure. Hoses must be tested to 1.5 times the working pressure. When not in use, the open ends of the hose must be taped, capped, or plugged. The connectors for the hoses must be made of corrosion resistant material and have a working pressure at least equal to the working pressure of the system. They must also be resistant to accidental disengagement (Fig. 2.9).

The pneumohose is used to hook up to a pneumofathometer at the surface so that topside can accurately determine and monitor the diver's depth at all times. The pneumoline must be hooked to a gas supply in order to operate the pneumofathometer. The pneumogas supply serves as an auxiliary breathing gas for the diver independent of the main breathing gas system. In an emergency, the diver can use his pneumohose as a secondary breathing gas supply. He can radio topside to turn on his pneumoline and feed the end through the neck dam in his helmet or mask. The pneumohose need not have the same ultimate bursting pressure as the main air supply hose since it is mainly used for gauging the diver's depth. A working pressure of 250 psi (pounds per square inch) is acceptable for the pneumohose. In an emergency, it can take the pressure required to get the diver home.

The communications wire is recommended to be a four-wire, stainless steel braided cable. This type of communications line has sufficient strength to double as a lifeline. However, in some cases, a separate lifeline is recommended.

The lifeline is used for many purposes besides a safety line. It is also a tool and a signaling device. Against a strong tide, the diver has no better friend than his lifeline to pull him in. When working on the bottom, a diver can use the lifeline to send for tools instead of surfacing. The tender can assist the diver climbing up the ladder by keeping a strain on the lifeline thereby removing some of the cumbersome weight of heavy equipment off the diver's legs.

Fig. 2.8.   Safety harness equipped with snap shackle for quick release. Photo by Wayne C. Tucker.

Fig. 2.9.   Breathing gas supply hose. Photo by Wayne C. Tucker.

Before scuba or even the telephone was invented, communication between diver and tender was accomplished by means of line-pulling signals. An experienced tender and diver could communicate effectively by this method and understand each other even where no signals had been established. If the tender knew what the diver's task involved, he would often anticipate the diver's needs without the diver having to signal to him. One positive aspect of working without the phones was that the tender kept a tighter rein on the lifeline and always had the feel of the diver. When line tending a scuba diver, the tender should therefore leave only a foot of slack and remain alert and aware of what the diver is doing.

Lifelines. For purposes of safety, it is sometimes wise to use a lifeline separate from the diver's umbilical. In commercial applications, the lifeline is taped to the diver's air hose which avoids straining the diver's air supply line. In addition to the umbilical, it is sometimes advantageous to use an additional safety line. The separate line can be used to send tools and objects back and forth from the surface to the diver. If the diver wishes to send an object from the bottom to the surface, the tender can tie a square mark onto the separate line so the diver knows exactly how much line to pull down.

When an object is stuck in the mud, or a heavy object needs to be moved, the diver can tie his separate line to the object, and the tender and crew can give him a hand. If the diver's umbilical gets fouled, the separate lifeline can be used to pull the diver to safety after he has severed his umbilical. With the modern equipment, the diver would notify topside, switch his air to the bail out bottle he wears on his back, pull his snap shackle, cut his air hose and communications wire, then ascend on the separate line. With the old hard hat gear, the diver would close his exhaust valve before cutting the air hose, thereby trapping sufficient air within the suit to get himself to the surface.

When using the old hard hat, a separate lifeline was a necessity, because it was impossible to make a free ascent without cutting yourself out of the suit. I was working at the Philadelphia Navy yard during the construction of a drydock in eighty feet of water. The diver on the shift before me had cut nine steel H pilings. As the piles were cut, an inch or so of steel was left uncut to keep the piles upright until removal. I was removing the piles by a wire sling with shackles tied on at six-foot intervals. I fastened the shackles to a hole in the top of each pile. I had shackled all but the last pile which had fallen over. Calling for more slack on the sling, I went down to shackle the last pile. A slight pull on

Fig. 2.10. Double-lock recompression chamber. Photo courtesy of Naval Coastal Systems Center, U. S. Navy.

the cable then caused several of the pilings to fall over against an uncut pile. Unfortunately, my air hose and communications wire were caught between the piles and severed, leaving me without communications or air. The tumbling pilings came to rest just inches above my back as I was leaning over to shackle into the last pile. Fortunately, the separate lifeline was clear and I signaled my tender to raise the load on the crane. My tender knew something was wrong because of the air boiling to the surface from the severed air hose. He signaled the crane operator to pick up the load. I hung onto the pilings until I was sure my lifeline was clear. In this instance, I was fortunate; had my lifeline been taped to my air hose, my lifeline would have been severed and I probably would not have survived.

The umbilical is made up in a bundle and generally taped every two feet. Beginning at the diver's end, it must be marked in ten-foot increments to one hundred feet and in fifty-foot increments thereafter.

Air Supply

The air compressor system used to supply breathing air to a diver must have a volume tank that is built and stamped in accordance with ASME (American Society of Mechanical Engineers) code. There must be a check valve on the inlet side, a pressure gauge, a relief valve, a drain valve, and the tank must be tested after every repair or modification.

The intakes for the compressor must be located away from areas containing exhaust fumes or other hazardous contaminants. The compressor must be lubricated by a mineral or vegetable oil with the same SAE (Society of Automotive Engineers) weight required by the compressor manufacturer so as not to contaminate the diver's air supply with petroleum fumes. The system must also have a filtration system to separate moisture, oil, and contaminants from the diver's air supply. Commercial filtering systems are available through diver's supply shops, but a good homemade filter can be fabricated with pipe fittings for shallow water diving and stuffed with Kotex as a filtering element. A better filtering system can be fabricated from pipe fittings, but requires some airtight welds and drilling and tapping. A good machine shop can make up this system (Fig. 2.11). The first pipe separates moisture and the second pipe is the filter. The filter is stuffed with activated alumina, activated charcoal, or Kotex or any combination of the three. However, for deeper diving, either activated alumina or activated charcoal or a mixture of both is recommended to make up at least fifty percent of the filter.

Air Flasks. For surface-supplied diving, larger air flasks such as the 300-cubic-foot bottles used for industrial air can be charged with breathing air. There are numerous times when these can be used instead of a compressor: in refineries where gasoline engines are not allowed; when the noise from compressors interferes with communications; or when compressors won't start. Air flasks also make a fail-safe backup system for the diver. The air is already compressed and filtered and each bottle is charged to pressure before the dive operation. Compressors can fail for any number of reasons, but a bank system of high pressure air flasks is highly reliable. In addition, scuba bottles can be charged from the bank system.

Tanks should not be stored without some pressure inside to keep moisture out. When corrosion takes place inside a tank, oxygen inside the tank is used to support the corrosion process. The amount of oxygen depleted from a tank used for storing breathing air can be significant, especially when the tank is only partially filled.

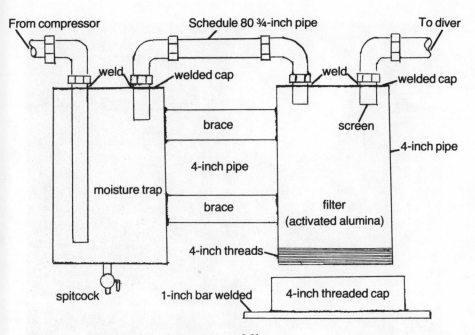

Fig. 2.11.   Homemade moisture trap and filter.

Visual inspection is required annually of scuba tanks to assure there is no corrosion inside the tank. Tanks should be stored in an upright position so that any moisture will settle in the bottom of the tank where the metal is thickest. Tanks which have not been used for extended periods of time should be exhausted, inspected, cleaned, and tumbled if necessary, then recharged.

If tanks are to be transported by airplane, the law requires they be exhausted prior to being loaded. A fully charged tank is a potential rocket or bomb if the valve is accidently broken off.

Manifold system. A means of distributing the primary air and aux-iliary air supply (pneumoline) to each diver and one standby diver must be inserted between the filter and the umbilicals (see Fig. 2.12). The manifold should have pressure gauges for the primary and secondary airlines. In addition, the pneumofathometer calibrated in feet of seawa-ter should be plumbed properly into the auxiliary airline so it may be shut off and purged. Ninety-degree ball valves are recommended for manual shutoffs and should be placed at the inlet of the primary and

Fig. 2.12.   A manifold system.

secondary air supplies and at each outlet to each diver. Finally, check valves should be placed at the umbilical hookups.

All fittings must be corrosion resistant and of sufficient internal diameter to support the air flow required to maintain the diver's demands. Topside can monitor the diver's air supply status and depth with a good manifold system.

Tools for Commercial Diving Jobs

Frequently, a commercial diver will be asked to perform a task requiring special tools which are either unavailable commercially, or too expensive to justify for one job. You may also need an item which will make your job faster or easier. When this occurs, it is usually possible to fabricate a satisfactory tool at a reasonable cost. Also, if the need for the tool arises in the future, you will have it handy and can charge rental fees for it (See Chapter 1).

The Diver's Ladder

Two types of ladders are recommended for commercial diving operations, each with a specific use. The commercial diver may work on one job site for an extended period of time, or he may go from job to job on a daily basis. According to the job, the diver will want either a portable ladder, or one that is built in place for the long job. Figs. 2.13 and 2.14 illustrate the two types of diver's ladders.

The ladder shown in Fig. 2.13 is the most practical type of portable diving ladder. It can be made up in two sections either six feet or eight feet long which are bolted together on the job site. The rings at the top allow the ladder to be tied onto a cleat, bitts, or railings on piers, barges, or anything handy on site. The two struts hold the ladder out at an angle in order to facilitate climbing with heavy gear. Without a standoff on the ladder, it will position itself against whatever it is tied to, often making it impossible to step on the rungs or forcing you to climb against a backward incline.

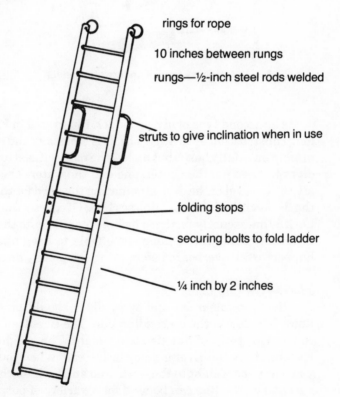

rings for rope

10 inches between rungs

rungs—½-inch steel rods welded

struts to give inclination when in use

folding stops

securing bolts to fold ladder

¼ inch by 2 inches

Fig. 2.13.   A light, sectional, portable diving ladder.

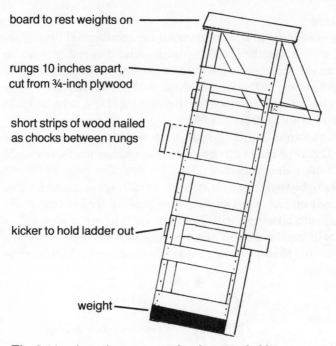

board to rest weights on ⎯⎯⎯⎯⎯⎯⎯⎯

rungs 10 inches apart, ⎯⎯⎯⎯⎯⎯
cut from ¾-inch plywood

short strips of wood nailed
as chocks between rungs

kicker to hold ladder out ⎯⎯⎯⎯

weight ⎯⎯⎯⎯

Fig. 2.14.   A stationary type of underwater ladder.

The second type of diving ladder, illustrated in Fig. 2.14, is used on long construction or salvage jobs. It is too heavy and cumbersome to lug around on a daily basis, but makes the most satisfactory platform for the diver to dress on, then enter, and exit the water. The two top rungs are above the level of the deck eliminating the need for the diver to kneel on the deck while the tender dresses him. Of course the diver should have his lifeline securely fastened before stepping onto the ladder especially if he is wearing any equipment unable to keep him afloat should he happen to fall overboard before being completely dressed.

The Descending Line

Every commercial and sport diver should be familiar with and know how to use the descending line. The line itself is made up from a convenient piece of line tied to a weight. The weight is lowered to the bottom where the diver is going to descend. When you reach the bottom, you carry the weight to the work area and tie it to whatever is handy, if necessary. The line can be used for a variety of purposes, for example, line signals can be relayed to the surface and knots can be tied at certain depths to indicate decompression stops. Your rate of ascent can be judged when surfacing. Currents can be negotiated more easily. When descending or ascending, use a descending line to hang onto. Prior to descending, you can estimate the depth of the water and speed of the tide or current. By slacking off on the descending line, you can search around the weight on the bottom. Also, you can use a clump weight tow to search on the weight near the bottom (See Chapter 3).

Tide Gauge

The tide gauge illustrated in Fig. 2.15 is ideal when working in muddy waters or if you are required to raise the gauge above the water for better visibility. Readings obtained from this gauge will also be more accurate in choppy waters than a conventional gauge.

To set the gauge, let the indicator float freely and set the board (fastened to a piling) to the indicator with an accurate tide reading. The indicator pole will slide through the pipe at the bottom of the board rising and falling with the tide.

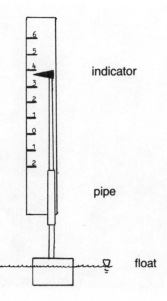

Fig. 2.15.   A tide gauge.

Airlift

An airlift illustrated in Fig. 2.16 is simply a pipe with an air hose stuck in the bottom. There are a variety of methods of fastening the airline to the pipe, depending upon how much time is allowed for fabrication. The principle behind the airlift is: the air entering the bottom of the pipe will naturally want to rise toward the surface. As it does, it will draw water through the bottom of the pipe to accommodate the rising air. The resulting suction can be used to suck mud, silt, sand, or soft concrete from any area the diver wishes to work in. Such a device is useful for excavating soil from a cofferdam in bridge construction, laying pipelines, removing laitance (soft concrete mixed with seawater) when pouring concrete in stages, uncovering objects buried in the mud, and laying submarine cables as well as many other uses.

In many construction applications, the airlift pipe will reach the surface. An elbow usually will be placed at the discharge which will throw the water and mud away from the excavation area. The deeper the water, the greater the suction is at the bottom of the pipe. Consequently a larger compressor is needed as the depth increases (for further discussion refer to Edward M. Brady's *Marine Salvage Operations* in Useful References).

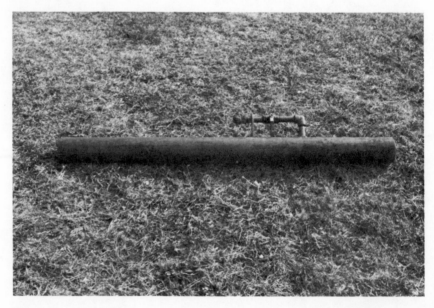

Fig. 2.16.   An airlift.

The airlift used in conjunction with a water jet will provide the maximum efficiency for the diver when excavating. The diver with a water jet can blow mud or sand to be excavated directly toward the airlift thus avoiding the situation in which the airlift simply digs a series of "post holes."

If the diver ties a line to the airlift, he can work out from the lift in any direction with the jet and direct the flow of mud or sand to the lift. A continuous flow of material is then directed to the lift allowing a large volume of material to be moved as fast as the lift will take it.

The airlift shown in Fig. 2.17 is easily fabricated for a job of short duration. The air hose is tied to the pipe and fittings at the bottom allow the air to escape into the pipe.

Fig. 2.18 shows a permanent airline welded to the airlift pipe. A hole is burned in the side of the pipe about a foot from the bottom, and an

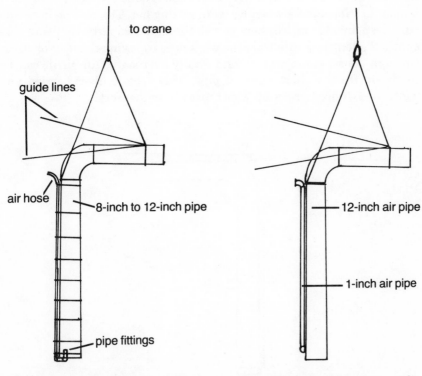

Fig. 2.17. An airlift fabricated for a job of short duration.

Fig. 2.18. A permanent airline welded to an airlift pipe.

elbow is welded to the pipe allowing air to enter the pipe. Guiding lines are tied to the airlift pipe to direct the flow of material discharged from the pipe. The topside crew accomplishes this by pulling on the lines.

A heavy-duty airlift is illustrated in Fig. 2.19. It is used to break up the bottom by repeatedly dropping and lifting it with the crane. Pipe fittings as shown on airlifts in Figs. 2.17 and 2.18 would break off. The air chamber at the bottom is a larger pipe welded over the airlift pipe which surrounds a series of small holes burned through the airlift pipe all around. This allows air to enter the pipe from all sides creating a more efficient airlift.

The air supply line is a two-inch pipe with a fitting for a two-inch air hose. An angle iron is welded to the top of the pipe to fasten the slings used to raise and lower it. Holes are burned in the bracket where two slings will hang the pipe level.

Airlifts do not have to be fabricated from pipes. For special applications, they can be made from a suction hose of any diameter. The suction hose can be bent to get into tight areas and around corners. I used them inside the *Normandie* when we were raising her. The suction hose was run deep inside the sunken vessel through compartments and discharged a long distance from the work area by laying the hose on deck, through doors, passageways, and finally overboard. An airlift can be made up from a short piece of pipe. This type is diver carried and controlled. It discharges a few feet away from the work.

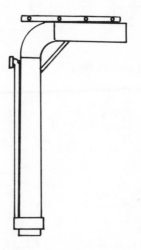

Fig. 2.19.   A heavy duty airlift.

Caution should be exercised when starting the large airlift. It begins with a kick. I usually climb up the airlift a few feet until it settles down.

The Jetting Nozzle

The choice of a jetting nozzle used for a particular job depends upon the type of work and the amount and density of the material to be moved. The nozzles used are: the back pressure type, where the force of the jet is balanced by the back pressure; the straight nozzle, in which weights help keep the nozzle from pushing the diver all over the bottom; and a two-way swivel nozzle which can be made up from pipe fittings, where the two nozzles are opposed, providing a balanced force under the diver's control.

The back pressure nozzle illustrated in Fig. 2.20 can be purchased at a diver's supply store. It is a good choice where the pump pressure is high, because the back pressure overbalances the forward pressure making it possible for the diver to handle the nozzle without getting thrown backwards. It is excellent for tunneling also because the back pressure tends to give the nozzle a light forward thrust causing it to bury itself if not restrained.

The straight nozzle is used when there is not much water pressure from the pump (Fig. 2.21). When used in conjunction with the airlift, the

2½-inch hose   balancing jets

trenching jet

pressure from pump up to 200 pounds per square inch

Fig. 2.20.   The back pressure nozzle.

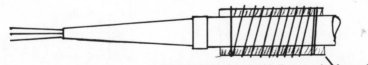

pieces of steel tied with line or wire for weight

Fig. 2.21.   The straight nozzle.

diver can hang onto a line from the airlift and direct a strong flow of water along the line to the lift. The straight nozzle will move dense stiff soil in greater volumes than the back pressure nozzle, the main drawback being the tendency for the straight nozzle to push the diver backwards. If the pump pressure gets too strong, the diver will have to hang onto something or switch to the back pressure nozzle, or the two-way swivel nozzle.

The two-way swivel nozzle is illustrated in Fig. 2.22. This type of nozzle is made up from pipe fittings by the diver. The nozzle can spin in any direction by leaving the fitting loose between the 2-inch elbow and the 2-inch tee. The pipe is reduced to a ¾-inch nipple on each end as a nozzle.

The two-way swivel nozzle will take all the pressure a pump can put out and can be left on the bottom unattended. Unlike the back pressure nozzle or the straight nozzle, the two-way nozzle is perfectly balanced. The back pressure nozzle unattended will bury itself and the straight nozzle will fly off in any direction. The two-way nozzle is excellent for cleaning inside cofferdams where H piles have been driven. The flow can be maneuvered up and down the piles to clean them. Along sheet piling it can be directed up with one nozzle and down with the other. When used for trenching, the diver does not have to bend a stiff hose to direct the flow up and out of the trench.

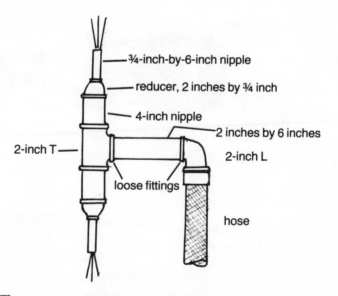

Fig. 2.22.   The two-way or 90-degree swivel nozzle.

Air Tools

In cold weather, a common problem with air supply is moisture freezing in the air hose and blocking the air flow. This seems to be due more to the humidity of the air supply than the temperature of the outside air. With a relatively dry air supply, it is possible to dive in subzero weather with no problem. However, a high moisture content in the air supply will surely cause problems even when the temperature is barely at freezing. The diver's helmet is likely to encounter problems with ice at the control valve because it is metal, and the valve opening is smaller than the opening in the air hose. When the air starts to freeze, the diver opens his supply valve to allow any particles of ice to pass through into the helmet. The exhaust or chin button must then be adjusted to account for the heavier air flow. Any metal hose fittings will also be a likely spot for ice to form. Metal conducts the cold more rapidly than the hose and therefore causes ice particles to form more rapidly.

Underwater Chain Saw. A sharp chain saw which can be driven by either pneumatic or hydraulic power will greatly speed the diver's work. The size of the chips the saw makes is an easy way to judge how sharp the saw is. The chips should be about the size of the teeth on the chain. If the chips are small or powdery, the saw is dull. Also, when the saw is cutting well, light pressure is all that is required to operate it. If the saw must be forced, or if the saw cuts to one side, the chain is dull, or the guide bar is worn, or both.

When sharpening the saw, you must have gloves, the proper size, a round file, a flat file, and a gauge for the idlers. The idlers are the dull teeth which set the depth of the cut and are filed to the proper size with the flat file and gauge.

When sharpening the teeth with the round file, first tighten the chain as much as it will go and still allow movement. Next mark the starting point so it can be determined when all the teeth have been filed. File in one direction only, using smooth and even forward strokes. If the file is dragged backwards, it will become dull before sharpening is completed. Use the same number of strokes on each tooth unless a tooth is damaged. In the case of a damaged tooth, file that tooth until it is sharp, then file the tooth directly opposite with the same number of strokes so the saw cuts the same on both sides. After the teeth have been sharpened, place the gauge over the idlers. If the idlers protrude above the gauge, file them down with the flat file.

Fig. 2.25 illustrates a cross section of the guide bar groove in various conditions. Check the tip and rails of the bar for wear. If the inside groove of the guide bar rail is worn, replace the guide bar.

Fig. 2.23.   U. S. Navy Mark XII divers with underwater circular saw. Photo courtesy of Naval Coastal Systems Center, U. S. Navy.

Fig. 2.24.   Drilling steel underwater. Photo courtesy of Naval Coastal Systems Center, U. S. Navy.

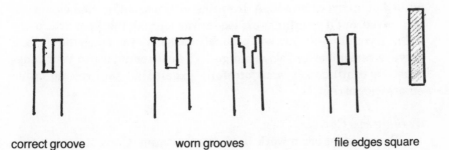

correct groove   worn grooves   file edges square

Fig. 2.25.   A cross section of the guide bar grooves. Check the tip of the guide bar often for wear. If the inside groove of the guide bar rail is worn, replace the guide bar.

Occasionally check the underside of the teeth on the blade for damage which could be causing undue wear on the guide bar. The wear is often due to lack of proper chain tension. At proper tension, the bottom of the chain is level with the guide bar.

There is an oiler on the underwater chain saw which must be filled with air tool oil to lubricate the chain during use. In addition, there is an air tool oiler which should be connected near the compressor and filled with oil. This will help the saw motor to operate smoothly. It is good practice to sprinkle oil on the chain each time it is brought to the surface, and run the saw for a few seconds to oil the blade and guide bar. At the end of the day, or when storing the saw, run kerosene or diesel fuel through the saw and the motor to insure that the saw will not rust.

Methods for Commercial Divers

Emergency Ascent

I worked with a man who was a "sand hog"* during the construction of the Holland Tunnel in New York. He was in the tunnel when they had a blowout in the roof. The man was sucked up with the escaping air underwater and rose to the surface in the air bubbles. He suffered no ill effects from the incident. During World War II, there were survivors from sunken submarines who reached the surface safely with nothing but a life jacket on.

If men have escaped from sunken submarines and have been blown out of tunnels, a diver who runs out of air should be able to reach the surface safely if he does not panic. The real danger from loss of air supply is not suffocation or drowning, it is panic which causes you to ascend while holding your breath. A drowning victim or suffocation victim can be revived, but if your lungs explode or you force air into your arteries by holding your breath, you will probably die before you reach the surface. Always remember to "blow and go." The expanding air in your lungs must be continuously and forcefully exhaled all the way up on an emergency ascent.

Working in a Current

Divers must often work in a strong current. Currents present an exhausting and potentially dangerous situation. I was working in nine-

---

* A "sand hog" was a name given to a man who in the 1930s and 1940s worked in a compressed air chamber in tunnels under river beds. Sand hogs were paid according to the depth of the underwater operation.

ty feet of water in the Potomac River in 1940 during the construction of the Potomac River Bridge. I was sent down to remove wooden pile cutoffs after they had been severed by a circular saw rigged up in pile driver leads. The pile cutoffs had to be removed from the bottom so a template could be set on the bottom and steel H piles driven through the holes in the template. If the pile butts were not removed, they would interfere with driving the H piles.

The crew had lowered a steel rail near the bottom as shown in Fig. 2.26. I was told to go along the rail and sweep to make sure there were no

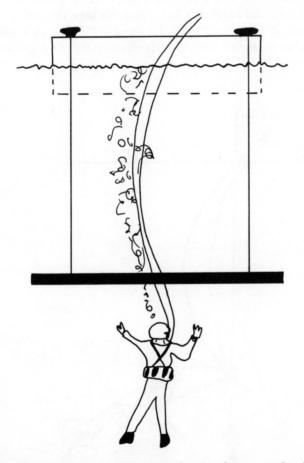

Fig. 2.26.   Diver working in a current showing heavy steel rail suspended under barge close to bottom. Diver ducks under the rail, allowing his air hose and lifeline to drag on the rail, keeping him from being washed off the bottom by the flow of the tide and the pull of his lines.

pile butts in the area. As I hit bottom, I encountered a strong current which made it impossible to let go of the rail. At best, all I could do was hang on. Then, I ducked under the rail leaving my air hose and lifeline beneath the rail which eliminated the drag on me and enabled me to locate and pick up over sixty pile cutoffs.

Fig. 2.27 shows another method of working in a strong current. Tie your air hose and lifeline with a ring above a headache ball. The ball is lowered by a crane. The ring loop can slide up or down the cable and therefore eliminates the drag on your lines. You are free to use both hands to work with.

When there is only a slow tide or slack water, a short line is tied to the cable above the headache ball. You can take the line in hand and work or search on orders from the foreman. Using this method, the search can be conducted from topside eliminating the possibility of your getting lost.

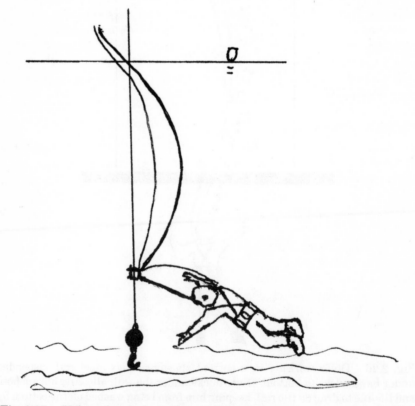

Fig. 2.27.   Using a headache ball to work in a current.

Other methods include lowering a set of pile driver leads with plywood secured to create a lee behind which you can work. Also, a clamshell dropped in the water ahead of the work area can create a lee. These methods work if the water is not too deep and the current is not too strong.

Making Underwater Measurements

By knowing the width and length of your hammer and diving knife, you have two measuring devices with you at all times. By cutting notches in the handle of the hammer one inch apart, many small objects can be measured to a fair degree of accuracy. If you know the measurement of one finger, two fingers, three fingers, and so on, the width of your hand with fingers spread, the distance from the tip of your fingers to the elbow, and to the middle of your chest, and with arms spread apart, you can give measurements without a rule in dark, muddy waters.

Where very accurate measurements are required, other methods can be used including a nail through a line, notches on a stick, a rule, or nails through a stick. Try to avoid visual estimates of distance and size underwater. The magnification effect of underwater vision through the air-water interface created by your helmet or mask makes objects appear larger and closer than they actually are. The magnification factor underwater makes everything appear about thirty-three percent larger than it actually is.

Using the Shackle Pin

Construction diving often requires you to shackle into something underwater. A shackle pin can come unscrewed as the line or cable moves about from tides, waves, or current. To avoid having a shackle pin unscrew, you can pass a piece of wire through the hole in the pin and take a turn around the shackle. If the shackle is to be used in a lift immediately, it may not be necessary to wire the shackle, just tighten it with a wrench; but if the shackle is to be used on a system that will remain in the water for any length of time, or if the load will be subject to working, you will have to wire the shackle pin.

You may frequently be called to renew mooring systems or work on special buoys which are not removed for maintenance. Note that the shackle pin in any mooring system must be wired or it will be worked loose over time especially during heavy seas.

Some yachtsmen use stainless steel wire for the shackle pins on their moorings. I have found that a number 12 solid copper insulated wire (household wiring type) with the insulation left on works better than anything else and is easiest to install and remove.

Driving Nails Underwater

The four-pound diver's hammer is used to drive nails underwater. To start a nail, hold it between your thumb and forefinger with the forefinger pointing down the nail. If you miss the nail, your fingers will be pushed out of the way instead of being struck between the solid surface and the hammer.

Fig. 2.28 illustrates the proper way to hold and drive the nail. To finish driving the nail even with no visibility, place your finger tip on the side of the nail to locate it for each hammer stroke. With practice, the hammer will strike the nail and the finger can be retracted slightly with each hammer blow. To drive a large number of nails, it is best to use a small air hammer.

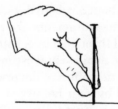

wrong way   right way   finishing

Fig. 2.28.   Driving nails underwater.

CHAPTER THREE

Search and Recovery Methods

ONE JOB frequently available for a diver is to recover overboard items and there are numerous methods of searching for them. Each method has a particular application. I have located and retrieved many lost objects underwater, including diamond rings, false teeth, toupees, outboard motors, and other unusual objects. When a small object is lost overboard, the owner can often indicate the location with reasonable accuracy. Where this is likely, you should drop a weighted line on the spot with a short search line attached (Fig. 3.1). Upon reaching the bottom, first pick up the weight and search beneath it by grabbing handfuls of mud or sand and carefully feeling for the object. Unless the visibility is very good, it is difficult to see a small object; therefore you must rely upon your sense of feel. After searching beneath the weight, use the search line to make ever larger circles around the marker weight. Where there is mud, take care to grab every inch of mud and feel each handful carefully. With patience, you can usually locate the object.

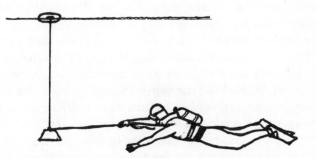

Fig. 3.1. Using a weighted line to search around and under a designated location.

Screen Search

If very small objects, such as keys or a diamond ring, are dropped in a known area (from a dock, for example), a screen and shovel can be used to sift through the area carefully. The best method is to mark off a sector to be searched with a weighted line, then sift through the entire area carefully. If the object is not found, move the weighted line so it partially overlaps the last area searched. Continue in this way until the object is found.

Grappling Lines

I was careless one time when I jumped onto the dock with some of my scuba gear and one of my regulators fell overboard. I had just finished a diving job, so I did not feel like dressing out again to go after the regulator. I had a grappling hook with me, and I decided to give it a try before I jumped into the water again. None of the dock workers thought I had a chance of picking up my regulator that way, but I was undaunted by their skepticism and with patient effort, I had my regulator back in hand. I actually retrieved the regulator in less time than it would have taken me to dress out again. Instead of looking like a bonehead diver, dropping my gear overboard, I impressed everyone by getting it right back without even going into the water!

Whenever I go on a search job now, I always bring along a grappling line. Often the object is something that can be retrieved or located that way. Methods of grappling are illustrated in Fig. 3.2. The sounding line, discussed below, is also handy as is a magnet for locating metal objects.

While working one day, the engineer of a Rhode Island sewage treatment plant lost a surveying rod in one of the holding tanks of raw sewage. He could not think of a way to get the rod out, and the sewage could not be processed because the metal rod in the tank would damage the machinery. Two days before I was going to be married, the engineer called to offer me the job of making a dive into the tank to retrieve the surveying rod. While I did not relish the thought of being quarantined on my honeymoon, I never like to turn down a diving job so I told him I would be over to take a look. On my way, I stopped off at a friend's house and borrowed a big magnet. I managed to avoid having to dive into the raw sewage tank by retrieving the rod with a magnet and line from the surface. Sometimes a little common sense will keep a diver out of raw sewage!

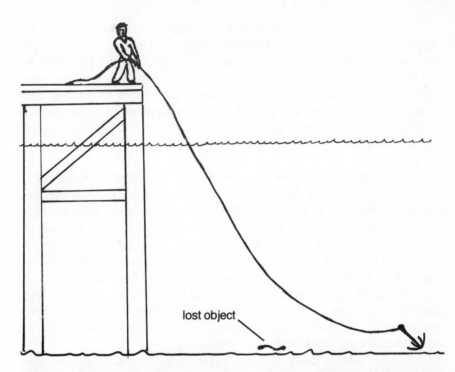

lost object

Fig. 3.2.   A grapnel as shown here can often be a handy tool to retrieve a lost object without the use of a diver. Or, a diver can save time by retrieving an object without having to dive. There are many times when such items as a chain saw, air drill, impact wrench, or other tools used on construction jobs, as well as an outboard motor, are dropped overboard accidentally. The grapnel will be useful to hook these objects, or, at least, to locate them. If the water is only ten to twenty feet deep, a competent swimmer can dive without gear to attach the line after the grapnel has located the object.

Weighted Line

Every search must be conducted methodically and carefully. If you simply jump overboard and swim around, your search will be spotty and often will end up in the wrong area. Distances over water can be very deceiving. When something like an outboard motor is lost, the owner will seldom have the presence of mind to take range sightings on shore so that he can put you near where the motor was lost. Often, the diver will be sent down hundreds of feet off target. In such a situation, you must change your method of searching to cover a large area.

First, drop a marker buoy (Fig. 3.3) where the owner claims the object was lost. Next, begin the search with a 200-foot line weighted on each end, with the line to the surface attached to a float. The 200-foot weighted line is dropped 50 feet to one side of the marker buoy and centered on the marker. Descend to the search area with another line fastened to an inner tube or float. The inner tube marks your location as a warning to other boats which may be in the vicinity. When the object of the search is located, tie the line from the inner tube to the object and surface.

If there is a current, start your search at the upstream weight on the 200-foot line and drift downstream searching on both sides of the line until the other weight is reached. At this point, be sure to pull any slack in the line tight, and then move the weight five feet toward the marker buoy in the center of the search area. Search, working back to the first weight on the tightened line. Then move the first weight 5 feet toward the marker buoy. The process is repeated until the object is found.

By beginning the search to one side of the lost object, and working towards it, you eliminate the possibility of starting just past the object and searching in the wrong direction. It is best to work into the area in order to make certain the object is not missed.

This method is also useful for making sure an area is cleared. For example, if a pier collapses, you must cover a large area to make sure all debris has been removed. When pilings are cut, you must survey the area to clear all the pile butts. Using scuba and flippers, you can pull yourself along the line to cover a large area in a short period of time.

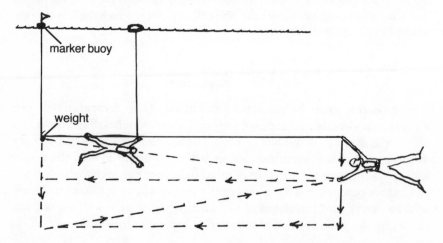

Fig. 3.3.   Diver moves line five feet on each sweep, keeping line tight on each move.

Running Jackstay

Another method of searching a large area is with the running jackstay (Fig. 3.4). Four weights are dropped with floats to mark the four corners of the search area. Lines at the opposite ends of the search area are strung between the weights. Each of the end lines is used to move a weighted line in the search area. Two divers can be used, one on each side of the weighted line. The buoys can be left in place to mark the area searched if the object is not found. New marks are then dropped on one of the four sides of the last area searched and the search can continue to expand this way until the object is found.

The running jackstay is also an excellent method for surveying the bottom. Occasionally a boat yard or marina will require a harbor survey

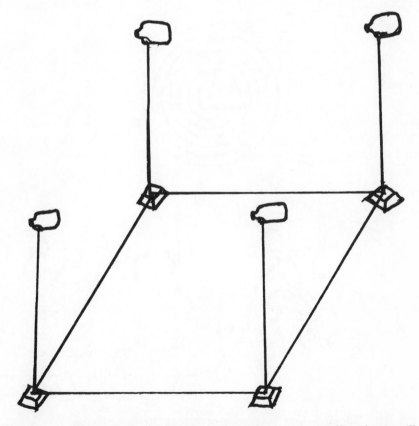

Fig. 3.4. A running jackstay. The floats shown here are one-gallon plastic milk containers. Anything that floats can be used, such as a life jacket, a plastic inner tube used in swimming pools, or a five-gallon gasoline can.

to locate and identify all objects and describe bottom characteristics in their location. The boundaries and search lines can be marked to form a gridlike network which will accurately locate anything you wish to identify in your survey. Ranges on your marker buoys can be taken from shore by a land surveyor. Depth soundings can be taken by a cane pole or with electronic chart recorders. After all information is gathered and recorded, a drawing can be made up supplemented with surface and underwater photographs of important features. You should also include a written report of the complete findings.

Circle Search

The circle search (Fig. 3.5) is my favorite all-purpose method of searching. It can be used with one diver or with many divers. The circle search

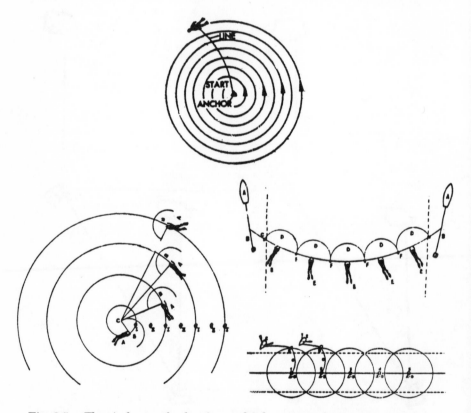

Fig. 3.5.   The circle search, showing multiple patterns for its use.

is conducted by dropping a weight with a buoy where the search is to begin. A search line is fastened to the weight at the bottom and you search around the weight in ever-widening circles, groveling in the mud with both hands around and around the weight overlapping areas already searched each time around. When you reach the end of the search line, the center mark is moved but the next circle must overlap the first.

I once located a lost sailboat mooring for a woman who said she knew exactly where it was and all I would have to do was to jump in the water and tie a line to the chain. I was experienced enough to know better, so I came prepared to conduct a circle search. I went down for a quick look where the woman *said* the mooring was, but I wasn't lucky. I then dropped a weight at the spot and began a circle search. Four hours later, one hundred yards from where I began searching, I found the lost mooring. I also found some diving gear which the diver she previously hired had lost when he was unable to find the mooring. I have never been unsuccessful when hired to retrieve a lost object. Perseverance and the right method have always paid off.

Planing Board and Clump Tow Search

In clear waters where a large area has to be covered, you can be towed underwater by a boat. For the best visibility, use the planing board (Fig. 3.6) towed in midwater which will allow you to go up and down to look over a large area from above, then descend for a closer look. You should be towed at about the speed you would normally swim.

The clump tow search (Fig. 3.7) tows the diver by a weight on the bottom. Again, good visibility is required, but the boat with the clump weight may tow a little faster, up to five knots

Locating Lost Objects in Strong Currents

An object dropped overboard in a current will land some distance from where it entered the water (See Working in a Current in Chapter 2.). In order to determine the location of an object on the bottom, you must know what direction and how strong the tide was at the time the object entered the water. If the current was due to tidal flow, the date and time of day will determine what the tide was when the object was lost. To locate the object, estimate the speed and direction of the tide at the time the object fell overboard. Then estimate how far the object might have

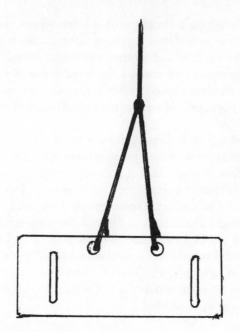

Fig. 3.6.   The planing board and its use.

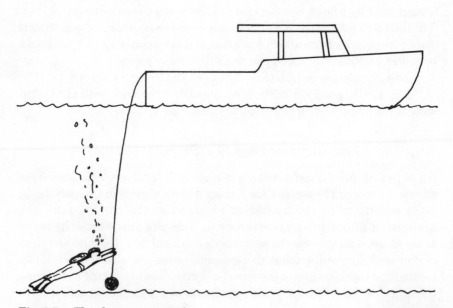

Fig. 3.7.   The clump tow search.

drifted in the tide. Drop a shot line at the spot determined and begin searching.

Just how far an object drifts with the current depends on the strength of the current, the depth of the water, and the density and shape of the object. A piece of thin aluminum plate might drift some distance in a current whereas a large lead ball will almost always go straight down. If the lost object was small and light, and if the water is deep with a strong current, then an object of the same size and weight should be dropped with a thin fishing line attached (light line reduces the drag which would push the object farther). When the test object reaches the bottom, a heavy weight and line is dropped to mark the search area which should be very close to the lost object. To be certain the tide is close to the same, add one hour to the time the object was lost for every day passed before beginning the search. (There is approximately one hour's difference in the tide each day.)

Finding and Retrieving a Lost Anchor Chain

Unless the location of the lost chain is fairly certain, I recommend the use of a special grapnel made up to the size of the lost anchor chain. Diving for a lost chain can be a waste of time if the diver is not fairly close to the area where the chain was lost. However, grappling for the chain can cover large areas in a short time.

The grapnel is made up from steel plates (Fig. 3.8). The plates are cut to form four hooks as shown. The hooks are welded to a piece of stock

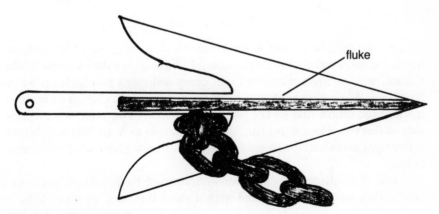

Fig. 3.8.   The grapnel.

with a hole cut for shackling. The hooks must be designed for the size links on the lost chain so that the chain will be caught in the flukes of the hook.

When towing the hook, the points of the flukes must be kept pointing down into the mud. A heavy weight is attached to the towing cable a short distance in front of the grapnel hook in order to keep the cable close to the bottom and allow the hook to point down. A small boat or tug can sweep the area and locate the chain. You can descend and follow the chain to one end where you fasten a cable. The crew topside can then raise the chain through the hawse pipe and on deck in the normal manner.

Searching with a Sounding Line

To locate a large object in flowing waters, you can use a sounding lead from a small boat. The boat is allowed to drift with the tide as soundings are taken allowing the sounding line to remain straight up and down over the sounding lead. When the lead strikes metal, wood, or some object, you will feel it through the sounding line. Depth soundings are achieved at the same time. Accurate soundings are not obtained from an anchored boat in a running tide because the current drag on the sounding line lifts the weight off the bottom.

When sounding, use a heavy weighted line with a marker buoy to mark the spot when the object is located. You can also use the heavy weighted line as a descending line. In order to locate the heavy line accurately, take sightings with the sounding line. The heavy line is then sounded until it strikes the object.

River Diving

When searching in a river, start downstream as far as possible. Look for bends in the river where the object might have been caught. Search into the current because a current will carry sediment you kick up away from you. Work toward the place where the object was lost. You can use a weighted trunk line on the banks of the river. Two men, one on each side of the river, can move the line for the diver to work side to side and move upstream with each pass. The trunk line is also useful in narrow lakes.

Fig. 3.10 illustrates another system used to search in river currents. Two weights are bridled with a short line, and an inner tube is

Fig. 3.9. Ice divers. Photo courtesy of Naval Coastal Systems Center, U. Navy.

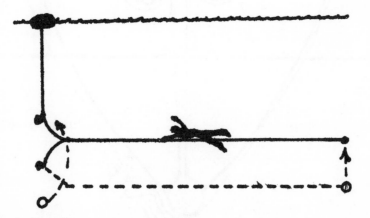

Fig. 3.10. Searching in a river current.

tied from the surface to one of the weights. A trailing line from the short line is allowed to drift downstream. You can move one weight at a time across the current and make a search along the trailing line. You can drift downstream with the current and pull yourself back against the current on the line.

A weight or knot secured at the end of the trailing line warns you that the end of the line is near. Without the weight, you can let the current sweep you from side to side as you slip down the line with the current.

Hogging Line Search

For surveying ship bottoms or for locating damaged areas, a hogging line (see Fig. 3.11) is passed under the ship. You move back and forth on the hogging line, and the topside crew moves the line forward or aft with each pass. In this way, you can relay information topside, and locations of damage or specific thru-hull fittings can be mapped by the crew. You

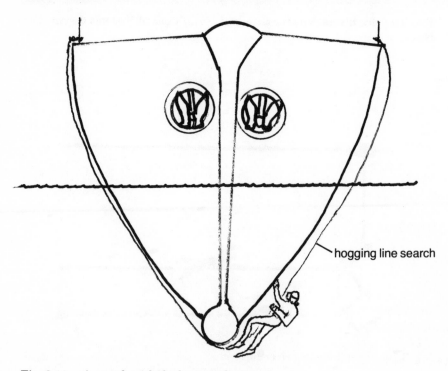

hogging line search

Fig. 3.11.   A search with the hogging line.

Fig. 3.12.   Divers making a hookup. Photo courtesy of Naval Coastal Systems Center, U. S. Navy.

can also work on specific areas or move back and forth with magnets (see also Chapter 4).

Body Search

One of the less appealing jobs of a commercial diver is seaching for a body. If the body was lost in moving water, one method used is to let a neutral weighted diver be carried by the current from the last known position of the body. Other methods of locating a body include those mentioned above.

Other Methods

Compass searches and metal detectors are used with limited success for special applications. In general they are not very effective because of extraneous metal objects already lying around which throw off the readings. Furthermore, the diver is looking at his compass or metal detector and may swim right by the object he is looking for.

CHAPTER FOUR

Making Ship Repairs

DIVERS ARE often called to work under the hull of a ship. In some cases, the ship's hull may be resting on, or near, the bottom. In many cases, however, the diver must find a way to work in midwater by attaching himself to the work area or by neutralizing his buoyancy. The methods used for working on the hull of a ship are discussed in this chapter along with specific procedures for making repairs.

Use of Magnets

Magnets are an essential part of the diver's equipment for ship work. When called to work on a steel ship, you should bring two thirty-five- to fifty-pound magnets. The magnets should have handles (Fig. 4.1) with a six-foot line tied between them and another line which runs to the surface. By taking two magnets down, one for each hand, it is possible to walk the magnets by hand in order to move under the ship. If it is necessary to surface, you can follow the line from the magnets to the surface. When there is no visibility, you can follow the line back to the magnets and continue working where you left off. Also, since you can readily become disoriented under the hull of a large vessel, it is safer to have a line going directly to the surface so that no time is wasted determining the surface direction in an emergency.

When working in scuba gear under a ship, you should wear a lifeline. You can easily get lost under a large ship and not know where the side of it is. Establish signals with the tender before going down. If the scuba tank has a J valve for the air reserve, check it periodically to make sure it has not hit the bottom of the hull and put the tank on reserve. Better still, use a pressure gauge on the air regulator which can be monitored continuously instead of relying on the reserve valve.

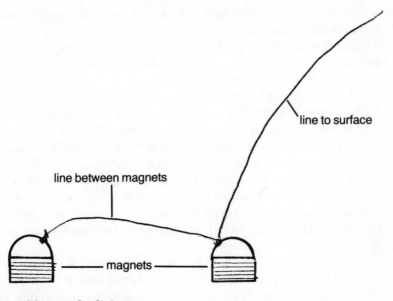

line to surface

line between magnets

magnets

Fig. 4.1. Magnets for diving use.

The Collision Mat

The collision mat is a large section of canvas which can be pulled under a ship to cover the damaged area. By attaching a line to each corner of the mat, the patch can be pulled underneath the ship to the damaged area. With the patch in place, the pumps may be started. The suction will pull the patch securely over the hole, and the leak will be slowed. In an emergency, a collision mat can be anything that is handy—a mattress, raincoat, boards, plywood, life jackets, etc. Anything larger than the hole that will be sucked against the ship can be used to slow or stop the leak. A collision mat can be used as an emergency patch to stop a leak. It can also be used as a temporary patch to raise a wreck.

In the summer of 1973, a drunken captain ran a brand-new sixty-foot Chris Craft aground on the rocks at high tide in Narragansett beach, Rhode Island. We had to pull the ship off the rocks and tow it to a marine railway for repairs. Since damage to the hull was enough to sink her in deep water, we had plenty of big pumps going when we pulled her off. As we began towing, however, it became apparent that the pumps were not going to be able to keep the craft afloat. I stationed four men with lines on a large canvas on each side of the ship, then I jumped in the water with scuba gear and pulled the canvas underwater over the damaged area. The topside crew tied off the canvas, and the pumps began to gain on the water rising in the bilge. We would have lost that ship if we did not use the collision mat.

I was diving on the Potomac River Bridge near La Plata, Maryland, in the winter of 1940. The wooden pile driver barge sprang a leak about 11 P.M. when it struck the top of a steel piling. In no time, I donned my helmet and weights and was overboard with a piece of plywood which I shoved towards the hole to slow the leak. With rags, I stuffed the small leaks and slowed the influx of water enough for the crew to build a wooden box around the hole from the inside of the rig. The box confined the rising water to its interior instead of allowing the leak to run inside the barge. The pumps were then able to control the leakage inside the rig.

The box around the hole had no top. In effect, it was a well which allowed the water to rise inside the box to the level of the waterline on the outside of the rig. Spud wells serve the same purpose. A pipe sleeve is run from the deck through the bottom of the rig. The water can then only rise inside the well to the level of the waterline on the outside of the rig. Spuds can then be run through the deck onto the bottom of the ocean to hold the barge in place.

A steel barge sitting on the bottom of the sea can be difficult to patch if the hole is also on the bottom. Your best approach is to place a pipe which has been cut to the contour of the inside of the hull over the hole. You can weld the pipe to the bottom underwater (see Chapter 7). And you can weld a cap to the top of the pipe thereby containing the leak inside the pipe. After the water is pumped out, you can do a better weld around the pipe or weld a larger pipe over the first one.

The Tooker Patch

During World War II, the *Normandie,* the largest ship in the world at that time, rolled over in New York Harbor. In order to close all the portholes that were facing the bottom, Captain Tooker, who was in charge of the project to raise the ship, designed what has been since known as the Tooker patch, essentially, another method of patching a hole in a ship or barge from the inside (Fig. 4.2). The patch is made to fold in half, allowing it to be passed through the hole. The two halves are unfolded, and the patch pulled against the hole from the outside. A toggle is then put on the bolt followed by the nut which is tightened to secure the patch.

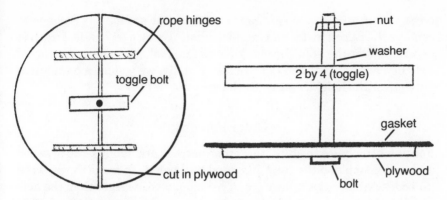

Fig. 4.2.   The Tooker patch.

AUG. 4. All pumps were working full blast on the Normandie (U. S. S. Lafayette) at 5:30 P. M. Wednesday. Two-inch cables, operated from winches ashore, kept the ship's hull in place under control as it began to clear the bottom . . .

Fig. 4.3.   With all pumps working full blast and with two-inch cables steadying the hull, the *Normandie* began to clear the bottom.

I was called to raise a steel barge that had sunk in shallow water. The decks of the barge were awash at high tide and above water at low tide. The damage to the barge was a hole punched through the bottom about three inches by eight inches. The puncture left raised metal around the hole, and the hole was against the bottom of the ocean. Working from inside the sunken barge underwater, I used an oxy-arc torch to cut a hole fourteen inches in diameter around the damage to remove the raised metal and round the hole. Using a jet nozzle, I washed an area under the hole big enough to pass a Tooker patch, then pumped out the barge at low tide to raise her. Finally, we welded a permanent patch over the hole to restore the barge.

Other Patches

For patching holes in ships, two other patches are handy—the plywood and cork patch and the steel and wood hull patch. To make the plywood and cork patch, cut a square out of ¾-inch plywood larger than the hole and a piece of cork or rubber the same size as the plywood. Use roofing nails to fasten the cork (⅛-inch thick) to the plywood. Next drill a ¾-inch hole in the center of the plywood. Use a ¾-inch threaded rod 4 feet long and put a nut and washer on each side of the patch. Pour tar over the nuts on each side. To install the patch, use a strong back on the inside of the hull made from ¼-inch steel channel with a hole drilled to match the threaded rod and fasten with a nut and washer.

The steel and wood hull patch is made from 1-inch exterior plywood. The hole is measured and marked on the plywood topside. A doughnut of caulking and canvas is made up to fit around the outside of the hole and holes are drilled in the plywood to accommodate L-bolts which fit inside the hole and are tightened snug against the doughnut.

Restoring an Old Barge

Old barges rusted through in spots can often be purchased at a nominal cost. You can restore such a barge and put it back into service for several more years by pouring concrete over the bottom from the inside. First you must thoroughly clean the bottom with a chipping hammer and wire brush to insure proper bonding of concrete to steel. Then lay a wire mesh across the bottom and up the sides for one to two feet to reinforce the concrete. Finally, three to four inches of concrete are poured over the entire bottom inside the barge.

To facilitate pouring the concrete evenly over the entire inside surface, cut holes through the deck in several places. Concrete is then distributed more evenly across the bottom. After pouring the concrete, weld the deck holes closed.

Many barges have a tendency to rust through at the waterline. A hole in the side of the barge can be patched by using a quick setting cement such as Water Plug or Speedcrete. Prior to patching, clean the

Fig. 4.4. Coauthor John Malatich (second row, second from left) with three diving companions and workmen while preparing to raise the Russian ship *Illitch*, in Portland, Oregon, November, 1943.

Fig. 4.5. Diver cleaning a propellor with underwater pneumatic brush. Photo courtesy of Naval Coastal Systems Center, U. S. Navy.

Fig. 4.6.   A salvage project at the U. S. Navy diver training facility. Ship is submerged then refloated. Photo courtesy of Naval Coastal Systems Center, U. S. Navy.

area around the hole thoroughly with a chipping hammer and wire brush. You need two men to complete the patch: one on the inside of the barge and one on the outside. Each man presses the quick setting cement from his side and the two parts are bonded together.

Minor repairs can be made on a ship or barge in the water by using the system shown in Fig. 4.7. You build a wooden box with a suction hose attached to the bottom and an air vent on the top. Where the box makes contact with the ship, use a softener made of rubber or cork to make a watertight seal. By using line from the surface, you can pull the box into place over the hole or damaged area underwater. You can do the final positioning after you have thoroughly cleaned the area of any growth which could prevent the box from sealing or cause it to slide. After positioning the box, you can tack angle plates to the hull and make the box more secure.

When the box is pumped out, it will have significant buoyancy which will press the seal tightly against the hull. The vent is necessary to allow air into the box as the water is pumped out; otherwise a vacuum

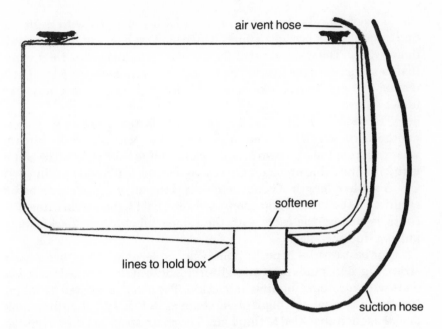

Fig. 4.7.   Making repairs from inside the ship.

is created inside the box. When the pump stops drawing water, a seal is made by water pressure and the hull may be burned or welded in the dry to make necessary repairs. By continuing to run the pump, welding and burning gasses can by exhausted to keep the air clear. You can use this method for installing intakes, discharges, and other thru-hull fittings as well as leaks or damage.

Methods of Removing a Line or Cable from a Propellor

Any ship which fouls its propellor with a piece of line or cable will usually call upon a diver to remove the disturbing agent. This job can take just a few minutes for a small piece of line or it may take considerably longer for problems like cable or chain or a lot of line which has melted onto the shaft. Polypropylene line will form a solid plastic ring around the propellor shaft if the ship continues to run with line in the wheel. A good sharp knife is handy for removing loosely wound line from the propellor blades and shaft, but a hacksaw is the choice for cutting line tightly wound around the shaft. If line has melted onto the shaft, or there is not enough room to use a hacksaw, a hammer and chisel will do the job very nicely. I use old knives which I sharpen with a file for underwater work because a finely honed blade will not cut line very well underwater. The water acts to lubricate the blade and instead of cutting, it slides over the rope fibers. The file not only roughens the edge it also makes it very sharp, like a saw blade, and easy to cut any line underwater.

The stopper hitch (Fig. 4.8) is used to fasten a line to a cable or another line which is fouled in the propellor. Notice that the hitch is wrapped from the top down over the cable or line to be pulled. The result is to kink the cable or to pull the line so that the hitch will not slip.

A six-foot length of chain can be used to pull on a cable with better results. The chain will grab more easily and hold tighter than a line. The chain is tied on the cable with the stopper hitch, then shackled to a pulling line or cable.

For best results in pulling on a line, cable, or steel rod, use a chain strap (Fig. 4.9), made up of an eight-foot length of chain joined at the two ends with a connecting link or shackle. The strap is secured by taking two turns through the bight of the chain as in Fig. 4.10. A pulling cable or line is then shackled to the chain. The chain strap has the advantage of being both simple and easy to secure and detach quickly.

I set out to remove a line from the wheel of a tug on one job, but when I got underwater, I found cable wound around the wheel and shaft instead of line. The cable was wrapped so tightly around the shaft, it could not be pulled by either of the methods already discussed. Since I had expected to be cutting line, I was not equipped with burning torches to cut cable.

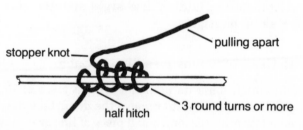

Fig. 4.8.   The stopper hitch.

Fig. 4.9.   A chain strap.

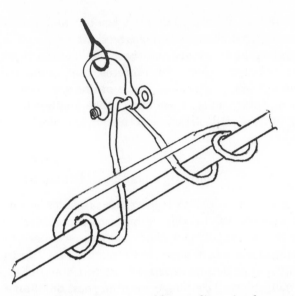

Fig. 4.10. To secure a chain strap on a cable or a line, simply pass one end through the bight of the other end as shown here; the turns of the chain on the cable will then bind and hold as strain is imposed on the cable.

Fortunately, there was a welding machine on the site, so I wrapped some 3/16-inch welding rods with masking tape, turned the machine up to 400 amps, and melted the strands of the cable. Ordinarily, underwater burning is done with the use of oxygen (Chapter 7) which is blown on the molten metal to oxidize it and provide a rapid cut. However, as in the case of the cable in the tug propellor, it is possible to cut thin steel and nonferrous metals by using a high amperage on an ordinary welding rod wrapped with tape. As discussed in Chapter 7, you can electrocute yourself if you use an AC welding machine for welding or burning underwater. Therefore, be sure you know how to set up and run the underwater welding equipment before you try it.

In my opinion the hydrogen gas or Mapp gas torch (with a special tip for underwater) is the most practical setup for small jobs in shallow water because it requires no source of electricity and no large machinery to operate. It can be loaded on a boat by hand and operated away from the dock. It has the added advantage of being able to burn nonmetallic material such as nylon line whereas the oxy-arc torch requires electrical contact to burn. Also, when burning cable from the shaft of a propellor, the gas torch will not cut into the shaft. In order to burn the shaft with a gas torch, it would require preheating the shaft for some time before it could be cut into. On the other hand, just touching the shaft by accident with the oxy-arc torch can damage the shaft.

A tugboat and crew are a costly operation to be disabled. By cutting a line or cable out in just a few minutes, you can enhance your reputation among tugboat captains. Tug captains are always talking to one another on their radios. They know when another tug is having troubles. By doing a good job for one of them in trouble, the word will spread to all.

Repairing a Damaged Propellor

Divers are often asked to inspect the propellor when vibrations are evident throughout the ship. Vibrations are generally due to an imbalance in the propellor or shaft and can be caused by line wrapped around the blade, a bent blade, or a broken blade. Vibrations can also be caused by a worn cutlass bearing, a warped shaft, loose connections for engine mounts, muff couplings, a stuffing box, the shaft at the transmission, a jackshaft, or a strut.

To remedy a damaged blade, the other blades must be cut to match it. By cutting all the blades to match, the propellor will be balanced again.

In order to cut each blade the same, make up a template by clamping a piece of wood to the damaged blade and drawing the cut on the wood. Then cut the wood to form a template and clamp the template on the other blades and cut each blade to match.

A welding machine of at least four hundred amps is required to cut the blades, along with an oxy-arc torch. Propellors are generally made of nonferrous metal and cannot be burned. They must be melted with the torch. The molten metal is blown out of the cut with the oxygen. The process is slow, so it is necessary to cut as little as possible to balance the blade. High spots or bumps on the edge of the blade can also be melted down. The job should be planned carefully to minimize the amount of cutting. If there is a lot of cutting to do, two welding machines can be used to get more heat (see Chapter 7).

Changing the Propellor

Determine the size of the propellor (also called a wheel) to be removed and obtain a wheel puller for that size. Without the appropriate wheel puller, it will be virtually impossible to remove the propellor from the shaft. On large diameter propellors, it is often necessary to use light explosive charges (see Chapter 8) to nudge it off the shaft. You can often rent wheel pullers (Fig. 4.11) from marinas or shipyards. You'll need a large wrench to remove the nut from the end of the shaft behind the propellor. You also must have a smaller wrench to tighten the nuts on the wheel puller, a pair of pliers to remove the cotter pin going through the nut, a diving hammer to tap the propellor, a block of wood to secure the propellor while removing the nut (on larger propellors it will be necessary to use a chain stop from one blade of the propellor to the keel and sixteen-pound hammers to drive it off), and a small line tied to the propellor to keep from losing the propeller as it slides off the shaft.

The procedure for removing the propellor is as follows: first, tie a line from the surface to a blade on the propellor. The line serves several purposes: on it you can run tools back and forth; it assures you that the propellor will not be lost if it is dropped; and you can use it to haul the propellor when ready to come to the surface. Second, remove the cotter pin from the shaft with the pliers and put the block of wood between the hull and propeller blade. Turn the propellor until the block is held between the hull and the blade. Put the large wrench on the nut and loosen, but do not remove, it. Place the wheel puller on next and tighten the nuts until there is a good strain on the propellor. If it does not come off, tap it from behind with the hammer, being careful not to damage the blades. The propellor will pop out to the nut. Third, remove the wheel

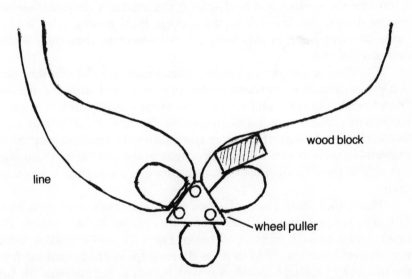

line

wood block

wheel puller

Fig. 4.11.   A wheel puller used to remove a propellor from the shaft.

puller and the shaft nut. Carefully slide the propellor until the key is exposed. Remove the block of wood and turn the propellor until the keyway is facing up. Carefully remove the key, if possible as the propellor is slid off the shaft. (If the key is stuck in the keyway, leave it there, but be careful not to knock it off when putting the propellor back on.) Now you can haul the propellor to the surface with the line attached to the blade.

To replace the propeller, start it on the shaft to the edge of the keyway. Insert the key carefully and slide the propellor over the key. Start the nut on the shaft, replace the block of wood between the blade and the hull (opposite side this time) and tighten the nut. Replace the cotter pin and the job is complete. If anything is dropped while working on the propellor, a line with a weight on it can be draped over the shaft and dropped. The weight should land near the lost object, and it may be retrieved.

Cleaning Intakes

The intakes on a ship draw water for the cooling systems in the main and auxiliary engines. Occasionally, an intake will become clogged or in need of a general inspection. If the engineer cannot shut down the power during the dive, the intakes will be operational while you are working. Of course, this is a potentially dangerous situation because you can get caught by the suction and held against the intake. Your umbilical can also be drawn into the ship by the suction. If the examination is to be made at night or in muddy water, it is imperative that you exercise extreme caution.

If you use scuba gear, a lifeline is necessary for safety. In the event you get caught, the crew topside can pull you away from the suction. Search with a magnet and a line to the surface and establish a search pattern by climbing up and down the line. The line should be moved six feet each time toward the bow or stern. With the magnet, you can be reasonably certain you will not be caught in the suction by examining one side of the line with both hands before moving it to an unexplored area.

The tender should be well to one side of the intake with your lines. This assures you that the lines will not be caught by the suction. The lines should be kept tight at all times. Fig. 4.12 illustrates the proper way to avoid suction. Note that the diver keeps his body well out from the intake by holding himself away with his knees and one hand. By this method, the water can enter the intake without being blocked by the

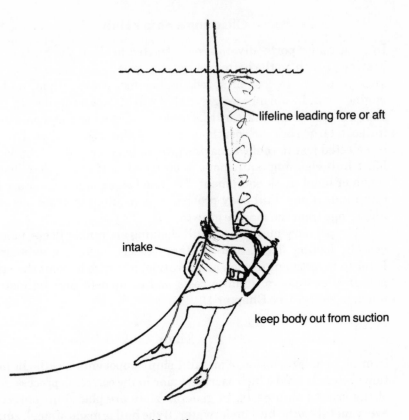

lifeline leading fore or aft

intake

keep body out from suction

Fig. 4.12.   The proper way to avoid suction.

diver. If the intake is a large one, take one flipper off and use one foot and your hands to keep away. The lifeline and one flipper are sufficient for surfacing when necessary.

I used to travel to Thule, Greenland, once a year to clean the intakes on a ship used to power the military base. Obviously, the ship could not be shut down for this operation since the entire base depended upon its power. I used hard hat gear on the job because of the cold water. (The polar ice cap was only a few miles away.) The tender was positioned aft of the intakes and instructed to keep a tight strain on my lines. I then placed both feet against the intake grating and held my body away from the intakes. I cleaned the intakes while they were operating allowing power to be continually supplied to the base. I was able to accomplish a potentially dangerous job safely by careful planning.

Cleaning a Ship's Hull

In most major ports, divers are contracted to clean the hulls of ships. Marine growth on the bottom of the ship greatly increases water resistance resulting in loss of speed, higher fuel consumption, and more engine wear. In warmer waters, a ship will have to be drydocked twice a year because of marine growth. Drydocking, cleaning, and painting the hull of a large ship can cost thousands of dollars. Quite often divers will be selected just to remove marine growth in order to avoid drydocking. Most hull cleaning equipment is designed so it can be handled with scuba or band mask equipment. The band mask is safer because of the communications. Full body protection is required to avoid lacerations and stings from the marine growth.

The primary markets for hull cleaning are tanker fleets, merchant vessels, fishing fleets, and military vessels (including submarines). Prior to investment in such an operation, it is wise to scout the area for potential customers. Itemize costs and equipment and estimate how much to charge (see Chapter 1).

Zincs

In order to halt corrosion of metallic ship components, a cathodic protection system is used which sacrifices zinc in the corrosion process instead of the crucial ship parts. In general, zincs are placed in contact with every metal on the hull underwater. If the hull is made of steel, zincs are placed in contact with the hull in many locations all over the bottom. Zincs are also mounted on the propellor shaft, the rudder, keel coolers, intake structures, and any other key metallic parts.

On steel hulls, zincs are usually welded on the bottom. The zinc used to protect the propellor and shaft is a zinc collar which is split and screwed together with stainless steel allen screws.

Whenever you work on the bottom of a ship, always check the condition of the zincs. It is important for the owner to know the state of his corrosion-protection system, so he can avoid serious damage.

I have often replaced zincs underwater when it was necessary. The shaft zinc requires an allen wrench and if it is a large shaft, the zinc may have considerable weight and you can tie some flotation to each half to help you get the zinc on the shaft. Zincs can be welded on underwater to the hull or rudder (see Chapter 7). Some zincs are fastened with screws to wooden hulls and a wire is run from the zinc to an intake screen or keel cooler. Other times, stud bolts are welded to the structure, and the zinc is fastened with nuts.

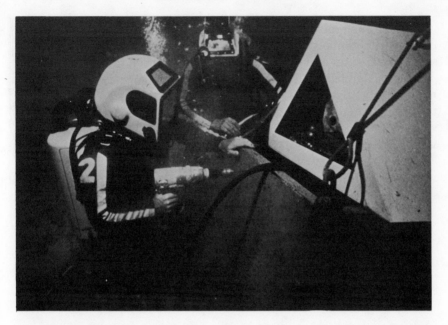

Fig. 4.13.   Mark XII divers drilling. Photo courtesy of Naval Coastal Systems Center, U. S. Navy.

Rudders

From time to time, the owner of a ship will call you to remove the rudder of the ship for repairs. The rudder is fastened with a bolted flange at the top whereas the bottom of the rudder sits in the pintle. To remove the rudder, you must unbolt the flange. Often the flange bolts are welded to the flange so they will not vibrate loose, and also the flanges may be welded with straps. If this is the case, it will be necessary for you to burn the bolts and straps but this must be done *carefully* so as not to damage the flanges or the rudder shaft (see Chapter 7). After unbolting the flanges, you can slide the rudder back and lift it out of the pintle. On a large ship, you'll have to rig the rudder with lines for lifting over the stern of the ship, and extend a line to either side to tip the rudder back so that you can lift it out of the pintle.

The shaft above the rudder goes through the hull and is bolted to the quadrant used for steering. If it is necessary to remove the shaft, it will be necessary to remove the rudder first so the shaft may be slid down and out. If it is not necessary to pull the rudder out of the water at the same time, it may be hung over the side or lowered to the bottom until it is time to replace it.

When you replace the rudder, put it into the pintle first, then raise it into position for bolting the flanges. Make certain that the quadrant is set at dead center and that when you line up the bolt holes the rudder is positioned amidships. If you are off by one bolt hole, or if the quadrant is not properly aligned, the ship will have more steerage to one side than the other. When replacing the flange bolts, use new stainless steel bolts with nylon locking threads (Nylock). Do not use the old bolts and lock washers because they will vibrate loose.

CHAPTER FIVE

Salvage Operations

DURING World War II, the German submarine wolf packs were sinking ships along the coast. If there was not enough water over the wrecks, they became a danger to shipping. I was captain and salvage officer in charge of dynamiting wrecks along the east coast of the United States. We had dynamited one ship off the coast of Florida that contained a lot of lead. After the war, one of our divers got together with a local contractor and spent about three weeks at sea salvaging the lead. When they returned to port, the local sheriff was there to meet them with a charge of piracy.

Although the lead had been on the bottom of the ocean, it still belonged to the owners who knew the lead was being salvaged without their consent. The owners allowed the diver and his associates to bring up all the lead which was worth several hundred thousand dollars, then seized it when the barge came to port. The owners benefited greatly by recovering all the lead from the bottom of the ocean at no cost to them. The diver and his associates wound up losing their time, expenses, and the lead; but they were lucky they did not have to go to jail.

Admiralty Law

According to admiralty law, even though a vessel is sunk, abandoned, a derelict, or aground, it and its cargo belong to the owners (usually an insurance company) who must be notified prior to any salvage attempt. If an agreement is not made before salvage, the owners can claim everything recovered and charge the salvor with piracy. Whatever is salvaged from a wreck must be documented with an admiralty court. The court will normally award the salvor more than if the goods were illegally sold. Besides the owner's claim, the state, and sometimes foreign governments have a claim where their jurisdiction applies. Of course, there will also be income tax due on whatever is recovered as well. All things considered, salvage is a risky venture that can involve numerous legal delays before compensation is made.

Underwater Vessel Survey

Before any salvage attempt is made, you should conduct an underwater survey. The survey should include the weather conditions of the area, the currents due to tide, wind, waves, or other factors. Observe also the ranges of high and low tide.

Note the visibility underwater and the type of bottom along with the lay of the vessel. As the diver for the operation you must carefully prepare a complete and accurate damage report, including any information you feel is valuable to the salvage program. Note whether the cargo has shifted and whether or not it must be removed. The condition of the vessel itself, its power source (gas or diesel), what material the hull is constructed of, how long the vessel has been on the bottom, and possible number of airtight compartments are the kinds of information you should include in your survey.

Locating Owners

A large ship has its name on the bow, stern, ship's bell, or on a plate on the side of the bridge. Vessels registered with the Coast Guard or a state bureau will have a number painted on the bow, or a name painted across the stern. Documented vessels will have a number stamped on a main beam, or, on a wooden vessel, the number will be carved or burned into the beam (usually located in the engine room).

The U. S. Bureau of Shipping (Washington, D.C.) or the regional district office of the Coast Guard maintains ships' records. Either of these agencies should be able to assist in locating the owners if proper information is supplied.

Wreck Diving

The craft from which you work must be securely anchored to insure the winds or changing tides do not move the boat away from the wreck. If the surface support vessel moves, you can wind up with a long swim back at the end of your dive, or worse, the descending line can be severed by the boat's shifting. If scuba diving on the wreck, you should carry a whistle for signaling. It may become necessary to surface some distance from the boat, and if the tide is running against you, you may need to signal for assistance.

The descending line is tied to the wreck where you are going to work, or carried along as the wreck is examined and tied off where you stop to surface. It is easier to go hand over hand on a descending line than it is to swim to the bottom, and if you travel between the wreck and the surface frequently, the descending line can conserve a lot of energy. If the dive is deep, tie knots on the descending line at the appropriate decompression stop depths.

Always use a penetration line to dive inside a wreck. The line is tied off to the work area making it easy to exit by pulling along the line, and also easy to return to the same spot. Where there is poor visibility, which is most often the case inside a wreck, a lifeline is used with scuba gear. If you become confused and lose the penetration line, you can follow your lifeline to exit. This line should be tended by another diver outside the wreck.

Inside a wreck underwater, the darkness, ship's list, and limited visual references can cause you to become disoriented. You must take careful note of your surroundings as you enter. The sense of touch is used in the same manner a blind person might orient himself in a room using familiar objects as reference points from which to launch himself into unknown areas.

Wherever tides or currents are prevalent, a trailing line should be set out on the surface prior to descending. The trailing line consists of a line with a float tied to one end which is let out to trail in the tide. If you ascend behind the boat, you may swim over to the trailing line and pull yourself back to the boat rather than swim against the tide. On the bottom you will find a stronger current at the bow and stern of the wreck which may wash you away. If the visibility is poor, you may lose contact with the wreck and be forced to surface.

As a wreck diver you should always carry a sharp knife to free yourself from lines which are readily snagged on a wreck by fishing hooks and lures.

Lifting Small Craft with Air

Oil drums* are secure containers for use in lifting with air. Some drums can be put inside the wreck in the bow section. The bung holes must be placed down and are used to fill the drums with air. Once in place, the drums must be secured so they do not roll allowing the bung hole to face up and let the air escape. Other drums can be placed in the cabin, but must be secured to the floor bracing beneath the floor boards. Drums not

* Check with your local department of environmental management about regulations concerning the clean containers.

secured in this manner may damage the cabin or lift it off the boat. Secure drums to the outside of the wreck by passing lines beneath the wreck and securing them to the cleats on the wreck.

When using oil drums for lifting, you need to consider the depth of the water. If the boat is in less than twenty feet of water, the only hole that is needed to exhaust the expanding air as the drum rises is the bung hole. A drum in good condition should withstand a ten psi rise in pressure without rupturing, which is about how much to expect on a twenty-foot rise to the surface.

If the water is deep, the drums should have a series of one-inch holes burned in the bottom, as in Fig. 5.1 or one large hole as in Fig. 5.2. As illustrated, these drums may be prepared for use upright, or on their sides. There are circumstances where the drum lying flat is the best position for hoisting, inside the cabin, for example, or beneath the counter of the boat where two drums can be tied together with one line behind the propellor and the other line beneath the shaft. The engine is the heaviest part of the boat. Therefore, when the boat surfaces, it is necessary to keep the drums as low as possible to attain maximum lift. Drums beneath the counter will help keep the stern above water when the boat surfaces enabling pumping operations to begin. If the stern is not above water when the boat surfaces, it will not be possible to pump it out.

The cable going through the drum positioned to lie on its side passes through the bung hole on one end and through a hole burned in the bottom on the other end. There are two cable clamps secured close against the drum to keep the cable from sliding into the drum. A short tail on the cable will help insure that the cable does not slide. The drum prepared for use in the upright position is prepared in the same manner by burning the holes for the cable on the sides of the drum near the bottom.

To position the drums around the outside of the wreck (Fig. 5.3), your topside crew ties a line to a flooded drum. Then you pass an end of the line through the block secured near where the drum is to be fastened. Sometimes it is better to pass the line under the wreck and bring the end back to the surface. At this point the crew pulls the drum down and holds it in position until secured. Be sure to place the drums at the stern first where most of the weight is, then put enough air into each drum to be sure it remains in proper position. Proceed with the rest of the drums around the outside of the wreck in the same manner. When all the drums are in place, fill them one at a time, but be sure to balance side to side and bow to stern. If all the drums are filled on one side first,

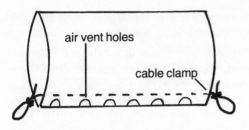

Fig. 5.1.   Drum with series of one-inch holes.

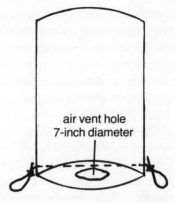

Fig. 5.2.   Drum with one air vent hole seven inches in diameter.

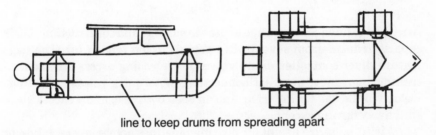

Fig. 5.3.   Positioning drums.

the wreck could roll, come up bow first, stern first, or on its side. Each fifty-five-gallon drum will lift about five hundred pounds.

It is important that the drums do not slip or slide out from the cables or lines holding them down. The wreck can be lost if one or more should escape during ascent. Even worse, a loose can full of air could strike the bottom of the support vessel on the surface and sink it.

If the wreck has been down for some time, there may be mud inside. This can be removed by a water jet or airlift (see Chapter 2). If the wreck lies in mud, the mud will create suction on the bottom of the boat which will have to be overcome before the wreck will start to rise.

The lift required to break ground will exceed the amount required to raise the weight of the wreck. Therefore, once ground is broken, the wreck may rise too quickly. It is better to lighten the wreck with sufficient air to raise it through the water and break ground by hauling from the surface on one side of the wreck to rock it free.

Raising a wreck with air can be tricky and is potentially dangerous if adequate control is not insured. When filling the drums with air, you must be very sure that the wreck will not surface too near the surface support. If the wreck should come up beneath the surface craft, the entire operation could sink.

If a wreck is upside down, or can be rolled upside down on the bottom, air can be pumped into the wreck and trapped inside the water-tight hull. When the wreck rises to the surface, it can be towed upside down into shallow water. Patching can be completed and the ship can be righted. If the wreck is towed to shallow water near shore, it can be rolled with cables from a tow truck or a bulldozer, then pulled onto the beach and repaired.

Lift Bags

Airlift bags have a wide range of uses in salvage and construction. Their capacity ranges from seventy-five pounds to ten tons of lift. The bags feature diver controlled dump valves for releasing excess air and controlling buoyancy, air inlet connections with quick release couplings welded in the bag for inflation, and an open bottom to allow excess air to spill away during ascent.

Airlift bags are useful for floating pipelines across rivers, lakes, or out to sea. You can dump the air and control the buoyancy of the pipe as it is lowered to the bottom. If the pipe is not in the right location after being lowered, you can pick it up again and move it by reinflating the bags.

Cofferdams in Salvage

A cofferdam is simply a box built around a hatch or an opening on deck. The box extends from the deck of the wreck to the surface and is made watertight. After the rest of the wreck is patched to make it watertight, the hoses from the pumps are put through the cofferdam. It may be necessary to steady the wreck with a rig to keep it level as it comes up. Some wrecks tend to be top heavy and will flip over if not stabilized during lifting.

Fig. 5.5 shows a cofferdam fastened to the deck of a barge, and the barge being pumped through the cofferdam. Notice that as the wreck is pumped, the air space inside allows the full weight of the water above to

Fig. 5.4.   Raising a block of concrete using airlift bags. Photo courtesy of Naval
Coastal Systems Center, U. S. Navy.

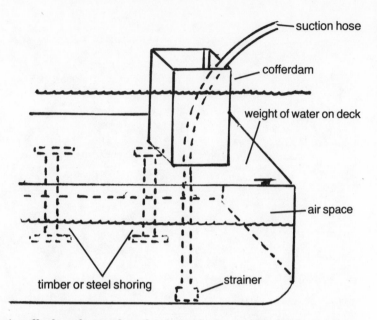

Fig. 5.5. A cofferdam fastened to the deck of a barge showing barge being pumped through the cofferdam.

exert its force on the deck and sides of the barge. In general, if the water above the deck is ten feet or more, it will be necessary to shore the deck and possibly the sides with timbers.

Fig. 5.6 illustrates a method for pumping out a sunken barge. After patching all the holes, one of the hatch covers is brought to the surface, and two holes are burned in it. One hole takes the suction hose from the pump, the other hole takes an air vent pipe to the surface to allow air to enter the barge as it is being pumped out. The vent pipe must not extend farther than just below the deck of the wreck, otherwise the pipe will be below the air pocket and create a vacuum under the deck which will put added pressure on it and make pumping difficult. The vent pipe should be at least one third the diameter of the suction hose to allow sufficient air flow.

On a small wreck it is advisable to use several small three-inch pumps. The smaller pumps are easy to handle and can be moved by hand. If a barge has several compartments, the pumps will have to be moved several times. The small pumps are handy in this case also since they do not require a crane to move them around. I raised a sunken tugboat by inserting the suction hose down the smokestack which ex-

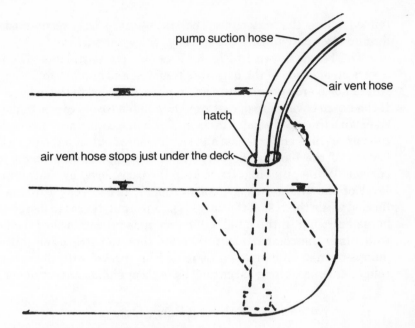

Fig. 5.6.   Pumping out a sunken barge.

Fig. 5.7.   Salvage pumps at U. S. Navy diving school. Photo courtesy of Naval Coastal Systems Center, U. S. Navy.

tended above the waterline. The stack served as a ready-made cofferdam after patching all the openings below the surface.

The barge shown in Fig. 5.8 has four compartments. The hatch covers on one side of the barge are removed and brought to the surface, where holes are cut into them and pipes are welded to the hatch covers. If the hatch covers are of cast iron, new hatch covers can be made from steel with the pipes welded to them. The hatch covers are then replaced, the barge checked for leaks, and suction hoses put into the pipes to the bottom of the barge. The barge is then pumped and brought to the surface. While pumping, try to keep the barge level by controlling the level of the water in each compartment. If one compartment stays flooded while the rest of the barge is pumped out, there is a danger of the barge buckling in the middle. If patching is needed to slow the flow of water into the compartment, take the time to patch it, or shift more pumps to that compartment to bring it near level with the rest of the compartments. A long barge may have six or eight compartments.

Rolling a Barge Over

Dump scows and sand barges sometimes roll over bottom up without sinking. A sand barge can be rolled back right side up by taking the sling completely around it (Fig. 5.9). The sling is run under the barge first, then over the exposed bottom and down the side to the deck cleats underwater. In this way, the sling will pick up one side of the barge, stand it on edge, then flip it over. Dump scows have pockets in the middle which are loaded, then dumped. An inverted dump scow which is loaded may be too heavy for the rig to flip. By flooding the compartments on one side of the scow, the other side will come well up out of the water. The scow can then be righted by the same method illustrated in Fig. 5.9. The compartments can be flooded by removing the plugs in the bottom of the scow and pumping water into them.

A small barge can be rolled over by taking two tugs with slings over the bottom to the deck cleats on the far side away from the tugs. By pulling on the barge, the backwash from the propellors will tend to sink the side of the barge facing the tugs and the slings will pull the other side over. The larger barge must be slung as in Fig. 5.7, otherwise there is not enough slack in the slings to allow the barge to flip completely.

Use of Slings on a Wreck

When pulling slings under a wreck or a heavy object underwater, it is often easier to drag a small messenger cable or line under the wreck

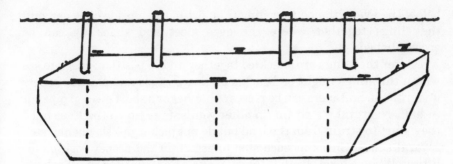

Fig. 5.8.   Raising a large steel barge.

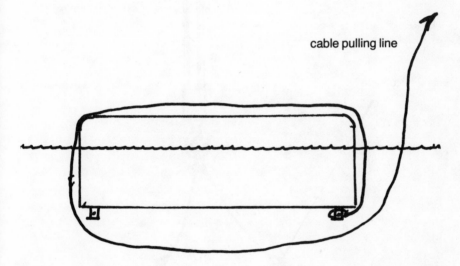

cable pulling line

Fig. 5.9.   Rolling a barge over.

first. You can use the messenger to pull the heavy sling cable under the wreck. Pulling the sling under the wreck can then be accomplished with the use of a crane if necessary. The messenger will sometimes have to be "sawed" under the wreck by taking a lead fore or aft on it. Then, by pulling on alternate sides in a sawing motion, the cable will work its way under the wreck to a point where the slings will not slide up and off the wreck when strained.

Shackling slings together underwater can be difficult. By passing a small line through the eye of the top sling and tying it about six feet below the eye of the bottom sling (Fig. 5.10), the topside crew can pull the slings together where the eyes meet and shackling can be accomplished.

After the slings are shackled together and in position, check to see where the slings might be bearing on sharp edges and place softeners under them. Softeners can be pieces of lumber or a short piece of pipe cut in half. Next, take a strain (in other words, take up on the lines until they start to strain from the load but do not pick it up) slowly and stop several times. Check at each stop to ascertain the proper position for lifting. When a good strain is taken, make a final check to be sure slings are in the proper place. Tie them to the cleats or bitts to keep them from

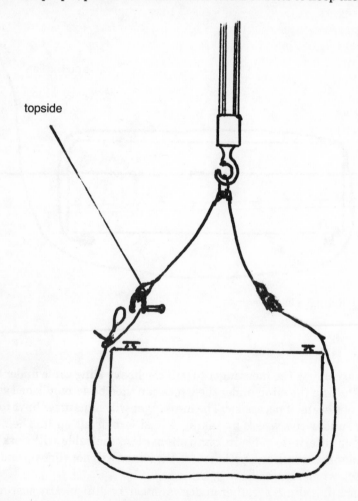

topside

Fig. 5.10.   Shackling slings underwater.

slipping. When all is well, you can surface prior to lifting. Be sure to be
well clear before a full strain is taken to avoid catastrophe if the slings
part.

Tunneling under a Wreck to Place Slings

It is sometimes necessary to tunnel beneath a wreck in order to place
slings. I was boss of diver operations and in charge of tunneling under
the *Normandie* in 1942. In this case, it was necessary to tunnel under
the ship in order to place slings to hold patches that were placed over her
elevator shafts.

We used a six-inch rubber suction hose as an airlift and a water jet
hose to wash the soil into the airlift. The depth of the water at high tide
was sixty-five feet. The tunnel was over a hundred feet long (Fig. 5.11).
At the outset, this might have appeared to be a dangerous job, but in
reality there was no danger of the top of the tunnel caving in since it was
the bottom of the ship. (The sides of this tunnel were made wide enough
so there was no danger of them caving either.) It took us about four
weeks to tunnel under the *Normandie* because of its size.

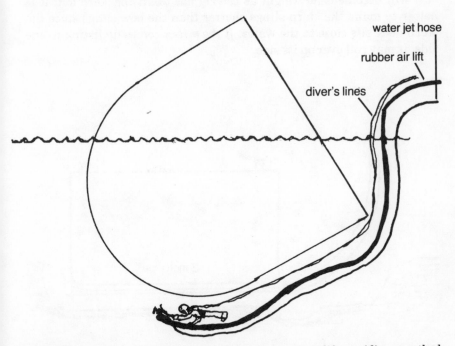

Fig. 5.11.   A six-inch rubber suction hose used as an airlift providing a method
of tunneling.

There are times when a pipe can be washed under a wreck by hooking a hose to the pipe and using the pipe as a jet nozzle (Fig. 5.12). A one-inch diameter pipe is all that is required. When the pipe has washed a hole to the opposite side of the wreck, a small diameter cable can be passed through the pipe in order to pull it out. After the pipe has been removed, the heavy sling is shackled to the messenger and pulled under the wreck.

When slinging a wreck for lifting, keep in mind that the slings are bridled and if one rig is used to lift with, all four slings come to a point at the block. All slings will therefore pull at an angle (Fig. 5.13). Notice that in the illustrations, the slings are pulling at right angles to the curve of the bow so they will not slip. Also, slings should be secured to cleats, if possible.

It is important to raise the wreck on an even keel. Notice that the sling under the counter makes it appear that the bow will be raised first; you must adjust this before the lift commences. The stern is, however, broad in comparison to the bow, and this will compensate in part for the difference.

If the wreck is brought to the surface with the stern underwater, the bow will become dead weight as the rig has to lift the stern out. It is better to make the stern slings shorter than the bow slings since the stern deck sits close to the water. If the wreck comes up listing to one side, it may roll over on its side.

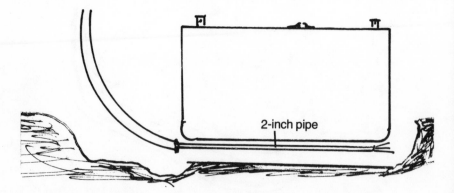

Fig. 5.12.   Using a pipe under a wreck as a jet nozzle.

A

right

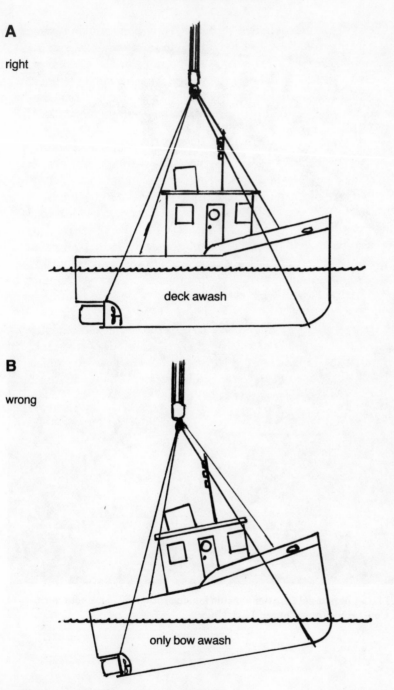

deck awash

B

wrong

only bow awash

Fig. 5.13.   (A) is the correct way to sling.

Fig. 5.14.   A personnel transfer capsule for saturation diving. Photo courtesy of Naval Coastal Systems Center, U. S. Navy.

Fig. 5.15.   Divers making hookup for lifting. Photo courtesy of Naval Coastal Systems Center, U. S. Navy.

CHAPTER SIX

Pile Driving

PILINGS are used in marine work to support structures and as temporary and permanent forms for concrete work, and are often in need of under-water repair and maintenance. Wood piles are used to support piers, docks, and bridges as well as for dolphins for securing large vessels or fending off vessels from a dock or pier structure. Concrete and steel pilings are used in construction of larger structures such as bridges and long piers. Steel sheet piling is driven in interlocking pieces which can form a cofferdam, permanent bulkheads along shore, temporary and permanent forms underwater, and a variety of other uses (see Fig. 6.1).

Pilings are driven into the bottom with a pile driver rig which can be a simple mechanical hammering device for small wooden pilings or a large hydraulic or pneumatic hammering device for heavy jobs. Most pile driving jobs are done by dock builders and pile drivers who will often use divers for some of their work. The union is generally involved with most of these jobs, so it is advisable to check with the superinten-dent to get a clearance card or show your log book to the union steward on the job. It is a good idea to check in with the local hall anyway (see Chapter 1).

Sawing Piles Underwater

On such a job you will saw piles to grade underwater with the use of a pneumatic or hydraulic saw (see Chapter 2). You should take the saw underwater with the air turned off, otherwise you could be injured by an accidental activation of the saw before you are ready to cut (during descent, you're often off balance creating a hazard from an uninten-tional starting of the saw). When you are in position and ready to use the saw, the tender should take up the slack in your lines to make sure the lines are clear. Then you are ready to have the air to the saw turned on and to begin cutting.

Fig. 6.1.   Steel sheet piling. Photo by Wayne C. Tucker.

Fig. 6.2. Diver ascending. Photo courtesy of Naval Coastal Systems Center, U. S. Navy.

When sawing piles with a long cutoff, first shackle the pile with a cable pulling the pile away from the cut. In this way, the pile will open as the cut is made and not bind the saw. The pile is lifted out with the cable as the cut is made. If a pile should bind the saw in the cut, insert a small wooden wedge in the cut to open it, or if possible, you can put your shoulder against the pile and push as the cut is finished.

Short cutoffs are left on the bottom, and a long line is taken down and tied to each cutoff. The whole string is then pulled to the surface where the topside crew removes the cutoffs one at a time. If you are called to cut only a few pilings and an air saw and compressor are not available, it is possible to use a small two-man hand saw (farmers used them before chain saws). When cutting piles by hand, use grade battens (see Sawing Piles to Grade Underwater below); otherwise, it is not possible to get a straight cut. It takes fifteen to twenty minutes to cut a pile by hand if the saw is sharp. Proper footing is also essential for cutting piles by hand. It is not possible just to hang onto a pile and cut. You must stand on the bottom or on the battens nailed to the piles, or you will tire rapidly on the first piling.

When I began diving, air saws were not very common, and we often cut piles by hand. One diver could cut an average of fifteen piles per day. Two divers on a two-man saw could cut more than twice that amount. For some jobs, the hand saw has some distinct advantages, including savings in hauling and renting a compressor, fuel used, and fewer mechanical breakdowns.

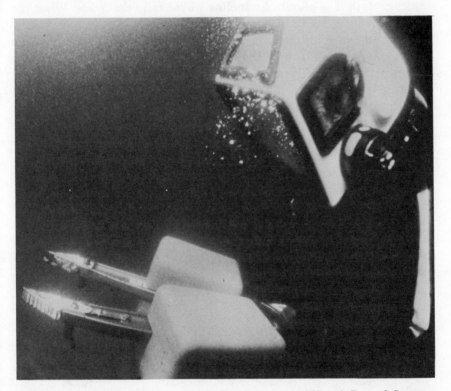

Fig. 6.3. Underwater bolt cutters. Photo courtesy of Naval Coastal Systems Center, U. S. Navy.

While diving on the Potomac River Bridge in Maryland in 1939, I was cutting wood pilings in ninety feet of water in a strong tidal current. The job was not going fast enough, so the contractor made up a circular saw with a long shaft and put it in the pile driver leads. The leads were lowered close to the bottom with the saw beneath. The shaft came to the surface and was driven by a motor. The saw was moved into the pilings by pulling the rig on its mooring lines. Two extra anchors were put out, in addition to those at the four corners of the rig, one out ahead of the rig and one behind it. The foreman could pull the rig straight ahead on one line or straight back. After the piles were cut, I went down and removed the cutoffs to clear the area.

Sawing Piles to Grade Underwater

Establishing grade on piles requires a long grade pole and an engineer's transit to shoot the grade on the grade pole. When using a grade pole, make certain it is plumb. An incline would raise the grade. When the grade pole is at the right elevation, drive a nail partway into the pile leaving enough nail sticking out so that a grade batten can float up under the nail and be held there by flotation (Fig. 6.4). Then nail the batten to the piling. The grade is shot on both sides of the piles, and nails are driven on both sides to establish a straight cut across the pile. When grades are shot, they are done on many piles at a time to avoid the necessity of setting up too often. When there are many piles close together, grade is only shot on a few intermittent piles, and the grade battens span the intermediate piles as shown in Fig. 6.5.

Fig. 6.5 shows four grade nails used for marking sixteen piles. They are driven into the piles above grade determined by the width of the one-by-three-inch batten. The grade battens are then floated beneath the nails and held in place by flotation until they are nailed. The bottoms of these two battens will then be at the proper grade. The other

Fig. 6.4.   Four grade nails.

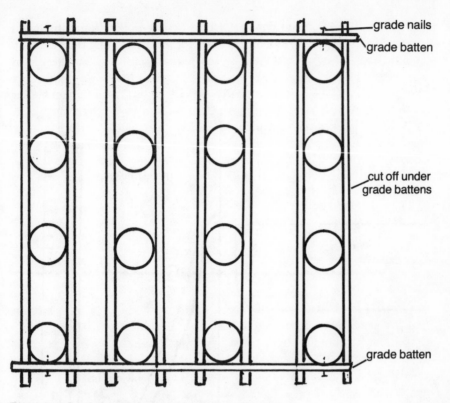

grade nails

grade batten

cut off under
grade battens

grade batten

Fig. 6.5.   Grade battens spanning intermediate piles.

battens are floated beneath the grade battens and nailed in place. After
the grade battens are removed you can begin cutting piles off at the top
of the battens which are at the proper grade.

   With the rig illustrated in Fig. 6.6 you do not have to take grade on
the pile before you cut it. There are no battens to be nailed to the piles as
guides for the saw. Grade is shot by the marking on the H beam and the
arms take the place of grade battens. You can easily assemble the rig
from an H beam, two angle irons, a bolt, and four-inch-by-four-inch
softeners on top of the angles. Fasten the softeners with bolts through
the angle irons countersunk into the wood. The softeners keep the saw
blade from contacting the steel angle irons. Weld one arm solid to the
beam in a horizontal position, bolt the other arm so it may swing to a
vertical position, and then be lowered to a horizontal position when the
rig is in place. Weld a horizontal angle stop below the swing arm to hold

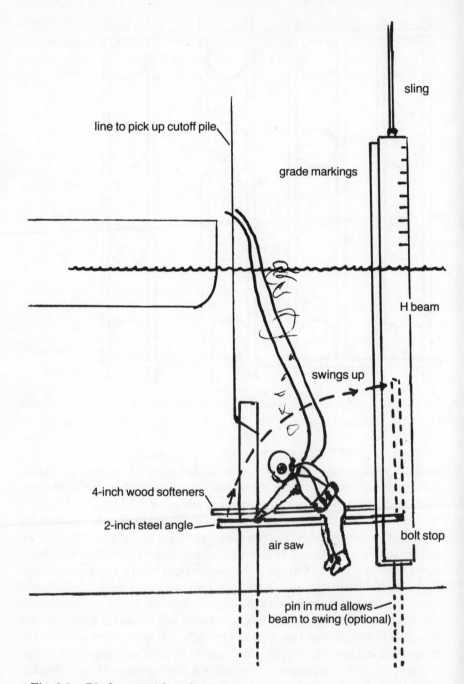

line to pick up cutoff pile

sling

grade markings

H beam

swings up

4-inch wood softeners

2-inch steel angle

air saw

bolt stop

pin in mud allows
beam to swing (optional)

Fig. 6.6.   Rig for use without battens.

it in a horizontal position. Set the steel pin in the mud and lower the beam to grade. Swing the beam around until the solid horizontal arm hits a pile. Then lower the other arm so that the pile rests between the two arms. You are in a position then to sit on the arms with the saw and cut the pile to grade marked by the arms.

Securing Pile Caps to Piles Underwater

A pile cap is usually a twelve-inch-by-twelve-inch timber that sits on top of a row of piles to create a foundation for the decking of a pier or bracing for pipelines. During construction, a drift pin is driven through the cap into each piling to secure the cap onto the pilings. Before a cap can be set on piles, you must take measurements to locate where the holes are to be drilled by the crew topside before the cap is sent down, since you would have a difficult time drilling through the cap underwater. As Fig. 6.7 illustrates, the piles are seldom in a perfect line. A one-inch-by-three-inch batten is nailed across the row of piles in the best line to locate the center of the holes to be drilled in the pile cap. A nail is driven to mark each hole, and the batten is sent topside where the crew will lay it on the pile cap and drill holes where the nails strike the cap.

When the cap is lowered underwater, it has weights on it to sink it as shown (Fig. 6.8). Once the cap is positioned properly on the pilings, toenail it onto the pilings to hold it in position while you drill through the holes in the cap and into each piling to the proper depth marked on the drill bit by the topside crew to accommodate the lengths of drift pins. You will then drive through the cap and into each pile. Drift pins are not spikes, they are round steel rods cut to lengths. The drift pins are set into each hole with a few blows of the diving hammer, then driven home with the jackhammer.

Once the cap is secured, loosen the set screws on the weights holding the cap down and send them topside. You can rig a system for the drill and jackhammer suspended on a line to the crane's number two cable. The crane operator can then lower the drill tied off at the end of the line while you drill the hole. The jackhammer can be suspended on another line tied off five feet above the drill. After you drill the hole, the crane can lower the cable until the jackhammer is handy. Your tender can send a drift pin down to you on your lifeline and you can set the pin with your diving hammer, and drive it home with the jackhammer. The crane can raise the drill and hammer and move to the next piling where you begin the procedure all over again. Using this method, you can secure a pile cap on four piles in fifteen minutes.

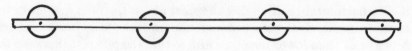

Fig. 6.7.   Setting caps on piles.

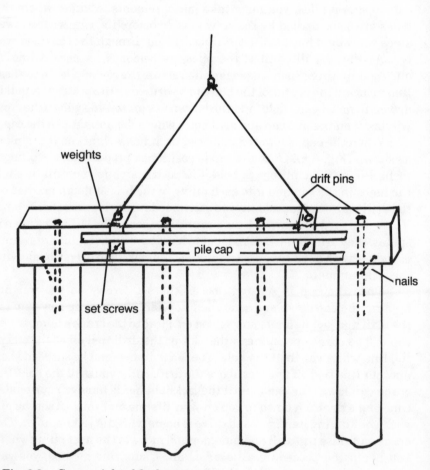

Fig. 6.8.   Caps weighted for lowering.

Often a pile will shift to one side of the pile cap and split away from the drift pin. The drift pin will usually be sticking out of the pile or the pile cap and must be burned off with a torch before the pile can be brought back into position under the pile cap. You must bring the pile back into position under the pile cap with the use of a come along. Usually two chains with hooks on the end about 6 feet long are used to secure the come along around the pile to be pulled and around a solid pile to pull on.

Once the pile is back in proper position, two angle plates made of one-half-inch-by-four-inch galvanized plates are nailed to the pile. There should be a nail hole in the angle plate as shown in Fig. 6.9. Holes are then drilled into the pile through predrilled holes in the angle plate for the lag screws, and the lag screws are driven into the pile with the air impact wrench. The two clamps are nailed onto the pile through the nail holes as shown in Fig. 6.10. The clamps are positioned above the lugs on the plates to keep them from sliding down the plates as shown in Fig. 6.11. The clamp bolts are then snugged up with the air impact wrench. Be careful not to tighten the clamps to the point where they bend or break off. Finally, drill holes into the pile cap through the predrilled angle plate and drive the lag screws into the pile cap securing the pile to the cap again.

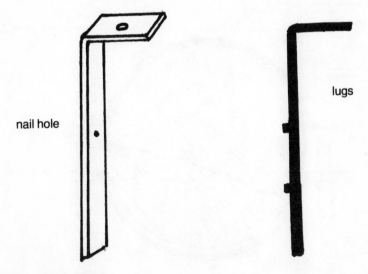

nail hole

lugs

Fig. 6.9.   Angle plate.

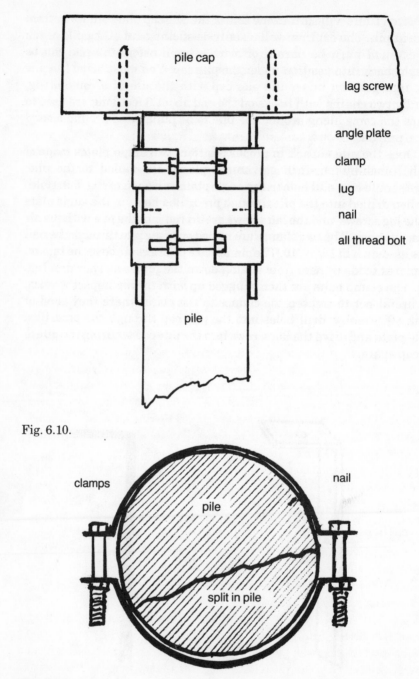

Fig. 6.10.

Fig. 6.11.

Many times new piles are driven under old piers and must be secured to the pile cap by a diver. The method just described can be used for placing new piles under an old pier. A good diver can average about two to three pilings a day using this method.

Drilling

Before you take a drill underwater, make certain that the bit is very sharp and that the motor is well oiled. Before connecting the air hose to the drill, pour a little oil into the hose at the drill, hook up the hose, and run the drill topside to make sure it is running smooth and is well oiled before taking it below.

Underwater, you must have a suitable platform to work from while drilling. If you cannot stand on the bottom and there is nothing to steady you as you drill, nail a board to the pilings so that you have a place to stand or sit while drilling. You will not be able to drill a straight hole by hanging free in the water and trying to swim while you drill. If the bit sticks and you are not steady, you can bend or break the drill bit or jam yourself against the piling.

When drilling, you can usually run the drill bit the full length of the auger. The auger will force the chips out of the hole until the solid steel shank enters the hole. Once the steel shank enters the hole, the chips will pack above the auger, and the bit will get stuck in the hole. If this happens, try running the drill in reverse, then forward for short bursts to force the chips down from the shank and under the bit. If this does not work, you'll need a pair of vice grip pliers or a pipe wrench to twist the bit out counter-clockwise.

Drill bits for wood come with a worm on the end that screws into the wood to start the hole. I have found it necessary to cut the screw tip off and sharpen the drill without the tip because drilling a deep hole requires periodic reversing of the drill to clear the hole of chips. Reversing the drill draws the screw out of the wood, and before it will bite back in, you will have to force it back in with several hard shoves. Often, however, no matter how hard you shove, the bit will not cut again. The bit must then be pulled out, the threads of the screw cleaned thoroughly, and the same procedure tried again.

When drilling a deep hole, therefore, it is easier to use a barefoot bit without the screw. The barefoot bit will cut as soon as it touches the wood. By pressing forward for three or four seconds, keeping the drill in forward, and withdrawing it to clear the chips you can drill a hole with much less effort than with the screw tip. If you are going to drill a deep hole through two piles, or through two timbers, take a board down with the same size hole drilled through and nail it to the pile where you wish to drill. The board will steady the barefoot drill bit to start the hole. If there are many holes close by to drill, start them all with the screw tip bit and finish them all with the barefoot bit.

The hole that is drilled for drift pins and spikes must be very close to the diameter of the pin or spike. If the hole is too small, the resistance of the material and the water inside the hole (which is incompressible) will keep you from being able to drive the pin all the way. A pile cap will rise from the piles beneath, or the pin will stick up above the cap. The hole should allow a snug fit but not be too tight. A square spike will fit into a round hole one-eighth inch smaller than the spike. The water can escape at the sides of the spike while it is being driven, but the fit will still be snug.

Driving Fastenings

A jackhammer is used to drive spikes or drift pins underwater through a pile cap and into a piling. A bit for driving is made up from an old bit cut off short to which a nut or washer cut from thick steel is welded. The nut or thick washer will create a pocket for the head of the spike to sit in as the spike is driven with the jackhammer (Fig. 6.12).

Always make it easy on yourself by attaching a line to the jackhammer which runs topside to the crew or the crane. The jackhammer is heavy and cumbersome to move around especially if you have to climb a pile with it to get into position. With the line, the crane can hold the jackhammer up for you and move the hammer from pile to pile eliminating a lot of unnecessary hard work.

Sometimes it is necessary to drive spikes or drift pins underwater when there is no compressor or jackhammer available with which to drive them. A sledge hammer is not always the best alternative. A ramrod (Fig. 6.13) can be made up to do the job quite nicely.

Pulling Steel H Piles

Steel H piles often rust at the waterline or become so deteriorated that they must be removed to clear an area for a replacement pier. To pull the piles, use a vibratory hammer which can be set on any part of the pile that has solid steel for the jaws to clamp onto without tearing the steel. The web or the flanges can be used to pull on. Some times the pile must be cut down to where there is enough solid steel to do this. Many of the

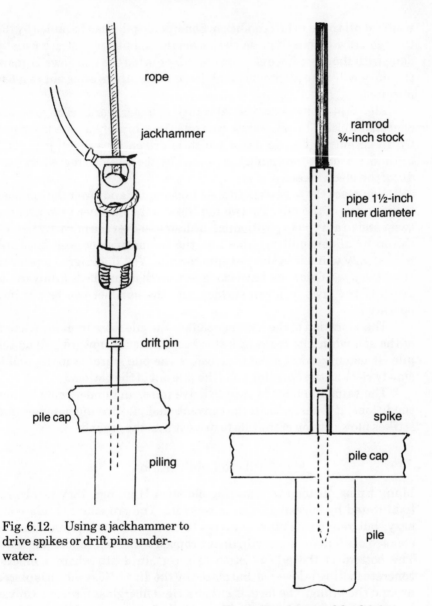

Fig. 6.12. Using a jackhammer to drive spikes or drift pins underwater.

Fig. 6.13. A ramrod for driving spikes underwater.

piles can be cut by the dock builders at low tide since the piles usually rust out between high and low water with the portion of the pile underwater at all times in fair condition. Some of the piles can be pulled by the topside crew before the tide rises over them, but the rest are usually done with the assistance of a diver to work during the tide flows. Some of the piles will take all day to break loose while others come out in a few minutes.

Fig. 6.14 shows how the vibratory hammer works. The jaws are operated topside by an electric control. The vibratory action is created by an eccentric electric motor which is driven by a diesel generator topside. Careful attention must be paid by the topside crew when handling the electric cables.

You place the jaws on good steel underwater and lower the hammer to sit on top of the pile. Tie two tag lines to the hammer to control the twist and to aid you in positioning the hammer over the piles. By having the dock builders pull on either line, the hammer can be positioned and held steady while it is lowered onto the pile. You then signal topside to close the jaws. Once you have made certain that the pile is firmly in the grasp of the jaws, you can surface, and the hammer can be put into operation.

The vibration of the hammer shakes the pile loose from the friction of the soil while the crane operator keeps a steady upward pull on the pile. It usually takes some time before the pile starts to move, and it slowly rises as the operator pulls the pile out of the bottom.

The same hammer is used to drive piles, and under some bottom conditions, it is faster than the conventional pile driving hammer that strikes blows on top of the pile to drive it into the ground.

Pile Rehabilitation

Many times, instead of removing old steel H pilings, they can be rehabilitated by encasing them in concrete. The procedure is relatively easy, but requires a crew of divers to carry out. Each piling must be cleaned of all marine growth, then wrapped with steel reinforcing wire. The bottom of the pile is jetted to a certain depth where a precast concrete footing is lowered and placed by the diver. Next a form is placed around the piling. The form is either a rigid fiberglass form or a canvas bag type. Finally, the form is pumped full of concrete, and the forms are stripped after the concrete is set (see Chapter 9).

We did a job for the Navy in South Carolina using this technique. When the pier was first built, the Navy had rolled a huge crane out to the end of the pier on rails. Thirty years later when the Navy wanted to bring the crane back, it was determined that the steel pilings had rusted

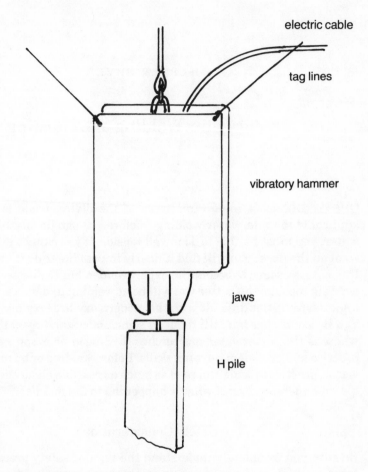

Fig. 6.14.   The workings of the vibratory hammer.

to the point where they would no longer support the moving load of the crane. We ran a crew of ten divers for two years encasing all the steel pilings in concrete. Many bridges and causeways have also been rehabilitated by the concrete encasement technique.

CHAPTER SEVEN

Underwater Welding and Burning

ONE OF THE most important tricks of the diving trade is definitely applicable to underwater welding—before you can do anything underwater, you must be able to do it well topside. If you cannot weld or burn steel on the dock, you will find it nearly impossible to do it underwater. It is not necessary to become an expert welder, but the better you are at welding topside, the better you will be at welding underwater. Burning underwater is not difficult with the modern oxy-arc (oxy-arc acetylene) and Broco torches but still requires some understanding of the process, whereas the underwater gas torches (hydrogen or Mapp gas) require practice and proficient burning skills. Before welding or burning underwater, practice topside and read as much as possible about the process to get an understanding of what is happening to the metals.

Safety Considerations

Be sure you completely understand the regular safety precautions for handling high pressure cylinders and high amperage welding machines topside and that the dive team is also so informed (see Appendix B). In addition to the regular safety precautions, further safety precautions must be implemented when welding or burning underwater.

If you are in charge of an underwater burning or welding operation, it is your responsibility to insure that all equipment is kept in good shape. This requires constant vigilance. Cylinders must be properly secured, electrical leads must be properly insulated, and every precaution must be taken to lessen the chance of accidents to the divers and other workers in the area.

To reduce the possibility of electric shock, and to avoid voltage losses to the water, be sure that every electrical connection which is going underwater is waterproofed. If insulation is damaged anywhere

Fig. 7.1. A gas bank of helium. Photo courtesy of Naval Coastal Systems Center, U. S. Navy.

on the torch or the leads, it must be completely covered with rubber tape, then again with good plastic electrical tape. Use a safety switch of at least 200 amps with a positive mechanical breaking switch in the secondary circuit. A knife switch is the only acceptable type. Take special care to be sure the switch is not being shunted out. Make certain that the cable between the welding machine and the switch is fully insulated along its entire length, also that periodic inspections are made to insure that no damage to the insulation occurs. The knife switch should be located so your tender can operate the switch upon signals from you, the diver. The tender should not operate the switch unless specifically directed by you, and he should confirm each change with you after it has been executed. We recommend using the voice command, "Make it hot," and the reply, "It's hot," and, "Make it cold," and the reply, "It's cold."

When cutting or welding underwater, you should be careful *never* to place yourself between the ground connection and your torch or electrode holder. Since seawater conducts electricity, you would be placing yourself in the current path between electrode and ground and be subject to severe shock. Likewise, you should never point the torch or electrode holder towards yourself.

The staging you use for your divers should be light enough to be moved easily, and the parts in direct contact with the metal being cut or welded should be of wood or insulated to protect the diver.

Take proper precaution to avoid explosive gases when welding or burning underwater. A diver can encounter explosive gases or hazards from:

1. Gasoline, fuel oil, paint, and other petroleum products in gas or liquid form in sealed compartments

2. Ammunition or explosives

3. Decaying animal or vegetable matter which can build up gases in partially flooded compartments

4. Unburned gases from the torches, which can build up in a sealed compartment and behind sheet piling. If there is any doubt of what is behind an area being burned into, you should drill a series of holes to insure proper venting of the compartment or space.

For performing underwater welding and burning operations, your wet suit or dry suit must completely insulate your body. In addition, you must have boots and rubber gloves. I generally wear a pair of dishwashing gloves underneath my wet suit mitts. The dishwashing gloves offer good insulation from shock if you wear a hole through your regular gloves. Best protection is obtained from a hard hat and suit. However, a full face mask is acceptable for such operations. Scuba is not recommended for underwater welding and burning because of the lack of communications, and the possibility of losing your air supply if you are knocked unconscious or are dazed.

Self-Consuming Technique

Welding underwater is accomplished by the so-called "self-consuming technique." You do not strike an arc with the electrode, but keep the electrode in contact with the work, allowing the rod to melt into the work. The rod consumes itself and the width of the bead can be controlled by varying the speed and pressure on the work. In most cases, the width of the bead is about the same as the rod.

You can expect underwater welds to have approximately a 20 percent loss in tensile strength and a 50 percent loss in ductility when compared with similar welds made in air. The loss in ductility is due to the hardening caused by the drastic quenching action of the surrounding water. In other words, the seawater cools the weld so fast it loses some of its strength and half of its flexibility.

Welding underwater is done with straight polarity from the welding machine which is set at a higher current than would be used for topside welding. Reverse polarity is conventionally used in topside welding, but is not used underwater. If reverse polarity is used underwater, electrolytic action occurs, and the metal parts of the electrode holder will be rapidly consumed.

Setting Up

For underwater welding, a direct current welding generator of at least 300 amp capacity is recommended (Fig. 7.2). To prevent excessive voltage drop and maintain the current required, cables should be furnished in 50-foot lengths (minimum) complete with a male connector and a female connector. Cables should be a minimum of 2/0 extra flexible welding cable except for the whip lead attached to the electrode holder. The whip may be a 1/0 welding cable to aid the diver in maneuvering the holder. Each additional length of cable and its connectors cause a voltage drop. All connections must be taped with electrical tape. To compensate for voltage drop and to maintain the current required. the

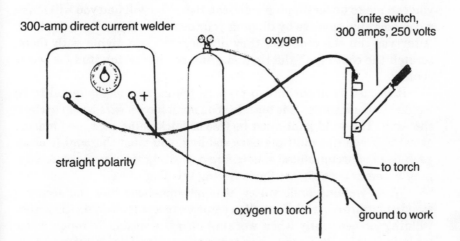

Fig. 7.2.   A direct current welding generator.

output of the welding power source must be increased by raising the open circuit voltage of direct current or by increasing the current setting in the other power sources. The electrode holder should be insulated, durable, and allow for easy changing of electrodes. It is desirable to send the diver only a few electrodes at a time since waterproofing protects the electrode covering for a limited time underwater. Fig. 7.3 shows an underwater electrode holder which can be made up by a machine shop.

It is recommended that fillet welds be made with 3/16-inch diameter rods except where the metal is too thin for that diameter. Tests have shown that single pass fillet welds made with 3/16-inch diameter rod average the same strength as 3-pass fillet welds made with 5/32-inch electrodes. By fillet welding with the 3/16-inch rods, only 1/3 of the welding time is required. No scraping or cleaning of the weld metal is necessary between passes, and the groove between the plates to be welded provides a positive guide in a single pass weld whereas in multipass welding, succeeding beads are inclined to wander due to the lack of this guide.

You can purchase rods which are waterproofed already, or you can dip your own rods. Commercially available products include: Sealac #30 from Duralac Chemical Co., Newark, N. J.; Ucilian from United Chemical Co., New York; and you can obtain sodium silica from any paint store. If you waterproof rods yourself mix one-half pound of celluloid in one gallon of acetone, or you can dip the rods in paraffin wax. You should dry out the rods in a stove prior to dipping them and allow them to dry for twenty-four hours after dipping. Fig. 7.4 shows a device you can make up for dipping your own rods. You will find you will make a considerable savings by dipping your own rods if you have the time. After you dip the rods and they are dry, prior to diving with them, scratch the coating off the tip and grind notches in the stud for better contact.

It is just as important to prepare the surface of the metal to be welded underwater as it is topside. You must have a wire brush to clean the area. The weld joint must be free of thick paint, rust, and marine growth. If you use multiple pass welding, you must thoroughly clean each bead of accumulated slag before depositing the next pass. A chipping hammer is necessary for removing this slag.

When welding underwater, it is recommended that you secure a steady platform to work from. You cannot expect to obtain a satisfactory welding job especially when working near the surface in rough water without it. Also, it is recommended that you attach the platform to the object to be welded rather than to some other equipment such as a ship

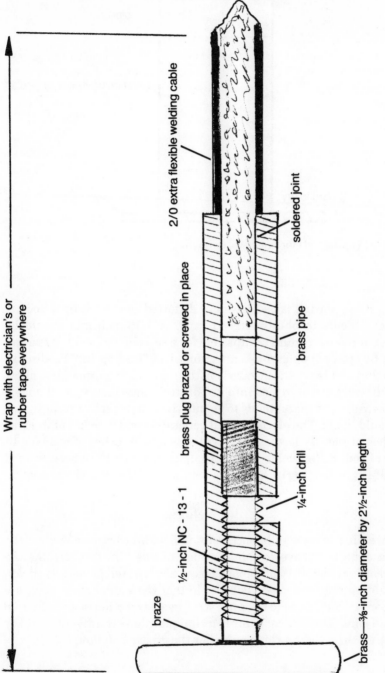

Wrap with electrician's or rubber tape everywhere

2/0 extra flexible welding cable

braze

½-inch NC - 13 - 1

brass plug brazed or screwed in place

¼-inch drill

soldered joint

brass pipe

brass—⅜-inch diameter by 2½-inch length

Fig. 7.3. An underwater electrode holder.

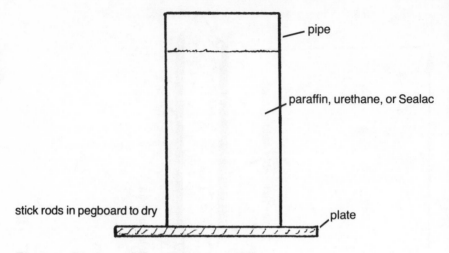

Fig. 7.4.   Dipping rods for underwater welding.

or float. If the plating is badly bent or distorted and the fit up is poor, it may be difficult to obtain a good weld. A 1/16-inch gap should be considered the maximum permissible for a satisfactory weld. If the gap cannot be closed, you can use a technique of "feeding in." Feeding in means that you leave the electrode in the gap area long enough to allow sufficient weld metal to feed into it. This technique is successful underwater because the metal tends to go into the gap instead of running out as it would in air. The electrode will generally yield 8 inches of weld for 10 inches of rod. By feeding in it will only give 6 inches of weld for 10 inches of rod. Fillet welds with gaps up to 1/8 inch have been welded successfully by feeding in, but the technique requires considerable skill.

Fillet Welding

Fillet welding is especially successful underwater because it gives the diver a definite groove to follow which allows him to overcome the limited or zero visibility problem he faces underwater. Generally speaking, welding requires good visibility in that the welder must pay close attention so that his bead does not stray even a fraction of an inch from the weld joint. The self-consuming technique allows the diver to weld by feel rather than sight as long as he has the groove to follow.

The following is the procedure to utilize for fillet welding:

1. Make sure the safety switch is open.

2. Fasten the ground lead to the work.

3. Clean the surfaces to be welded thoroughly.

4. Set the welding generator to deliver the proper current for the electrode and mode of welding to be used. The current is set from 0 to 30 percent higher than the topside current for the same electrode since the surrounding water absorbs the heat rapidly. (See Table 7.1)

Table 7.1 Current Settings for Underwater Welds

Electrode Size (Inches)	Position	Current (Amperes) (X)	Time for 12-inch Burnoff (Seconds)
5/32	H	170-210	56-44
5/32	V	170-210	56-44
5/32	O.H.	170-190	56-50
3/16	H	220-260	59-50
3/16	V	220-260	59-50
3/16	O.H.	190-210	66-61

5. Place the striking end of the electrode against the work so that the electrode is at an angle of approximately 30 degrees to the line of the weld. The angle may vary from 15 to 45 degrees depending on the type of electrode used and on the personal preferences of the diver.

6. Call for "current on." The arc should start when the tender closes the safety switch. If the arc does not start, tap or scrape the end of the electrode against the work until it does.

Once the arc has started, exert sufficient pressure against the work to allow the electrode to consume itself. Maintain the original angle between the electrode and the line of weld by moving the hand perpendicularly toward the surface being welded. Weld so that the bubbles generated from the stinger will interfere as little as possible with your visibility. Weld toward yourself. When the electrode is consumed, call for "current off" and keep the electrode in welding position until the tender has confirmed that the current is off. The tender must open the safety switch and keep it open while you change electrodes. Before you change to a new electrode, clean the end of the last bead. The next bead should slightly overlap the previous one. If a second pass is to be made over the first, the entire bead must be cleaned. Once the new electrode is in the stinger and in position against the work, call for "current on" and continue welding.

The same technique is used in the vertical position except that vertical fillet welding should begin at the top of the patch and work down. In the overhead position, the same technique is used also, except the current range is very narrow. Welds deposited using current settings outside this range will result in poor deposits or no deposits at all. Skillful divers can use a 35 to 55 degree angle of the electrode to work in the overhead position, and a steady rate of progression is governed by the diver. This requires considerable skill, but will produce fillet welds without undercutting which is involved when using the "self-consuming" technique. If you do not possess this skill, you should continue to use the self-consuming technique.

Repairing Cracks

Small cracks can be repaired underwater. You should locate the ends of the crack and drill or burn a small hole at each end to stop further cracking. Measure a plate to cover the crack and to fit to the contour of the base material. Then place the patch over the crack and weld around the edges until the patch is watertight. In a tight spot, you can strip a welding rod and beat it into the crack then lay a bead on top. However, a patch is preferable and yields a stronger repair job.

If proper fit up is accomplished, tests by the Navy have shown that a single pass 3/16-inch fillet weld can develop an ultimate tensile strength of approximately 10,000 pounds per linear inch of weld. When calculating the strength of a fillet weld, as shown in Table 7.2, a factor of safety must be incorporated. For static loading conditions, the factor of safety used is 6. In other words, the working strength of 1 inch of linear weld would be $10,000 \div 6$ or 1,600 pounds per linear inch of weld.

Table 7.2 Relative Strength of Underwater Fillet Welds

Electrode Size (Inches)	No. Passes	Strength lbs./linear inch	Factor of Safety—6	Strength to be Used in Calculating (Pounds)
5/32	3**	12,000	$\dfrac{12,000}{6}$	2,000* (1,400 for pad eyes)
3/16	1	10,000	$\dfrac{10,000}{6}$	1,600* (1,000 for pad eyes)

* Lower in overhead position
**Single pass weld with 5/32 inch electrode is too small to be reliable

If a pad eye is to be welded for lifting, the working strength is further reduced to account for the existence of unknown bending stresses which depend on the stiffness of the pad eye. Working strength for pad eyes is 1,000 pounds per linear inch of weld.

I patched a ship one time that was cruising around the world. The ship had settled on a stone at low tide which pushed the bottom plate up and cracked it. The crack was only a foot long, but the dent and the overhead welding position made the job difficult. The ship's captain assigned an expert welder to advise me as I did the job. I first welded a 1/8-inch plate to the hull just to seal the leak. Then, I put a 1/2-inch plate which was larger over the smaller 1/8-inch plate. After I finished, the crew was able to pump out the hold and put on another patch from the inside, close to the hull. After I had tacked it on, I welded a dog to the hull, then forced the plate down with a wedge (Fig. 7.5).

Cutting

Underwater cutting or burning is accomplished by three techniques. The oldest method of burning underwater was developed by Commander Edward Ellsberg of the U. S. Navy during the salvage of a World War I submarine. A bubble of air envelops the flame of hydrogen and oxygen underwater. Hydrogen is used as fuel because acetylene becomes unstable at pressures greater than 15 psi and is therefore unsuitable as a fuel at depths greater than 25 feet underwater. Another method of burning underwater is to use the oxy-arc torch which employs a tubular

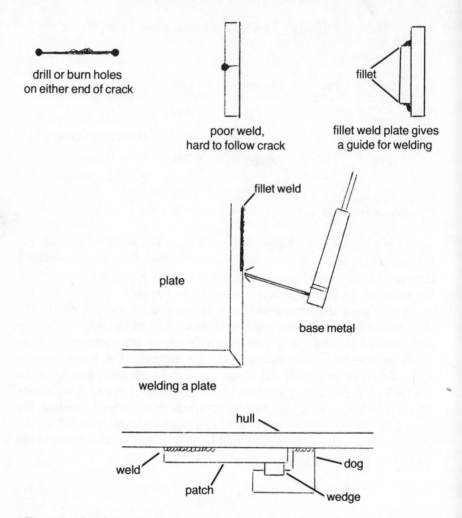

drill or burn holes
on either end of crack

poor weld,
hard to follow crack

fillet

fillet weld plate gives
a guide for welding

fillet weld

plate

base metal

welding a plate

hull

weld

patch

dog

wedge

Fig. 7.5.   Patching a hull.

steel electrode through which oxygen is blown to oxidize the molten
metal as the arc is struck. Oxy-arc is most efficient when burning steel
since nonferrous metals do not oxidize or burn when oxygen is blown on
the arcing metal and nonmetallic materials will not conduct electricity
to start an arc. The third type of underwater burning is accomplished
with the Broco torch. The Broco torch employs the principle of a burning
bar. Instead of being made up of tubular steel rods, the electrode consists
of several small solid steel rods and one magnesium rod encased in a

hollow tube through which oxygen is blown. Once the torch is ignited, it will continue to burn as long as the oxygen lever is depressed. The Broco torch burns anything once it is lit since magnesium continues to burn when oxygen is supplied whereas the oxy-arc torch will immediately extinguish itself if it loses the arc.

The Hydrogen Torch

The oxy-arch torch has almost completely replaced the hydrogen torch underwater because the latter takes considerable practice and experience to be able to cut consistently and rapidly underwater. The biggest problem with the hydrogen torch is adjusting the flame and keeping it lit underwater. In contrast the oxy-arc torch is lit by contact with the steel to be cut. Actually, the hydrogen torch cuts steel much faster and cleaner than the oxy-arc torch, is cheaper to use, and will burn through almost anything. (The Broco torch is the fastest of the three and is also easiest to learn.)

If you take the time to learn how to use the hydrogen torch and you already own one, you will find it irreplaceable for jobs such as cutting a cable out of a propellor in a ship or tug. The hydrogen torch will cut cable very fast, takes less time to set up, and has the added advantage that it will also burn nylon, manila, polypropylene, or sisal rope where the electric torch will not. There is also no need for a ground lead with the hydrogen torch. Cutting cable with the electric torch can be troublesome because the cable may be very greasy or rusty, preventing a good ground. In addition, if the cable has a rope core, which many do, you may have trouble cutting through with the electric torch if the arc goes out in the rope core. There is a danger, too, with the arc torch of cutting into the propeller shaft when working in muddy waters. There is little danger of cutting into the shaft with the hydrogen torch because of the amount of preheating that would be required to cut into a solid shaft.

Another advantage to consider with the hydrogen torch is the setup for an emergency job, or a job of short duration. The only supplies you need are gas—hydrogen, oxygen, and air. Everything can be loaded on a boat by hand, and with scuba gear, you can cut a cable out in no time. Compare this to taking a welding machine, cables, oxygen, switches, hard hat gear, and communications to the job site. Furthermore, the oxy-arc torch has to be staged from something capable of supporting all the necessary equipment.

In shallow water the hydrogen torch can be set topside before it is sent into the water. If it stays lit after it is in the water, it will probably burn a cable with no trouble. If it should go out, you can send it back topside and have the flame set a little higher before bringing it back down. In this way, you can burn without touching the torch settings in depths up to twenty feet. As you go deeper, you will have to keep setting the flame higher or it will go out. However, if you are diving in only fifty feet or so of water, set the gauge pressure shown on the chart (in Table 7.3) for that depth and set the torch to full flame and take it to the bottom. It should then have the proper setting for burning at that depth.

Table 7.3 Tip Sizes and Pressure for Hydrogen Torch

Steel Plate Thickness (Inches)	Tip	Initial Oxygen Pressure (Pounds)	Initial Fuel Pressure (Pounds)	Initial Air Pressure (Pounds)
Up to 3/8	1 UA 1 UH	25	3 to 5	1 to 2
1/2 to 3/4	2 UA 2 UH	25 to 35	5	1 to 2
3/4 to 1 1/4	2 UA 2 UH	35 to 50	5	1 to 2
1 1/4 to 3	3 UA 3 UH	50 to 75	7 to 10	1 to 2
3 up	4 UA 4 UH	75 and up	10 and up	1 to 2

Pressure Increases

Depth	Oxygen Pressure Increase (Pounds)	Fuel Gas Pressure Increase (Pounds)	Compressed Air Pressure Increase (Pounds)	Note
10	5	5	5	Pressure increases for
20	10	10	10	depth are at the rate of
25	12 1/2	12 1/2	12 1/2	1/2 pound increase for
50	25	25	25	each foot of depth.
75	37 1/2	37 1/2	37 1/2	
100	50	50	50	

Underwater, the hydrogen torch will burn as fast as an acetylene torch will topside. If you can burn topside with an acetylene torch, you can burn underwater with a hydrogen torch. If you have never used a torch before topside, try burning with the hydrogen torch on the surface. The hydrogen torch does not require changing rods underwater as the electric torch does; once the cut is started with the hydrogen torch, you can continue burning without interruption. I have used the oxy-arc, Broco, and hydrogen torches for many years. In my opinion, the hydrogen torch is faster than the oxy-arc torch, and the cheapest of the three to operate. Whenever I bid a lump sum contract for burning, I would use the hydrogen torch.

Burning with a Hydrogen Torch

When setting up a bank of cylinders for burning, follow this procedure (Fig. 7.6):

1. Place the cylinders in an upright position and where they will not be knocked over. Then secure them properly by chains or by lashing them in place.

2. Blow out the cylinder valves by opening the valve on the bottle for a short burst. This rids the outlets of any foreign matter.

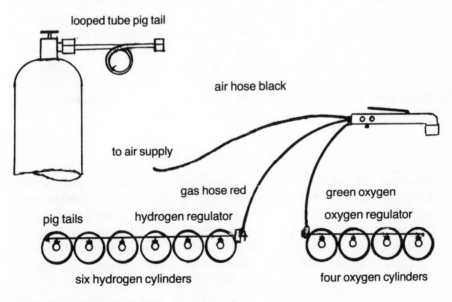

Fig. 7.6. Burning with a hydrogen torch.

3. Open the valves for a short burst to clear any foreign matter that may be in the hoses before you connect the torch after connecting the hoses to the gauges.

4. Select the proper tip size for the work you are doing from Table 7.3.

5. Use a striker to light the torch. Turn the torch away from everything and crack the hydrogen valve, then light it with the striker.

6. Turn up the hydrogen and turn on the oxygen and set the flame.

7. Turn on the compressed air and hand the torch to the diver if he is at the surface. If not, drop the torch into the water a couple of feet and see if it stays lit.

In shallow water with good visibility, the torch can be lowered to the diver. If you are using a lifeline separate from your umbilical, the torch can be tied to the line and you can pull it down. The torch is tied near the handle so the flame is beneath the line as it is lowered. You will see the light from the torch as it nears and can feel the knot where the line is tied to the torch. Grab the torch handle above the flame and you are ready to begin burning.

In deeper water, you must come to the surface to get the torch, because you have to adjust the flame as you descend or it will go out. Upon reaching the bottom, you can open the valves full blast and get good results if the gauge pressures have been correctly set topside. Otherwise, set the torch to where it suits you judging the sound and color of the flame. A pale blue is ideal when you have the visibility to determine the flame color. Table 7.3 gives the recommended gauge pressures at the surface for the hydrogen torch.

The Oxy-Arc Torch

Chances are you will use the oxy-arc torch more on long construction jobs where you work for a company. The oxy-arc torch works on the same principle as the hydrogen torch except the heat to melt the steel is created by the electric arc instead of the fuel from the torch. The oxygen is blown through the center of the electrode which is hollow. Table 7.4 indicates the performance of the oxy-arc torch on comparative steel thicknesses.

Fig. 7.7. A Mark XII diver on a welding project. Photo courtesy of Naval
Coastal Systems Center, U. S. Navy.

Table 7.4 Cutting Mild Steel

	Thickness of steel to be cut (Inches)			
	¼	½	¾	1
Minumum Cutting Speed (Inches per minute)	25	20	18	15
Tubular Steel Electrodes Consumed per 100 ft. of cut (Pounds/pieces)	21/70	29/100	29/100	33/110
Oxygen Consumed per 100 ft. of cut (Cubic feet)	250	300	350	400
Oxygen Consumed (psi)	20	30	40	50

To burn with the oxy-arc torch you will need a direct current welding generator of at least 300 amps connected for *straight* polarity. The leads should be 2/0 extra flexible welding cable in minimum lengths of 50 feet connected with male and female connectors taped over. An oxygen hose is taped onto the torch lead to supply oxygen to the torch. The other lead is the ground lead and should have a ground clamp fastened to the end. A knife switch rated over the maximum current you will be using is required. For example, it may be necessary to use a 600-amp machine for burning thick steel in deeper water. You should have at least a 600-amp knife switch for that machine. Oxygen cylinders, pigtails, and an oxygen regulator are also required.

The oxygen pressure at the gauge is set according to the thickness of the steel, the depth of the water, and the length of hose used to reach the diver. Use the table below to determine the basic pressure needed to cut the thickness of steel you will be working on, then add 5 psi for every 10 feet of depth you will be working and 10 psi for every 100 feet of hose used to reach the diver.

Oxygen Pressures for Cutting Steel

Plate Thickness (Inches)	Oxygen Pressure (psi)
¼	20
½	30
¾	40
1	50

If you are not certain of the polarity when setting up the torch, you may determine it by clamping a welding rod to the ground lead and placing one in the torch. By putting the two rods in a bucket of salt water about an inch apart, lots of bubbles will come out of the negative pole and very few from the positive pole when the switch is turned on. In other words, the rod in the torch should bubble profusely while the rod in the ground clamp should not. If this is not the case, switch the leads at the welding machine.

When you are ready to weld underwater, start the torch perpendicular to the surface you are going to burn (Fig. 7.8). If you angle the torch, you increase the thickness of metal to be burned and reduce your efficiency. However, if the metal to be burned is thin, then you may angle the cut somewhat to speed up your burning.

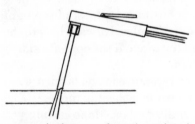

wrong (unless surface is painted, then lead into cut)

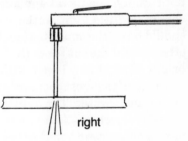

right

Fig. 7.8.   How to use the torch.

Burning with an Oxy-Arc Torch

When starting your cut, press the rod to the metal and signal for switch on. If there is no arc, pick up the rod a little or tap the metal with the rod until you get an arc. Then keep a constant pressure down on the metal and pull the tip along the line of the cut. If you get a flashback, stop and go back because the cut did not go completely through the metal.

Do not change rods until the tender has repeated your switch off command. Likewise do not signal for switch on until the rod is located in the cut and your fingers are not too near the tip of the rod, or you will get a jolt. I have been jolted many times by making these mistakes and can assure you it is not too serious, just unpleasant—you may lose feeling in your fingertips or taste every filling in your teeth as the electrolysis takes place, but these things pass.

When burning where you cannot see the cut, first make sure the switch is off, then with your left hand, put the rod where you are going to cut. Turn the switch on and keep your left hand on the rod. Hold the burning rod between your thumb and forefinger leaving your little finger on the steel (Fig. 7.9). Use your little finger as a guide on the metal to cut in a straight line by dragging it ahead of the cut.

Do not attempt to see your cut unless you are in an ideal position and you have good visibility. I look at the color of the light when I am in muddy waters. If the light is yellow on the side I am cutting, I know I am not through the metal and am getting a flashback from the arc. There should be little light on the side you are burning on. Most of the light should be on the opposite side. When I burn H piles, I always look to the other side of the cut to see the light from the torch. If the opposite side is bright, then I know I am burning through.

One of the most common jobs a diver is required to do is burn sheet piling underwater. The hardest part to burn in a sheet is the lock (Fig. 7.10). The lock is about two inches thick altogether. Make certain you have a good ground on the sheeting because rusty sheets can cause poor grounding which will reduce the heat on your torch. To cut through the lock, cut a one-inch piece out of the lock facing you. This will expose the male part of the lock and enable you to cut through it. Then, by pushing your rod through the male part of the lock, you can cut the other half—the female lock—with ease. Do not try to cut through the whole lock without taking out the first piece, or it will take you twice as long to cut the sheet and you will waste a lot of rods trying. Diver time and rods are expensive.

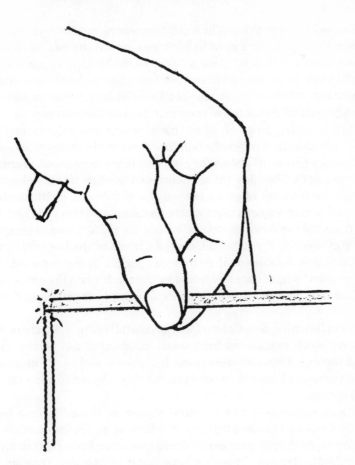

Fig. 7.9.   Burning when you can't see the cut.

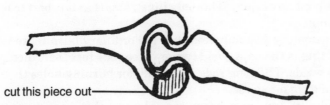

cut this piece out

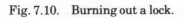

Fig. 7.10.   Burning out a lock.

You seldom get to burn in a position where you have visibility and can look through your cut to be sure you are taking out all the metal. Cutting sheets is usually done as close to the bottom as you can get so you will have to lie flat and keep your face close to the bottom while you are burning. When you burn sheets off a cofferdam, however, you will be burning them off at the top of the concrete pour (see Chapter 9).

When cutting ships or other objects where gas pockets may occur, there is always the danger of a buildup of gas on the opposite side of your cut. Torches throw off gas as they burn so there are certain precautions you must take (besides those mentioned earlier in this chapter) to prevent the buildup of gases behind the cut. Fig. 7.11 illustrates the right and wrong ways to burn where gases may be trapped. You should burn from the top down thereby allowing the rising gases to escape from the top of the cut. If you burn from the bottom or the low side upwards, the rising gas bubbles will form a gas pocket at the high side of the compartment which may be ignited by the torch when the cut is made in that location. The result will be an explosion which can cause danger to you.

When burning on a flat surface horizontally (Fig. 7.12) there may be frequent small explosions from small buildups of gas on the opposite side of the cut. This situation is not hazardous, and really unavoidable unless there is a high side where you can start the cut to allow the rising gas to escape.

These explosions can be quite strong at times. I have had my faceplate cracked several times by the force of an explosion while burning. The most violent one I experienced was when I was cutting up a ship in Portland, Oregon. The ship was lying on its side with an angle upward. I was burning through a bulkhead and built up a gas pocket on the other side. When my flames hit the pocket, I was thrown back and dazed from the force of the explosion. The topside crew felt the shock also and everyone thought I must have been hurt. When I came to the surface, my face plate was cracked in several places. I was lucky not to have suffered any injury. This only illustrates that it is best to follow all precautions.

Occasionally you may find that the ordinary burning rods are too short. If this is the case, weld two or three rods together, then put tape over the welds. The long rods are handy for burning holes through the bottom of a rig for spuds.

Spuds are put on a barge to replace anchors and lines used for working the rig into position. By putting spuds down, the barge is anchored in the precise location for working. To put spuds on a barge,

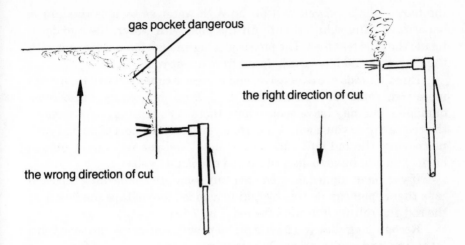

gas pocket dangerous

the right direction of cut

the wrong direction of cut

Fig. 7.11. Right and wrong ways of cutting to prevent buildup of gases behind cut.

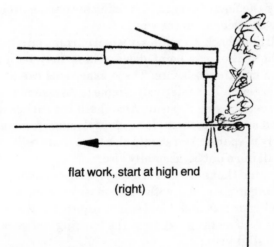

flat work, start at high end
(right)

Fig. 7.12. Burning on a flat surface.

cut a hole in the deck, then lower a pipe through the hole and weld it to the bottom of the barge from the inside and to the deck. Your next problem is to cut the hole through the bottom of the barge inside the pipe for the spud to go through. If you attempt to cut through the bottom of the barge, the spudwell will fill up with water as soon as the hull is penetrated. The solution is to fill the pipe with water, then go down inside the pipe feet first. The pipe is just big enough for you to squat with the long rods and burn the hole out from under you.

Burning rods are expensive, and there are times you will take down more rods than you will use that day. Often the coating will become damaged and may leave spots where there is no coating. Bare spots on the rod can give you a jolt. Also, when you get to the part of the rod with no coating, the rod will stick to the metal and you will not be able to burn. You will have to discard the rod and get a fresh one.

If you have some damaged rods, buy some sticky masking tape and tape them. You can do this by taking a wide piece of tape the length of the rod and rolling it around the rod (Fig. 7.13).

Recognizing that you have a problem with your torch can save you a lot of time and aggravation. One of the most common causes of trouble is slag that has backfired up into the torch and which reduces the amount of oxygen coming through the rod. You may realize right away why you are having difficulty burning. Whenever I notice that I am slowing down, I check the flow of oxygen by holding my hand in front of the torch and pressing the trigger all the way.

Slag will blow back very quickly when burning on a flat surface like the deck where the rods point down. There may be a lot of minor explosions as mentioned before. These explosions can send some slag into the rod or torch. It is relatively simple to disassemble the torch and check the screen for slag deposits. Also check the rubber washer inside where the rod sits in the torch. It needs replacing often and you should carry a supply of spares. You should also have spare collets for the torch since they will burn out occasionally also.

Keep in mind that seawater is a very good conductor of electricity. If you are burning in a wet suit with a face mask or in scuba, you will feel a tingle around your face and if any skin is exposed, it will tingle also. By keeping your face as far away from the burning rod as possible, there will be only a slight tingle.

You can get a shock underwater when you are not burning. I was using scuba gear to set an intake pipe through a wall of steel sheeting. All I did was touch the sheets and I got a jolt. I surfaced to find a welder working about fifty feet from where I was diving. There was a steel I beam from the deck of the steel barge to the sheets that the crew was using for a walk. The welder had his ground cable clamped to the barge. The current then passed from the barge through the I beam to the sheets which extended underwater where I was working. My being in the

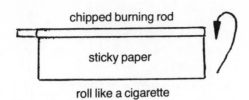

Fig. 7.13.   Dealing with a chipped rod to be burned.

water between the sheeting and the barge, with seawater as a conductor, put me in the field between the steel sheeting and the steel barge. Every time the welder struck an arc, I would feel the current. I stopped the welder from working until a wooden gangplank was put between the barge and the sheeting. Thereafter, I was no longer the object of stray electric currents.

Whenever you feel jolts underwater, look for welders working topside. If you are welding or burning underwater, look where you have placed your ground. If the ground is in back of you, then you have placed yourself in the field between the rod and ground and the water between the ground and your rod is carrying the current through you. This can be extremely dangerous! Make sure the ground is to your left or right, but not behind you.

Emergency burning rods can be made out of 5/16-inch steel tubing or 1/8-inch extra strong iron pipe in 14-inch lengths or longer if needed. Cover all except the grip end in 3 wraps of masking tape. When using the homemade rods, make sure you have good rubber gloves because they may give you a jolt. Use them only in an emergency.

To burn nonferrous metal, or to burn steel plate when no oxygen is available, use 3/16-inch welding electrodes and crank up the power on the welding machine. Cutting is accomplished by dragging and sawing with the rod. The technique is effective, but a lot slower than other methods of cutting. The metal is made molten by the heat and is pushed out of the cut with the welding rod.

CHAPTER EIGHT

Underwater Explosives

THE USE OF explosives under any circumstances requires competent licensed personnel. Since this chapter is not intended as a primer in the use of explosives, the information here is to be applied only by those who have prior experience or training in the handling and use of explosives.

Explosives are the most powerful tool you can have at your disposal. In a fraction of a second, it is possible to accomplish a task that would take weeks by hand or to do certain tasks that could not otherwise be accomplished at all. As an example, I was called on to remove a four-foot diameter propellor from a fishing vessel underwater. On dry land, this job takes yard workers all day with hydraulic pullers, heating the hub with a torch, and banging with sledge hammers. It is never an easy job; underwater it is presumed by many to be impossible. It so happened that a diving company had previously tried to pull the propellor using two divers working for two days with hydraulics. They were unsuccessful. I knew that Navy divers were able to do this job with ease. How? They did it the same way I did it—with a precise amount of explosive charge properly placed and tamped. I had the propellor off the shaft in less than one hour and was only in the water for five minutes.

Blaster's License

You do not always need a blaster's license for it is possible to work under the supervision of a licensed blaster. Again, however, anyone handling explosives must be properly trained. There are certain advantages in hiring a licensed blaster to work with you on a job even if you have a license of your own. Since an experienced licensed blaster makes his living by working with explosives, he is an expert at handling, storing, and transporting them. He also has all of the permits, equipment, and insurance required. For you to maintain and carry these, and keep all of

Fig. 8.1. Diver placing instruments on underwater staging. Photo courtesy of Naval Coastal Systems Center, U. S. Navy.

the records required (whether you use any explosives or not) would be too costly and time-consuming unless you were going to use explosives constantly in your diving business.

For most divers, explosives are used only on occasion. Even if you run into a job which will run for some time, or if you decide to specialize in underwater explosives, you still will need someone topside to assist in making up charges and handling the explosives. Besides, an experienced blaster can offer invaluable advice, and it is a secure feeling to know that your topside crew is competent in handling the explosives. A licensed blaster is the logical choice for the topside job for safety, insurance purposes, and for the invaluable advice he can provide.

I have held a blaster's license for over twenty-five years, but I always use another licensed blaster for transporting, storing, and handling the explosives topside whenever I do a blasting job.

Explosives

There are quite a few underwater explosives available but plastic explosives, and recently liquid explosives, have a wide range of use in underwater work, especially for making up shape charges and specialty devices such as chain cutters and well casing cutters. For information on specialized use of explosives underwater, contact the Broco Corporation (Pomona, California 91767).

C-4 (Composition-4) is the most commonly used plastic explosive. It is white in color, more powerful than TNT (trinitrotoluene), is not greasy, has no odor, and is relatively stable. Detonation velocity is 26,500 fps (feet per second). C-4 remains pliable in temperatures of −20 degrees F to 170 degrees F, it comes in a 2½-pound block which measures 11 inches by 2 inches by 2 inches. C-4 is good for cutting steel and breaching concrete.

TNT is one of the least sensitive types of explosives. It is reasonably stable in any climate and is not affected by moisture. Therefore, it is one of the most durable for underwater use. It comes in one-half-, one-, and eight-pound solid blocks usually packed in cardboard or in tin containers with holes in the ends for caps. TNT should not be removed from its container because of its highly toxic fumes.

Blasting gelatin travels at 23,000 fps and is generally made up from nitrocotton and nitroglycerin or ammonia gelatin. It is used for excavation underwater such as trenching. Gelatin dynamite is good for about 72 hours underwater.

Straight dynamite is made from wood pulp and nitroglycerin. It has a velocity of 19,000 fps and is fairly resistant to water. Dynamite is a good general-purpose explosive for underwater excavation and demolition, and it is inexpensive.

Tetrytol is composed of 75 percent tetryl and 25 percent TNT. It has many of the same characteristics as TNT, but is better for cutting and breaking. Tetrytol is stable in character with a velocity of 23,000 fps.

PETN (pentaerythritetra nitrate) is a white colored high explosive which is used as the explosive core in detonating cord and as a base charge in blasting caps.

Detasheet is an explosive made by the Du Pont Company, and it comes in sheets. It is very flexible, and is good over a wide range of temperatures. It is easy to cut with a knife, is waterproof, and safe to use. Detasheet also may be purchased in a variety of extruded shapes for specialty charges. It is made of PETN and an elastic binding. It can be ordered by writing to Chemical Products Division, Explosives Department, E. I. Du Pont De Nemours & Co., Inc., Wilmington, Delaware 19898. (Du Pont also publishes a blaster's handbook available on request, see Useful References.)

Triex and Quadrex are two component liquid-liquid and liquid-solid explosives with high detonation velocities. The components are stable individually and may be shipped by common carrier. Triex has seen considerable use recently underwater for specialty charges. Triex and Quadrex are available from Broco.

Effects of Water on Explosives

The presence of a water environment around an area to be blasted creates problems which are not present in topside blasting. Water visibility, surge, and currents hinder the planning, preparations, and placement of explosive charges. The effectiveness of the blast will be affected by the depth of the water as well as the resistance of the explosive to deterioration from submergence.

A charge shot underwater must move the water over and around the rock or material shot before the object can move. Underwater, it will take from two to six times the amount of explosive normally required to break and move rock on dry land. The deeper the water, the more weight there is on the particular surface to be blasted; therefore, more explosive will be required to break and move material at deeper depths than in shallow water.

Most explosives deteriorate when exposed to water. Some have a higher resistance to water than others and are preferred for underwater use. The resistance of any explosive to deterioration underwater is adversely affected by currents or surge action to the exposed part of the

Fig. 8.2.   Mark XVI mixed gas scuba divers. Photo courtesy of Naval Coastal Systems Center, U. S. Navy.

explosive. In still water, a charge placed in a bore may last for days, weeks, or even years, but when exposed to currents or surge action, it may deteriorate in a matter of hours. Most explosives, when submerged, lose some of their efficiency and may on prolonged exposure reach a point where they will not detonate.

Making Up Charges

Here again, this section will not deal with the specifics. Making up charges is covered in a basic demolitions course. The information given here is intended to supplement and add what is required for using explosives underwater.

The detonator (blasting cap) has lead wires which are connected to the blasting machine. When an electric current is applied to the two wires, the charge is detonated. Any stray current has the potential of accidentally setting off the detonator. For this reason, the lead wires and blasting wires must be shunted (twisted together) until the charge is ready to be detonated. Since seawater is an excellent conductor of electricity, it is of utmost importance that you exercise caution when using explosives underwater. Make certain there is no welding going on in the vicinity. Be sure radio transmission is halted topside. Anything that could introduce a stray current in air or underwater must be checked before making up charges. Electric blasting caps may be used underwater as they come out of the box. No special preparation is necessary.

Occasionally, you may choose to use a nonelectric cap to detonate your charge underwater. This is okay for a small job where control is not important (for example, in remote areas). The disadvantage, of course, is the lack of control you have over when detonation occurs. (You won't want any boat traffic in the area). You will also be running a higher risk of a hang fire. The advantage is you don't need as much equipment. To make up a nonelectric cap for use underwater, simply crimp the cap twice, 1/16 inch between crimps as illustrated in Fig. 8.3.

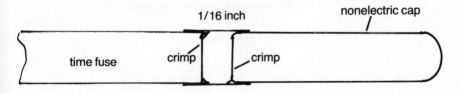

Fig. 8.3.   Safety fuse crimp for underwater use.

Using Detonating Cord

Detcord and Primacord are detonating cords which have a variety of uses underwater. The core of the cord in either product is a high explosive consisting of PETN. Detonating velocity is 26,000 fps. Slower and faster Detcord is available for specific applications, and is color coded by its velocity, the colors being yellow, orange, and pink. Pink detonates the fastest at 28,000 fps, orange at 26,000 fps, and yellow at 22,000 fps. The faster explosive is used for cutting, and the slower is better for pushing. For example, you would choose the faster explosive to cut pilings and the slower explosive to loosen a propellor from its shaft without damaging the prop or the shaft.

Detcord is also useful for detonating multiple charges with one cap. The cord can be run in one continuous length or branched with girth hitches to the charges. When running cord, avoid kinks or sharp bends of less than 40 degrees, otherwise the cord can shoot itself out. Fig. 8.4 illustrates the proper way to make up a charge with detonating cord and cap.

To cut timber or pilings underwater with cord, wrap a 3- to 6-inch diameter timber with 15 turns of cord (Fig. 8.5). Or, use dynamite or TNT-staggered charges as shown in Fig. 8.6.

To loosen a propellor underwater (Fig. 8.7), use one turn of low velocity detonating cord for each inch of shaft diameter. Tamp the charge with old manila line or sandbags tied securely. To blow off the propeller in order to salvage the material (this will destroy the shaft and prop), tie sticks of dynamite around the shaft and tamp as shown in Fig. 8.8.

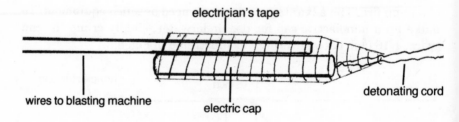

Fig. 8.4.   Detonating cord and cap charge for underwater use.

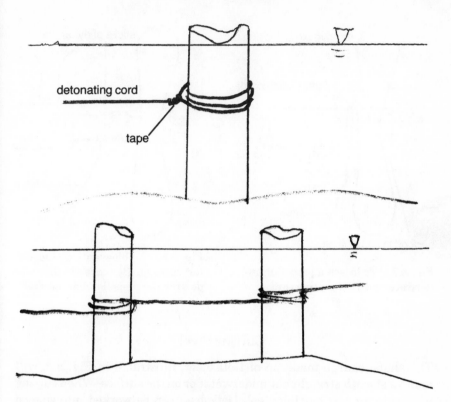

Fig. 8.5. Cutting pilings with detonating cord.

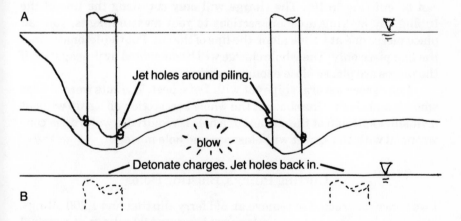

Fig. 8.6. Cutting pilings with staggered charges.

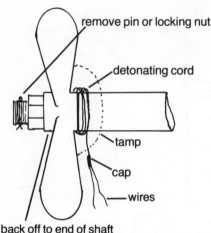

Fig. 8.7. To loosen a propellor underwater with detonating cord.

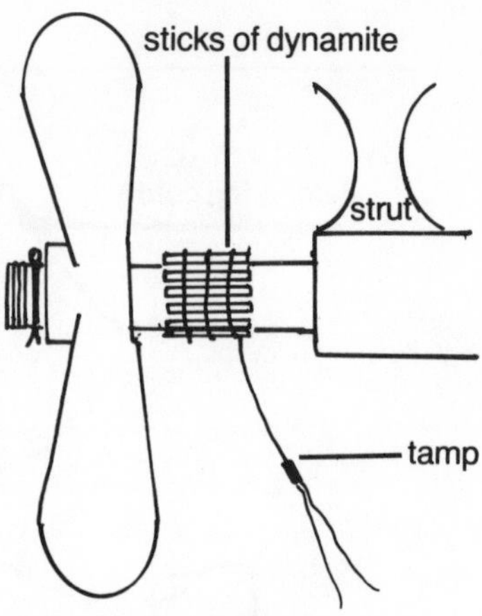

Fig. 8.8. To blow entire propellor
for salvage. *Be warned:* this will
destroy the propellor and the shaft.

Cutting Steel

The shape charge made up of Detasheet, illustrated in Fig. 8.9, will
make a smooth straight cut underwater or on the surface. When cutting
up a ship, or just cutting steel, Detasheet can be worked into shaped
charges or may be used unshaped. By bending copper tubing, any shape
can be cut (Fig. 8.10). The charge will only cut along the line of the
tubing. By making up short sections to your measurements, you can
place pieces one at a time along the line of the cut. Put the detonator into
the last piece only. The whole charge will be detonated by propagation if
the pieces are placed close enough together.

I have seen several ships cut with Detasheet. The cuts were always
smooth and clean. One shot cut the whole bow section off a ship without
a violent explosion at the surface. If a hole is required, a waterproof cone
wrapped with Detasheet will blast a round hole in steel.

Cutting Pilings, Blasting Holes

I was once contracted to remove an old ferry slip that had 1,200 pilings.
My procedure was to choke a long cable around 20 pilings at a time. I
hooked the cable to a bulldozer on shore which pulled the cable tight. By
using small charges, the 20 piles were cut off, and the bulldozer was able
to pull the whole bundle to shore where the pilings were trucked away.

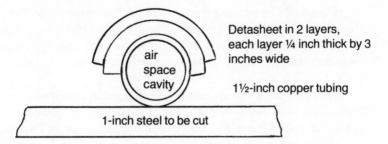

Detasheet in 2 layers,
each layer ¼ inch thick by 3
inches wide

1½-inch copper tubing

By closing ends of tube to prevent flooding of cavity, the assembly can be used underwater.

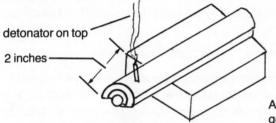

Allow 2-inch overhang to
get jet cutting started.

Fig. 8.9.   Using a shaped charge of Detasheet.

Plate can also be cut using only Detasheet and works in air or underwater just as well.

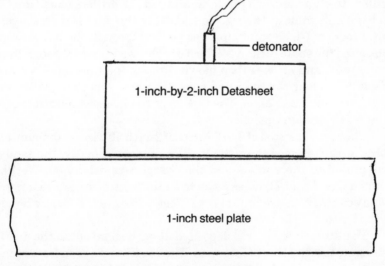

Fig. 8.10.   Using an unshaped charge of Detasheet.

I started the process from shore and worked out to the end of the slip. After I shot the first bundle, I had a hole which enabled me to shoot the rest of the bundles four feet below the mud line. This way no butts were left sticking out of the mud line which might be hazardous to small craft.

Another job I did required a hole to be dynamited through a concrete wall at a refinery pumping station. The purpose was to clear a space for a pipeline which was to run out to the river. The concrete was twenty-five years old making it so hard that a jackhammer had little effect on it. I drilled holes one foot deep and used one-quarter stick charges of dynamite placed in the holes one at a time and shot them. Using this method, I was able to chip through the wall without damage.

Blasting and Trenching Techniques

As supervisor of a pipe crossing job on a river which was 700 feet wide, I had to create a trench in order to place pipes below the river bottom. Two pipes were to be laid side by side. One pipe was a 6-foot diameter line, the other was a 10-foot diameter line. The pipes were fabricated from concrete 1 foot thick. Beneath the river bottom was shale rock which had to be blasted. To accommodate the drilling rig, five holes were burned through the deck of the barge at the rake of the bow. A 6-inch pipe was welded to the deck and to the rake under the deck. These holes were used to drill through. At the front of the barge, a platform was welded for the drillers to stand on. The platform allowed the drillers to add drill steel and work in front of the rig. To penetrate the mud and sand over the shale rock, a 4-inch sand pipe was pushed through the bottom until it contacted the shale rock. A 3½-inch drill bit was passed through the pipe to the mud, and air was then blown through the steel pipes containing the drill to clear the mud and sand. The hole was then drilled in the absence of mud and sand. The pipe kept the hole clean until the dynamite was placed in the hole.

Charges consisted of 5 to 7 sticks of 2-inch 40 percent dynamite. The holes were stemmed with small chips of stone. Finally, the sand pipe was pulled to the surface and the charge was detonated. Working 9 hours a day, I shot 12 holes a day to a minimum of six feet below grade. (Many contractors prefer to shoot 10 feet below grade to insure breakage at the bottom of the trench.)

The dug out shale was deposited at each shore out to the middle of the river, leaving the middle open. The result was a road from each side which was used to roll the pipes out with bulldozers. Pipes were then loaded to the rig for laying in the trench. The roads were also used to truck in stones to cover the pipes. When the pipe had been laid and bedded, the roads were used to backfill and stabilize the trench.

Excavation Techniques

Underwater explosive excavation for small jobs can be accomplished by one of three methods: contact blasting, snakeholing, and blockholing. Larger excavation techniques are beyond the scope of this book and require the assistance of blasting engineers. (For further information, consult *Guide to Underwater Explosive Excavation* which can be obtained from J. S. Brower & Associates, Inc., 2040 N. Towne Avenue, Pomona, CA 91767.)

Contact Blasting

This method is accomplished by placing an external charge on the material to be excavated or broken (Fig. 8.11). When used for breaking rocks, the contact blasting charge shatters the rock in a process called cratering. As the explosive detonates, it imparts a violent shock to the material in much the same way as a powerful sledge hammer would.

The most effective explosives for underwater contact blasting are those with the highest detonation velocities. The efficiency of contact

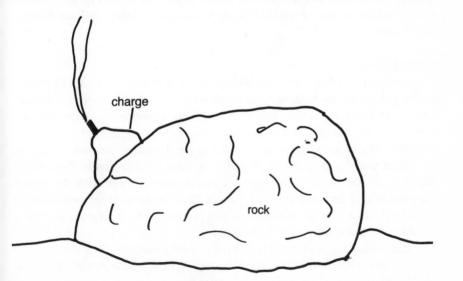

Fig. 8.11. Contact blasting charge.

blasting depends on how good the contact is between the explosive and the material to be blasted. Sand or water between the explosive and the rock will cushion the shock of the blast and reduce the effectiveness of the charge. The shape of the charge is also important, and special shape charges are available for contact blasting. If plastic explosives are used, a conical pile initiated at the top produces the best result as illustrated (Fig. 8.11).

When diver time is a consideration, contact blasting is the preferred technique. It requires the least amount of time for the diver to place the charges.

Since contact blasting breaks up the material but often leaves the shattered pieces in the same location, another method is usually required to remove the broken material. A linear rope charge placed directly over the broken material will blow the fractured material outward in both directions. The downward pressure caused by detonation washes the material from the area below and adjacent to the charge. Repeated charges of this type can be used to deepen and widen a trench effectively.

Contact charges are often undesirable in areas where waves, surge, or current effects are strong enough to move the charges from their desired locations. Weights or spike tie downs may be used to secure the charges in their desired locations, but caution must be used to avoid having the tie downs become unwanted projectiles. It may be preferable to use blockholing or snakeholing techniques under these adverse conditions.

Snakeholing

Snakeholing is used if boulders or formations are buried or partially buried in the bottom. It is a combination of internal and external charge techniques in that the explosive is confined by the surrounding mud, but the charge is still external to the rock being blasted (Fig. 8.12). Snakeholing is accomplished by drilling a hole under the rock in such a way that the charge may be placed in contact with the rock. The better the contact, the better the result. The hole may be jetted with the water jet pipe nozzle as indicated in Chapter 2, or by some other mechanical means. A charge is then made up and placed in the hole assuring that good contact is made with the boulder.

Snakeholing is one of the simplest and most effective methods of boulder or rock section blasting. However, it is only efficient where holes can be drilled quickly and easily under the rock so that direct contact can be made between the explosive and the rock to be blasted.

Blockholing

This method as shown in Fig. 8.13 is an internal charge technique based on drilling and loading one or more holes in a rock or ledge. It is used mainly for removing an obstacle. The charge required by this technique is less than that required by contact blasting or snakeholing

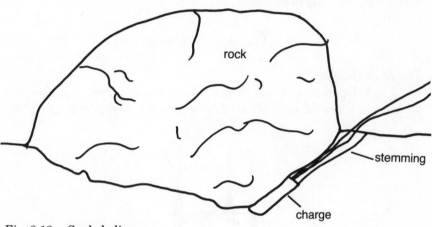

Fig. 8.12.   Snakeholing.

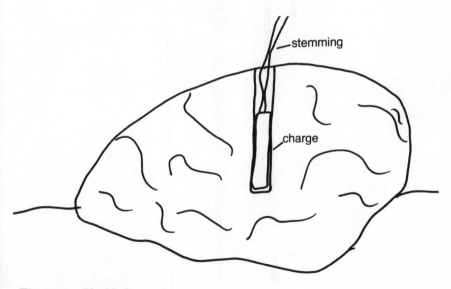

Fig. 8.13.   Blockholing.

because the confinement of the charge inside the material yields a higher efficiency. However, blockholing requires drilled holes in the material to be excavated, and drilling underwater requires additional equipment and diver time. Under some circumstances, it may not be possible to obtain the required drill holes. The explosives will be most efficient if the holes are drilled so that each charge is close to the center of the rock which is to be shattered.

Alternate Methods

The Rock Chopper

I developed this device (Fig. 8.14) to widen a trench underwater without the use of explosives. The trench we were working on was

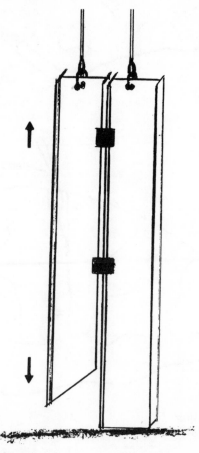

Fig. 8.14.   The rock chopper.

blasted to accommodate the two large pipes being laid (see Blasting and Trenching Techniques above). After blasting a trench through 20 feet of shale rock, it was determined that there were high spots and that the sides needed to be widened. Normally, divers must shoot the high spots and sides; but, on this job, there was too much to do. At this point I designed the rock chopper which widened the trench and cut down the high spots.

The rock chopper is made from two I beams two feet wide and one inch thick. One beam is the guide which sits on the bottom. The other beam is the chopper which slides up and down the guide. The chopper is fabricated easily by welding the guide clamps on the I beam.

The Hydraulic Rock Jack

Another valuable device is the hydraulic rock jack (Fig. 8.15) which can be used for splitting rocks or concrete without the use of explosives. The jack and shim are two inches in diameter, so a two-and-one-quarter-inch hole is drilled into the concrete or rock to be split. The jack is inserted in the hole and pumped by hand. The jack is capable of splitting large rocks and stretching or breaking reinforcing rods in concrete so that a torch can be inserted to cut the rest.

For best results, two rock jacks are used at one time. As with most hydraulic tools, the rock jack works as well underwater as it does on the surface.

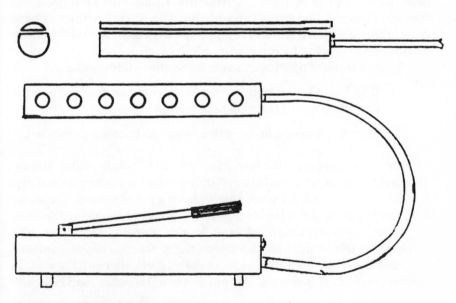

Fig. 8.15.   The hydraulic rock jack.

CHAPTER NINE

Underwater Concrete

CONCRETE has a wide variety of uses in underwater construction and repair work. Durability and low cost are primary considerations for the use of concrete in marine work. There are many structures today which are built exclusively with reinforced concrete as a constituent material. Many of the modern bridge designs use concrete for the entire structure with the foundations poured underwater and the superstructure fabricated from precast concrete which is later bonded to the foundation.

Tremie Pipe Method

Making a good concrete pour for a foundation underwater is critically important to the integrity of the structure. Bridges have collapsed and structures have failed owing to poor foundation work. Contractors have gone broke when core samples reveal improper concrete, and the entire foundation is rejected by inspectors.

Two methods of pouring concrete foundations underwater are:

1. Build a cofferdam which extends above the surface and pump it dry allowing the concrete to be poured in the dry.

2. Pour the concrete in the water using the tremie pipe method.

The first method (dry cofferdam) is limited to shallow water and requires a tremie pour to seal the cofferdam before it can be pumped dry. Fig. 9.1 shows a typical tremie pipe with a hopper at the top. The slings hold the hopper and the tremie pipe at the proper level during the pour.

Concrete is a mixture of sand, stones, cement, and water. The proportions of the mixture determine the properties of the hardened concrete. If too much water is added to the mixture, there will be voids in the concrete when it sets up. Too much water, therefore, will critically

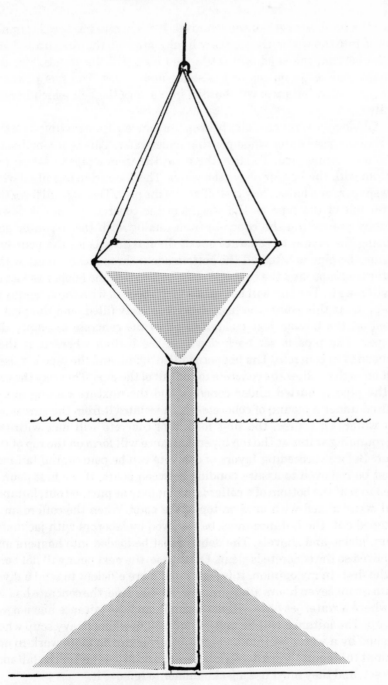

Fig. 9.1.   A typical tremie pipe.

alter the final strength of the material. If a concrete mixture is simply poured into the water, the stones will separate from the mixture and fall to the bottom, the sand will settle next on top of the stones, and the cement will settle on top of the sands and stones. The fine powdery cement, called laitance, will harden into a smooth shell which breaks easily.

Obviously, it is necessary to keep the concrete from mixing with the surrounding seawater when pouring underwater. This is accomplished with the tremie pipe. To start the pour, the tremie pipe is set on the bottom with the hopper above the water. Then, a burlap bag filled with newspapers or a bale of hay is stuffed into the pipe. The bag will force the water out of the pipe as the weight of the concrete pushes it down, thereby preventing the concrete from mixing with the seawater and causing the stones to separate out of the mixture. Once the pour has begun, the pipe is lifted off the bottom about three inches to allow the water to escape, and the concrete must be added to the hopper as fast as it will take it. The bag will be pushed to the bottom with the concrete on top of it. At this point, the hopper is completely filled, and the pipe is lifted off the bottom just enough to allow the concrete to empty the hopper. The pipe is set back down on the bottom where it is then embedded in concrete. The hopper is filled again, and the pipe is raised just enough to allow the concrete to run out of the pipe. This way the end of the pipe is buried under concrete and the mixture coming out is poured under a mound of concrete which isolates it from the surrounding water. Of course, the first mound of concrete will mix with the surrounding water at the top layer. Laitance will form on the top of the pour. Before succeeding layers of concrete can be poured, the laitance must be removed to assure bonding between pours. If the first pour is used to seal the bottom of a cofferdam so it may be pumped out, laitance will occur mixed with mud on top of the pour. When the cofferdam is pumped out, the laitance must be removed by laborers with jackhammers, picks, and shovels. The debris must be loaded into hoppers and removed so the concrete is clean. Otherwise, the next pour will not bond to the first. In my opinion, it is faster and more efficient to send a diver down about seven hours after the pour. At this time, the concrete has set to where a water jet hose will not harm it, and the laitance has not yet set up. The laitance will be mushy and will flow like heavy soup when washed by a water jet into an airlift. A diver can do more work in one hour at this point than a dozen laborers can do in a day after the laitance has set, and they must use a jackhammer to remove it.

Considering the cost of a rig, crew, and laborers, the price for a diver sent down before the laitance has set will save thousands of dollars later. Of course, if delays occur and the diver cannot go down before the laitance has set up, the laborers will have to be hired after all. The laitance can be removed easily from the seventh hour to the tenth or eleventh. After eleven hours, the laitance will be too hard to wash with a jet hose, and the job will have to be done in the dry.

Wherever cofferdams are being built, you, as a diver, should make the contractor aware of the advantage of letting you clean the laitance between pours before it sets up.

Excavating a Cofferdam

The fastest way to remove the buildup of soil from inside a cofferdam is first to dig each pocket between the cross bracing in the cofferdam with a clamshell. Then you can wash the soil to an airlift with a high pressure water jet. The back pressure nozzle made of pipe fittings described in Chapter 2 is a good choice. With this nozzle, you can twist the end and point a stream up the sheeting to loosen the soil that sticks in each bay of the sheets. Then by pointing the other end down and towards the airlift, you can clean a sheet in a matter of minutes.

By keeping a line tied to the airlift, you can always direct the flow of soil directly at the airlift and keep a good flow of soil through the pipe. You can also follow the line over to the airlift to assure its proper placement. With a line directly to the airlift, the volume of soil removed is greatly increased because you can wash the dirt directly into the airlift without actually being able to see the lift. Without the line or good visibility, you will simply move the dirt around with the jet and not remove it with the airlift. Divers are often called in only to inspect a cofferdam after the topside crew has attempted to do the job with the airlift and jet operated from topside. You can clean out a dam in less than half the time a topside crew can because you are able to direct the flow of mud to the airlift, whereas the topside crew mostly sucks up dirty water. If you are a good diving contractor you will be able to convince a contractor who is driving a cofferdam that using a diver can save him time and money on the job.

Checking a Cofferdam after Excavation

Piles are often driven inside the cofferdam for reinforcement, causing the bottom to rise above grade as the piling displaces the mud and soil. The cofferdam is excavated with a jet pipe and airlifted by the topside crew without the diver, and the diver checks the dam after excavation to make certain that all the mud is removed from between the sheeting and from inside the web of the piling. Sometimes you will find a mound of dirt around the pilings that will rise six to ten feet off the bottom. Here it is best to dig the bottom a little deeper, and bring it to grade by dumping stones around the piles after they have been driven. This will also eliminate some of the mud by stabilizing the soil with stones. Mud lodged between the sheeting may rise high off the bottom. Any of these situations must be remedied prior to pouring the concrete and it is imperative that you make a thorough inspection and correct any high spots before the pour is made to seal the cofferdam. Lives may depend upon it.

Suppose the bottom pour is to be eight feet thick in concrete to seal the cofferdam. If you miss a high spot of mud, it will decrease the thickness of the pour at that location causing a weak spot or a hole in the concrete seal. When the cofferdam is pumped out, the water pressure from beneath will blow the seal at the weak point. If the cofferdam has been pumped dry and workers are inside when the seal breaks, their lives may be lost. Make certain when making an inspection inside a cofferdam that you check every sheet and piling.

When the bottom pour is being made and there is a lot of silt and mud on the bottom, the concrete will sink through the mud causing the mud to rise above the concrete as the pour is being made. If the cofferdam is large, the pour will be started at one end and brought to grade as it is being poured. This means that there is a ten-foot wall of concrete plowing over the bottom causing the mud to rise ahead of it. By the time it reaches the other end of the cofferdam, there will be mud against the sheeting on the far end. The mud can accumulate to fifteen feet in thickness. Some of this mud will be compacted and trapped under the concrete causing an irregular thickness across the cofferdam. High spots of mud beneath the pour will weaken the seal as mentioned before. To counter this problem, it is best to slow the pour down and have divers descend with an airlift to remove the accumulating mud before the concrete is poured over it.

I was the diving inspector on a large bridge where a major contractor tried to pump concrete through pipes without using a hopper. The results were disastrous because the concrete had to be removed later at a cost of millions. When concrete is poured through a pipe without a hopper, the pipe can lose its seal and fill with water. The concrete poured through the pipe filled with water will separate and mix with seawater causing a layer of bad concrete in an otherwise good pour. When core samples reveal these layers of bad concrete, the entire pour must be removed or, if possible, the bad layers must be removed by tunneling through the good concrete to the bad layer.

When a tremie pour is being made, it is very important that the tremie pipe is on the bottom. It is a good idea to send a diver down to check the pipe in scuba gear before the pour is started. One of the most costly mistakes I have seen was when the tremie pipe caught on top of an H pile about seven feet above the bottom which resulted in hundreds of cubic yards of poor concrete which had to be removed by divers. This mistake cost the contractor over a million dollars. I have seen similar occurrences on other jobs.

Another situation which can cause a bad pour occurs when the tremie pipe is lowered on the tip of the mound from a previous pour. (There is always a mound where the tremie pipe was pulled out of the concrete as indicated in Fig. 9.2). This mound will not allow the pipe to make a seal to start a new pour because the concrete will slide down from the mound keeping the end of the pipe open and allowing water into the pipe. The result is a lot of bad concrete poured before the level is brought up to the pipe where a seal can be made. This suggests that a five-minute dip with scuba gear is a small price to pay as insurance against losing millions of dollars or jeopardizing the safety of a bridge pier.

Fig. 9.2. A typical pour. As shown, the concrete will mound and the laitance will settle on top of the concrete around the mound. The depth of the laitance can be found by estimating the length of the slope as if there were no laitance. If the slope flattens out around the tip of the mound, the depth of the laitance against the sheeting at the sides of the cofferdam can be estimated.

Lowering Rings inside a Cofferdam

The rings inside a cofferdam are made of heavy I beams which are stacked horizontally one on top of the other. They serve as a guide for driving the sheets and are later wedged inside the dam to reinforce the sheets against the water pressure as the cofferdam is pumped out. The top ring stays in place and the rings under it are lowered into position after the sheets are driven.

Sometimes the rings weigh more than one rig can handle and two rigs are used to lower them. There are also times when the cofferdam is so large that two rigs cannot handle the rings. When this is the case, the rings are lowered in sections and assembled underwater by divers.

There is a simple way of lowering a ring in one piece without the use of rigs. Fig. 9.3 shows a ring being held on two parts of the cable with cable clamps. A hole is cut into the sheeting. Then, a cable with an eye on one end is shackled into the hole. Another hole is cut in the ring

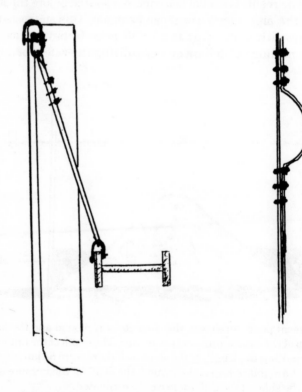

Fig. 9.3.   Lowering rings in a cofferdam.

which will line up with the hole in the sheeting and a shackle is placed in this hole. The end of the cable is passed through the shackle in the ring, up and through the shackle above in the sheet, and then dropped into the water as a loose end. The cable must be long enough to reach the level to which the ring will hang and back to the surface again since two parts of the cable will be used to lower the ring.

The two cables are then clamped together as shown until the ring is ready to be lowered. If you place two or three cable clamps close to the water under the clamps spaced three feet from the top clamps, you can loosen the top clamps and you can pull in a foot of slack in a bight as shown (Fig. 9.3). Tighten the top clamps again, loosen the bottom clamps, and the cable will render through the shackles and the ring will drop as the slack is pulled out of the bight in the cable. This can be done a foot or two at a time until the ring is in position. Cables rigged in this manner will have to be placed on all sides of the dam, and when the ring is being lowered, a dock builder will have to man each cable. In this way, all the slings can be slacked at one time smoothly.

If the cofferdam is large, you must drive soldier piles to keep the center bracing of the ring from sagging. Cables will also have to be put on these soldier piles and lowered as the ring is lowered. You can lower a ring in a matter of a few hours in one piece, rather than spending days or weeks assembling the rings underwater with divers.

Wedging Rings in a Cofferdam

The rings must be wedged tightly against the sheeting before the cofferdam is pumped out. The rings support the sheets against the outside water pressure as the dam is evacuated. If there is too much space between the sheeting and the rings, the sheets could bend or locks could tear due to the water pressure.

There are several ways to wedge out a dam; one is to take long planks down and do several sheets at a time, the other way is to wedge each sheet separately. I prefer to wedge each sheet separately because it is actually faster, and does a better job. To start, make up a stick with notches one inch apart to use as a ruler. Next, go around the dam taking measurements on every sheet and call each out for your tender to record. The tender relays the measurements and the number of the sheet to be marked on paper. The crew then cuts planks of proper thicknesses and nails a wedge to the plank as shown in Fig. 9.4. The plank is made up to take up all but one inch of the opening. Wedges are used to make up the last inch. One wedge is nailed onto the plank, the other wedge has two nails started by the topside crew and is tied to the block on the rig used to lower the plank. You take the plank and cut it loose from the block, then let it float up between the ring and the sheeting with the wedge underneath. Next, cut the second wedge loose and nail it to the top of the plank to secure it as illustrated. As you are placing one board and wedges, the crew topside can be making up the next set from the measurements recorded previously.

Fig. 9.5 shows you how to wedge sheeting with a long board that is weighted with angle irons nailed on top to keep it in place. It may be argued that this is a faster way to wedge sheeting, but there is a danger of the board being knocked loose when the water jet is used to wash out mud between the sheets as they are excavated. When each sheet is wedged separately, there is no wood between the bay of the sheets to get knocked loose by the jet pipe. The long board also presents the possibility of moving sideways causing a sheet to have no wedges. When this occurs, the lock could split from the outside water pressure as the cofferdam is pumped out. Divers have burned holes through the ring to secure the long boards after they had been knocked loose while the dam was being excavated.

Patching Concrete Underwater

For patching concrete pipes or cracks in concrete, or for general underwater repair work, there are several concrete products on the market

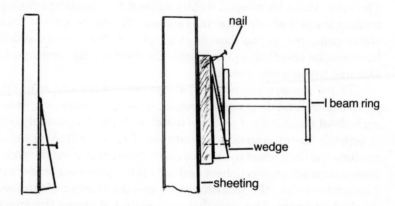

Fig. 9.4. Board sent down with wedge nailed on it which is floated up under the I beam and the sheeting.

Fig. 9.5. Wedge sheeting in place with top wedge nailed, securing blocking top and bottom.

which work very well. The trade names are Water Plug, Speed Crete, and Pour Rock. These products are fast setting. The rate of hardening can be controlled by the amount and temperature of water used to mix the cement.

Have a man topside mix the cement in batches about the size of a grapefruit with a consistency that just lets the cement hold its shape without much slumping. The ball is sent down in a weighted bucket which is perforated to let the water in. When you get the cement underwater, hold it in place with your hands until it sets up firmly in place. You will feel the cement get warm in your hands and it will harden shortly thereafter. If the water used to mix the cement is too warm, the mixture will harden before you can get it into place. If this is the case, the cement must be discarded. To remedy the situation, topside should use a little ice water to keep the cement cool while mixing it. When the water used for mixing is too cold, the cement won't harden for about five minutes. How soon you can get the cement in place will determine the temperature of the water used to mix the cement. In the winter, you will have to use warm water to mix the cement or you will be holding the mix in place for a long time before it sets up.

Sometimes it is advantageous to put the cement in baggies until you can get it into place. If you use baggies, you can have a softer mix which will not harden as quickly as the drier. This is helpful where the cement must take a longer trip underwater before it can be applied.

For larger patching jobs, a dry mixture of Portland cement and sand is shoveled into burlap bags. The bags are tiewrapped and loaded onto a pallet. The pallet is lowered to the diver who places the bags. The surrounding water will seep into the bags and wet the mixture. Also, where the bags touch each other, the mixture will diffuse through the burlap and bond the bags together. After placement, the bags may be secured further by mortaring them with quick setting cement. This method is used to fill voids in underwater structures and to armor structures on the bottom such as the diffuser sections of pipelines.

Pile Rehabilitation

When H piles on a pier have rusted between high and low water lines, concrete is usually poured around the H pile. This can be done with heavy canvas bags, fiberglass forms, or with pile cans as shown in Fig. 9.6. As indicated this pile can is for a plumb pile. The can comes in two halves. It is open at the top and the bottom has slots cut to fit around the H pile. The two halves have angle irons welded to each side with holes

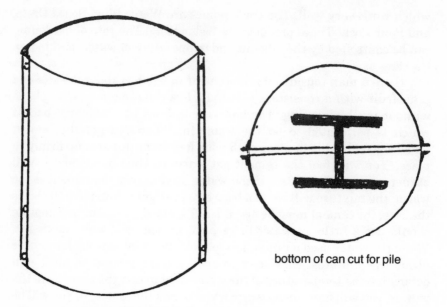

bottom of can cut for pile

Fig. 9.6.   Plumb pile can.

drilled for bolting them together. The two halves are hung to the proper depth and bolted together around the H pile. To keep the pile centered in the can, short pieces of reinforcing rods are welded from the pile against the top of the can. This is done by the topside crew at low water.

As concrete is poured into the cans, reinforcing rods are set in the cans from top to bottom through the freshly poured concrete around the can.

The concrete is poured with the use of a short tremie pipe that reaches the bottom of the can. Usually this is the rubber hose from the concrete pump which can be bent into the can under the pier.

Fig. 9.7 shows a plumb and batter pile can. The bottom of this can has no slots cut into it for the pile. The slots must be burned into the bottom of the can on the job site. When the plumb and batter piles are driven, the angle of the batter pile will differ from bent to bent (one series of piles to the next). Careful measurement must therefore be taken on each batter and plumb pile to determine where the slots will have to be burned.

To measure the batter, a carpenter's square is handy. By placing the square against the plumb pile, then measuring the vertical distance to the batter pile at the one-foot mark on the horizontal leg of the square, the angle of the batter is determined by the right triangle rule. (See Fig. 9.8).

To cut the slots properly, a template is made up from scrap H pile by cutting a one-half-inch slice. Place the template the right distance from the plumb part of the can so the batter will fit. It should be noted that the plumb piles and batter piles may not be in line. The plumb pile may lean slightly upriver and the batter pile may lean slightly downriver. This will cause the piles to move off-center in the cans. Measurements must be taken with the carpenter's level to determine how much the piles are out of plumb. Place the level against the pile, then measure how far out of plumb the pile is at the two-foot mark. Transfer the measurement to

Slots for H piles must be burned on job to measurement

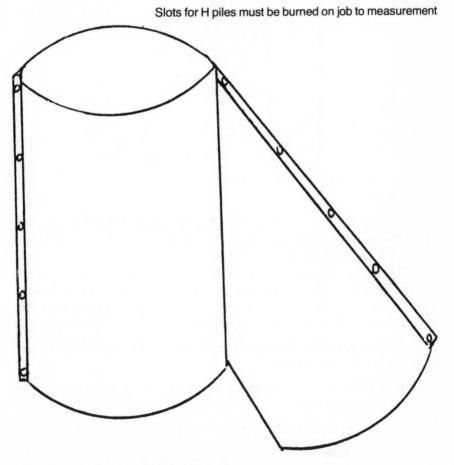

Fig. 9.7.   A plumb and batter pile can.

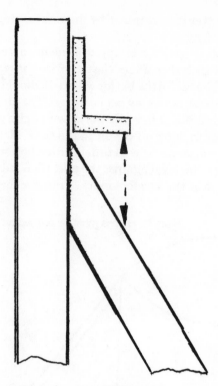

Fig. 9.8.   Using a carpenter's square to measure.

the length of the can. For example, if the pile is one inch out of plumb at the two-foot mark and the can is six feet long, the slot will be three inches off center at the bottom of the can.

The canvas bag and fiberglass form methods of pile rehabilitation differ from the pile can method in that the entire piling is usually encased in concrete from the bottom of the pier to below the mud line underwater. The procedure is as follows:

1. Jet around the bottom of the piling excavating two to three feet below the mud line.

2. Place a precast concrete footing around the H pile which will fit inside the form.

3. Place wire reinforcing steel around the piling.

4. Position form.

5. Pump concrete.

The forms may be later stripped, but are sometimes left in place as additional protection to the pilings.

Fig. 9.9. Navy experimental platform, Gulf of Mexico. Photo courtesy of Naval Coastal Systems Center, U. S. Navy.

CHAPTER TEN

Laying Pipes and Cables

UNDERWATER PIPELINES are laid for a variety of purposes, among them: water and sewer mains, intake and discharge structures for power plants, and supply lines for oil and gas. The types of pipe include concrete, plastic, and steel as well as combinations of these. Pipelines are usually buried well below the ocean or river bottom, but may be left exposed next to bridges or other structures. Pipe sections are joined by several methods including the bell and spigot joint sealed with O rings, flange joints, and welded joints.

Underwater cables are used mainly for communication purposes. Sometimes cables are buried, but when placed in the deep ocean, they may simply be laid on the bottom.

Pipelines

The general procedure for laying underwater pipelines is as follows:

1. Dig the trench in which the pipe will be laid along the proper line and to the proper depth below the pipe grade to allow for bedding stone or pilings.

2. Place the proper bedding or blocking for the pipe.

3. Lay the pipe to the proper line and grade, assuring good joints.

4. Secure the pipe for backfilling.

5. Install diffusers and vents when necessary.

6. Backfill the pipe, restoring the bottom to proper grade.

7. Cover backfill with stone armor when required (for example, where pipeline is laid in surf zone).

Fig. 10.1.   Mark V divers on underwater pipe. Photo courtesy of Naval Coastal Systems Center, U. S. Navy.

Range Markers

Range marker (or range board) is the common name for the marks used to align the pipe. More properly, range markers are bearing markers because they determine direction. However, when two sets of range markers are used, their intersection point determines the distance or the location of the pipe.

With the help of a surveyor, the range markers are placed on shore in such a manner that the crew can line them up by sight from the barge on the water. Generally, two plywood panels are painted as shown in Fig. 10.2. One half of the diamond is painted black and the other yellow. These two range markers are set on shore one behind the other in line with the bearing of the pipe. The mark closest to the shoreline is set lower than the mark farther behind. When viewed from the water, the range markers will appear as shown in Fig. 10.3. Using a second group of range markers set off to one side of the line of the pipe, the location of the end of the pipe is determined where all the range markers line up as shown. This method can be used to determine intermediate distances along the pipe also.

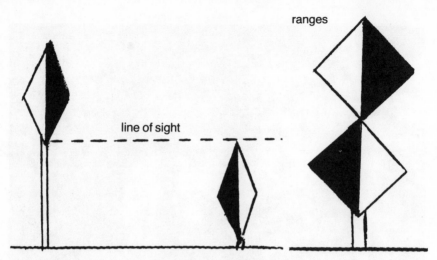

Fig. 10.2.   Using plywood panels for range markers.

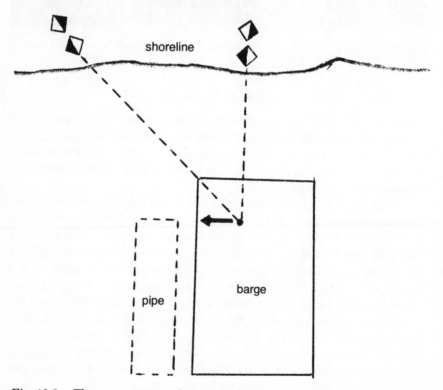

Fig. 10.3.   The arrangement of range markers.

Setting Pipes on Pile Caps

For setting pipes on pile caps a sounding pole of aluminum pipe is made up with grade markings for shallow water work where this kind of pipeline is set. Fig. 10.4 shows a typical concrete pipe set on a pile cap. The pipe has a saddle on the lower end which mates the pipe. Grade is taken by the water level indicated by the elevation markings on the grade pole. The sounding pole is placed on the pipe as it is being lowered into position. The foreman can then tell how far the pipe is off the bottom at all times. He can also bring the pipe up against the previously laid pipe section and feel through the pole when the two pipe sections touch. By plumbing the pole, he can get a true line and keep the pipeline straight. On many jobs, I have seen the foreman actually mate two pipe sections before I went down.

For deeper water, a sounding line can be used to check line and grade. In this case, you must tell the foreman topside when the sounding lead is directly over the center of the pipe. Topside then plumbs the line to obtain grade and alignment. A timber float stage is usually tied off to the rig as a work platform. The float allows the foreman to stand close to the water level and position himself directly over the pipeline where the soundings are taken. You can work off the float stage also if the water is not too rough.

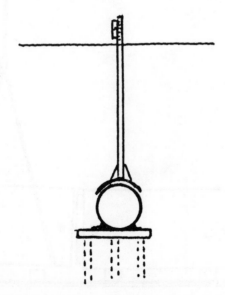

Fig. 10.4.   A typical concrete pipe set on a pile cap.

Joining Sections of Concrete Pipe

It is important that pipe sections are assembled properly and that the steps for doing so are followed in the proper order or the lugs may break on the pipe section. Fig. 10.5 shows a pipe section about to be placed. Note that it is tipped a little higher offshore. This is done to keep the pipe from dragging on the blocking from the previous section, and to facilitate the mating of the two sections. Also note that the spigot end of the pipe is facing offshore which allows the bell end of the pipe to be set on the spigot. By resting the bell on the spigot, the pipe may be maneuvered into position for entering.

Once the bell is sitting on the spigot, the pipe is lowered until it is entered by the previous section. When the two sections are thus mated, you can get the two bolts in on each side of the pipe. When the bolts are in, lower the pipe until there is a three-finger opening at the top of the pipe. Next, maneuver the pipe until you can get the two sides drawn in to three fingers on each side. When this is done, check to see that there is a three-finger opening all around the pipe. If the pipe is not sitting on the blocking at this time, check the offshore end to see how much more blocking is needed to permit the pipe to rest firmly on it. If the space is more than two inches, call for boards to bring the block up to grade. This

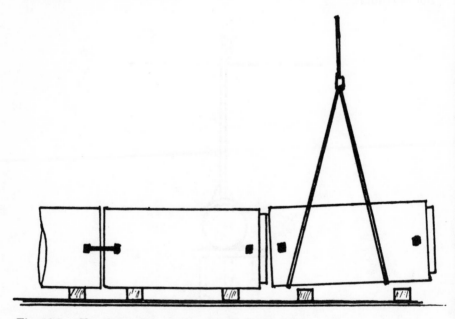

Fig. 10.5.   Showing a pipe section about to be placed.

step is extremely important. If you should take up on the two side bolts without blocking the offshore end and draw the pipe up tight, the bottom of the joint will close with all the weight on the two side bolts. This will damage the pipe or break off the lugs. When the pipe has three fingers all around and is properly blocked, tighten the bolts until the joint has two fingers all the way around. This makes for a good, tight-fitting joint.

If you find that the pipe has rolled on the bottom, the next section to be lowered should be rolled in the slings on deck so the bolts will line up when the pipe sections are mated. When slinging the pipes on deck, check the lugs for level after the slings are tight. Also make certain that all the bolts have been run up by hand and are well greased.

When joining pipes underwater, always check to make certain that the gasket has not rolled out of the joint. If it has rolled within the joint it may have been damaged and as a result will have to be replaced. This possibility can be minimized by making certain that the topside crew greases the gasket and the bell end of the pipe properly before lowering.

Fig. 10.6 shows a ratchet wrench commonly used to tighten the bolts. By tying a line to the end of the wrench, your crew topside can pull

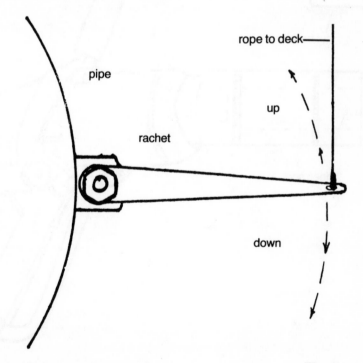

Fig. 10.6.   Using a ratchet wrench.

on the line by hand or winch. They can pull it up eighteen inches, then you can pull it down. The process of tightening the bolts is usually done with two divers. Each diver takes one side of the pipe and maintains communication through tenders with the other diver as to how much opening there is on the opposite side of the pipe. If one diver is ahead of the other, the pipe will be entering at an angle and will bind. It may then be difficult to draw the other side up tight.

Fig. 10.7 illustrates how an air impact wrench can be used underwater to tighten the nuts on the bolts. By taking a socket the right size

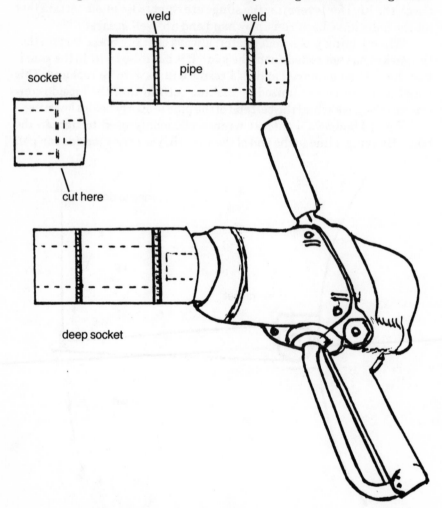

Fig. 10.7.   How an air impact wrench is used.

and cutting it in half as shown, a strong metal pipe can be welded between the two halves making a deep socket. This will make the process of tightening the bolts much faster and easier than using a ratchet. When the weather is cold, make certain that the crew topside stores the wrench in a warm place prior to sending it to you, otherwise it may freeze up when you try to use it.

If the pipe is being laid in cold weather, the metal on the bell end of the pipe will form a coat of ice on it. The bell will then be too small for the spigot to enter. This will occur if the metal is out in subfreezing weather and lowered into the water. As soon as the metal hits the water, ice will form but you may not be able to tell why the pipe sections do not join. Of course, eventually the surrounding water will melt the ice and time may be the only remedy in this situation. However, it is best to bring the metal on the pipe above freezing with a torch topside before applying the grease and lowering it into the water.

Never let the pipe start on a downgrade, or an upgrade, or go off line by allowing more than a one-finger difference in the opening from one side to the other or from top to bottom. Once the pipe starts off line or grade, it will take several sections to bring it back.

If this situation does occur and the line and grade cannot be corrected in a few pipe sections, you must go back and put slings under the previously laid sections and increase or remove blocking a little on each pipe section for several sections. It may sound like a lot of work, but with two divers it can be done in a few hours and really is a small price to pay to insure that there are no open joints that cannot be corrected later.

Unless a pipeline is a gravity flow line where accurate grade is very important, a tight joint is more important than the grade of a pipe. For example, sewage can be piped across a river with the line going up and down hills as though it were a rubber hose. As long as the line is forced (pumped) the sewage will still flow because it does not depend on gravity to make it flow. Intake and forced discharge lines are similar in that grade is not critical. As long as the end of the pipe is where it should be, it is not important if the grade is a little off.

After the pipe is made up and is sitting on the blocking, the foreman should check the line and grade with the grade pole or a sounding line. If line and grade check out all right, then you can place wedges on either side of the pipe and nail them securely (Fig. 10.8). If this is not done properly, the pipeline may roll while the trench is being backfilled. When the pipe section has been completed, the slings may be released. You must make sure that the slings do not foul on the bolts or the blocking, or bind under the pipe. If any of these mishaps occur, the pipe

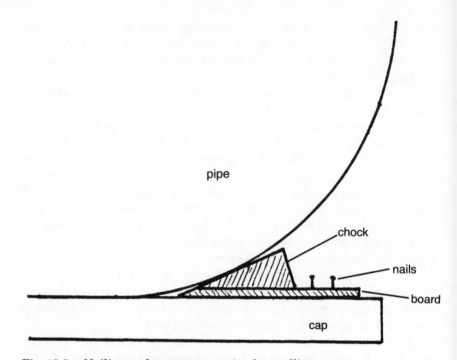

Fig. 10.8.   Nailing wedges to prevent pipe from rolling.

may roll or be damaged. It is best for you to stay with the slings until they are clear of the pipe. Finally, before surfacing, check the trench ahead to make certain that it is clear for the next pipe section to enter.

Soundings are taken on the next blocking before the next pipe section can be laid. If any extra blocking is needed, it can be sent down with the next pipe section by tying it to the lugs.

Setting Blocking

The frame shown in Fig. 10.9 is used to set blocking. The frame is easily assembled out of H beams. The blocking is first tied to the bottom of the frame using small rope lines that are passed through the rings as shown. The two ends of the line are then stapled to the blocking. The H beams on each side of the frame slide up and down and are used to level the blocking by driving the high side of the block down. At the same time, the line holding the block to the frame will be parted thereby eliminating the need for you to dive down to let the blocking go.

The two drop beams are affixed with grade markings to establish grade on the blocking after it has been set. If additional large blocking is

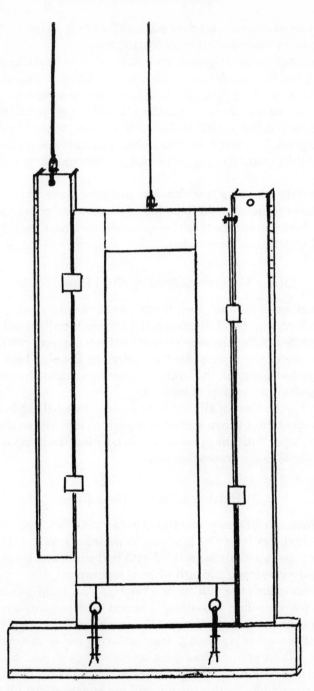

Fig. 10.9.   Frame used to set blocking.

needed, you will have to set the additional blocking on the first weighted block, then nail it to keep it from floating away.

Blocking can be weighted down with concrete by nailing a one-by-four-inch board on each side of the block as shown in Fig. 10.10. Nails are driven partway into the blocking before pouring the concrete to hold the concrete to the block. When the block is placed in the trench, the concrete faces down so that wedges can be nailed to the block after the pipe is in place. The block weighted with concrete is always the first to be placed. Additional blocking, if needed, is then nailed to the weighted block.

When the blocking is within four inches of grade, the extra boards are tied to the lugs on the pipe topside before the pipe is sent to the bottom. Then you cut the block loose and place it under the pipe after the bell and spigot have been mated.

Other Methods of Joining Steel Pipe Sections

A new method of joining pipes eliminates the need for bolts to hold the pipe together. Fig. 10.11 illustrates the hydraulic puller used to pull the pipes together. After the pipe section has been entered, two divers, one on each side of the pipe, place the pullers on the pipe lugs as shown. When the divers signal, the hydraulic pumps are activated and pull the pipes together in a matter of seconds.

Another method of joining steel pipes with a bell and spigot joint sealed with O rings uses a suction pump which is placed on the outboard end of the pipe. With the pipe sections in position, the pump is turned on and the sections are drawn together.

Pulling a Pipe across a River

If the crossing is for a sewer main or a waterline which is not more than a few hundred feet long, the pipe can be pulled across the river. In this case, the pipe is usually assembled with ball joints which are capable of withstanding a strong end pull without separation.

To accomplish the pulling, use two rigs with dragline buckets. The rigs are positioned on opposite shores and work towards the middle. If the rigs cannot reach to the middle, one rig will be used to pull the bucket of the other rig with a dragline to dig out to the middle of the crossing. When one rig has gone as far out as it can, the roles are reversed and the other rig digs while the first pulls the dragline. While digging the middle section, do not pull the bucket of dirt all the way to

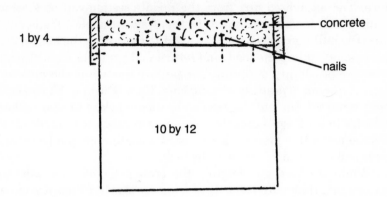
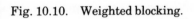

Fig. 10.10. Weighted blocking.

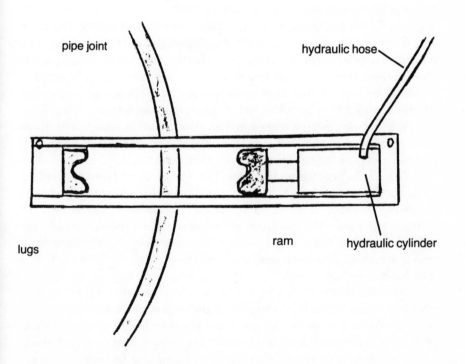

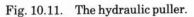

Fig. 10.11. The hydraulic puller.

shore. The excavated dirt from the middle section can be stockpiled within reach for later removal. In this way, valuable time is not lost while the pulling rig waits for the digging rig to drag the bucket all the way to shore, dump the load, and return to the middle. This also eliminates the possibility of fouling the pulling line while the digging rig drags it around depositing dirt onshore. Finally, while the stockpile is being removed, the pulling rig can be digging close to shore allowing both rigs to work continuously. A crossing around three hundred feet is possible using this method. However, if a floating rig can be used, it is faster and easier to accomplish the task.

While the rigs are digging, the crew assembles the pipe three sections at a time with the help of a bucket loader. Slings are made up using a quick splice or cable clamps. Each segment of pipe made up of these three sections must be rigged to be lifted in a level position. Each pipe section must have a sling, and the three slings are bridled at the top. Each end section of pipe should have the same sling length while the middle section is slung with the shorter sling.

To lighten up the first section of pipe so that the front end of the pipe does not dig into the mud as it is being pulled across the river, oil drums are secured toward the leading end of the first pipe section. The flotation will keep the end up and possibly floating slightly off the bottom. The manufacturer's literature on the pipe should indicate the weight of the pipe underwater. Each oil drum has a lifting capacity of about five hundred pounds. Using this information, an estimate of how many drums are needed to keep the end of the pipe up can be made. Usually if the pipe is under twelve inches in diameter, flotation is required. However, if the pipe is over that size, it is possible to float the pipe by sealing the end and making sure that no water enters it.

To pull the pipe across the river (Fig. 10.12), one rig does the pulling with its dragline while the other rig connects the previously rigged segments of three sections each. As each segment is connected, the pulling rig hauls the pipeline across while the other rig holds the following end off the ground and assists the crossing by booming down and giving the pipeline a lead towards the pulling rig. If the pipeline gets hard to pull, the loader can push on the pipe to help.

Once the line has been pulled across, the diver will have to check to make sure the line is in the trench. Soundings must be taken along the line to assure it is deep enough. Once this has been confirmed, backfilling is done in much the same manner as excavation was accomplished.

For laying the small sewer or water crossing in lakes or rivers where a floating rig cannot be towed into, a small float can be made up as

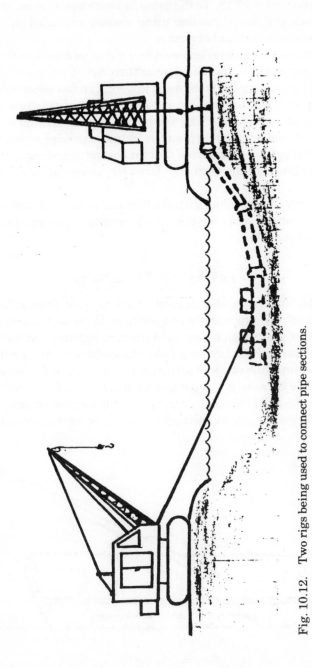

Fig. 10.12. Two rigs being used to connect pipe sections.

illustrated in Fig. 10.13. To dig close to shore use a crane or backhoe. Then trench the rest of the line using a water jet, airlift, or dynamite. One section of pipe is laid at a time.

The pipe sections are deposited by a rig on shore where the boom on the float can reach them. The float is then rigged to be pulled by hand back and forth along the pipeline. It takes only a few minutes to go back and forth with sections of pipe, and even if you only lay two sections of pipe a day including trenching and backfilling (backfilling is done with the jetpipe), you are moving along at forty feet per day which is not bad for a short crossing, considering that the costs of operating are way down after you eliminate the need for a large rig, an operating engineer, and an oiler.

If a crane is available, then the first few sections of pipe can be laid from either shore, and only the middle section of the pipe must be dug and laid by the diver.

Laying Pipe from a Barge

Fig. 10.14 illustrates the method of laying pipe from a barge. The segments of pipe are made up on shore in three sections as described above. After the trench is dug, load the pipe segments on the rig to one side of the barge. Next lay the pipeline from shore to the rig with the end of the pipe out of the water at all times. It is important that no water gets into the pipe because it will become too heavy.

With the end of the pipe sticking out of the water, attach a segment. As you add each segment, release the lines holding the pipe out of water,

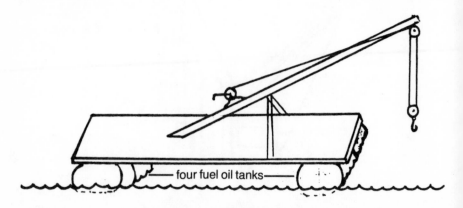

Fig. 10.13.   A small float using four fuel oil tanks. Water can be used in these tanks for ballast so that the end does not rise when picking up the pipe.

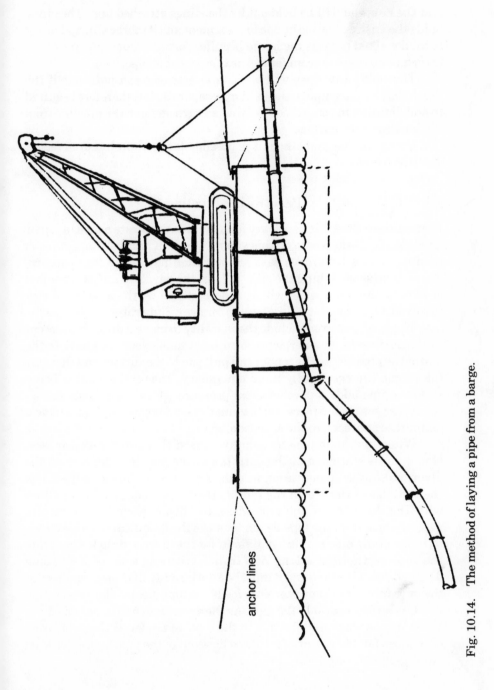

anchor lines

Fig. 10.14.   The method of laying a pipe from a barge.

and the new end will be held out by the slings attached to it. The crane holds the entire pipeline by the last segment and its three slings. The rig is then walked back as the barge is pulled forward along the line of the trench until there is room for the next segment of pipe.

The ball joint pipes will withstand a strong end pull, but if the pipeline is bent too much, the joint may separate. It is therefore required to add flotation in some cases to avoid a sharp angle in the pipeline from the bottom to the surface.

Using the barge method, it is possible to lay eight hundred feet of pipeline a day.

Penetrating Pipelines

From time to time it is necessary for a diver to penetrate a pipe to repair a break. If called upon to do this you must take a professional approach because it is a hazardous task. Penetration pay is the first concern. There is no sense taking the risk without the pay. You are paid per foot of penetration on a scale which is determined by the amount of risk involved. Check with the local union for prevailing rates.

The risks involved include the inability to make a direct free ascent to the surface in an emergency. You must make your way back to the end of the pipe before the tender can pull you to the surface and this may take some time especially in an emergency. The confinement of being inside a pipe adds a psychological pressure which compounds the already dangerous business. But again, the true professional will have a deliberate approach to the situation.

When making a penetration dive, insist that two divers are used. One diver is stationed at the entrance to the pipe in order to tend the diver making the penetration into the pipe. The umbilical will bind on the top edge of the pipe if the topside tender pulls directly on the lines with the diver inside the pipe. Also, the diver would have difficulty getting slack from the topside tender since the umbilical will ride on the top edge of the pipe making it difficult for the diver to drag his hose into the pipe. If there is a long penetration, there is a lot of hose being dragged down the pipe and it must be kept clear at all times. The diver at the entrance to the pipe therefore feeds the umbilical to the penetration diver as he proceeds into the pipe. As the diver returns, the outside diver takes up the slack and feeds it to the topside tender so the pentration diver does not have to drag all of the hose out of the pipe himself risking entanglement.

When using scuba gear, a lifeline is still required. Inside the pipe, it is dark and easy to get turned around. With a limited air supply, not knowing which way is out, the diver could swim to the wrong end to exit and wind up without enough air to get back.

Be extremely wary of the possibility of any flow in the pipe. Remember that you become an obstruction to the flow and it does not take much to create a powerful suction which you will not be able to fight against. I was called to a job where there was a large basin inshore which was connected to the sea by a four-foot diameter pipe. On the rising tide, water would flow into the basin. A one-way flapper valve at the basin then prevented the return flow at ebb tide. My job was to repair a break in the line, but I decided to wait until the tide was high and there was no flow in the pipe. The superintendent became impatient and insisted that I dive before I thought it was safe, and I was fired as a result of the altercation. Another diver was brought in who agreed to dive the pipe during the flow. In a hard hat suit his body nearly filled the pipe acting like a plug. The current took him into the pipe to the end of his lines where he had to stay until the tide turned. The crew on deck thought they had lost the diver and nearly gave up on him.

For a long pentration dive in a pipeline, scuba gear with a power scooter and a good underwater light is handy. A long swim can be tiring and cause you to consume a lot of air. With the scooter, you can concentrate on relaxing as it tows you through the pipe. The light is used for the inspection and to avoid any obstructions which may be present in the line.

Repairing Intakes at Industrial Plants

Occasionally you will be asked to clean intakes at plants along a river or lake. The intake is sometimes inside a wooden box with boards spaced across the front about an inch apart to allow the water to enter and still keep branches and debris out. Besides cleaning out the intake with a water jet hose, you may find quite a few loose boards where the nails have rusted out over the years. It is best to suggest to the owner that the entire structure be refastened because if some of the nails have rusted through, the rest will shortly follow.

Galvanized nails should be used for refastening. It is best to use a small air hammer to do the job, since it takes too much effort to swing a hammer underwater and you will wind up bending a lot of them. Often an intake structure has a backup which should also be refastened at the same time.

I have found ten-inch thin lag screws are better for refastening than nails. The lags can be set with the diver's hammer, then driven home with an air impact wrench which socks the boards up tight against the frame. The impact wrench can be borrowed from a service station or rented. If the wood is very hard, holes will have to be drilled one-eighth-inch diameter less than the lags.

Laying Submarine Cables

Before you contract to bury a cable, check the bottom carefully. Probe the soil and walk the area in scuba gear to be certain there are no obstructions that may require a rig to be moved. To check the trench line, stretch a line across the river between piers in line with the proposed trench. Pull a small boat along the line, dragging a shot line to which the diver clings as he walks the bottom. Also use a lifeline on the diver which can be used to signal the tender/boat operator to stop, slow down, or proceed. You can climb the shot line and describe any obstructions you may find while the topside crew records its location and description.

After a thorough examination of the bottom, you can make plans as to the type of equipment needed for the job. By probing the bottom, you can determine whether the cable can be buried with a jet hose, or whether an airlift or blasting is required. Also you can determine if a crane on a barge will be required.

Fig. 10.15 shows a method of laying cable between bridge piers. Lay the cable with a rig by spooling the cable from the top of the spool, under the rig, and into the conduit as shown. Move the rig slowly along the trench with the anchor lines and lay cable across the river. Pick up the bight of the cable and enter it into the other conduit. When the cable is laid, check the cable to make sure it is in the trench. If it needs moving, you can easily place it in the trench.

A small cable can be pulled across a river with a truck or bulldozer, then buried with the water jet hose using a back pressure nozzle. Cables are usually buried to a depth of two to four feet, but may not be buried if there is no river traffic.

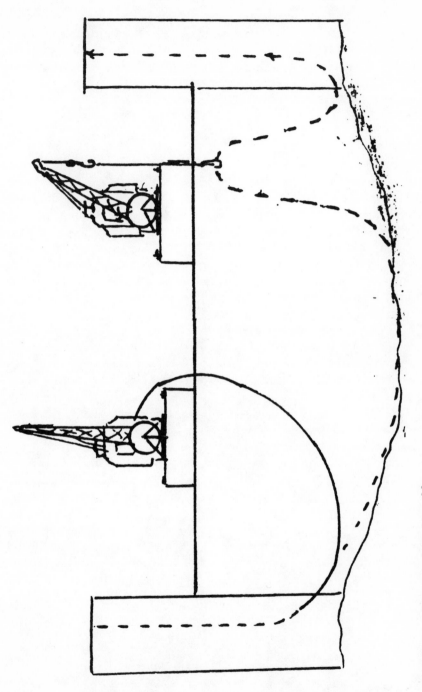

Fig. 10.15. Laying submarine cables.

Appendix A

1. Coast Guard Provisions for Commercial Diving Operations*

RULES AND REGULATIONS

[4910-14-M]

Title 46—Shipping

CHAPTER I—COAST GUARD, DEPARTMENT OF TRANSPORTATION

[CGD 76-009]

PART 197—GENERAL PROVISIONS

Commercial Diving Operations

AGENCY: Coast Guard, DOT.

ACTION: Final rule.

SUMMARY: The Coast Guard is issuing regulations governing commercial diving operations from vessels and facilities including vessels required to have a Certificate of Inspection; deepwater ports; and artificial islands, installations, other devices, or otherwise related to activities on the Outer Continental Shelf. Commercial diving exposes individual divers to many hazardous situations that can and have caused marine casualties. These regulations prescribe safety and health standards for commercial diving operations.

EFFECTIVE DATE: February 1, 1979.

FOR FURTHER INFORMATION CONTACT:

Commander Peter T. Muth, Manager, Underwater Sefety Project (G-MP-3/USP/82), Room 8234, Department of Transportation, Nassif Building, 400 Seventh Street SW., Washington, D.C. 20590, 202-426-2307.

SUPPLEMENTARY INFORMATION: The Coast Guard published an Advance Notice of Proposed Rulemaking (ANPRM) on August 11, 1975 (40 FR 33681), proposing to amend chapter I of title 46 of the Code of Federal Regulations (CFR) by adding a new subchapter prescribing marine occupational safety and health standards for vessels and facilities that are under Coast Guard jurisdiction. In this ANPRM the Coast Guard proposed to regulate all working conditions and work places under Coast Guard jurisdiction if they are determined to be hazardous to employees, and if the Coast Guard determines that the hazards encountered can be reduced or eliminated by the promulgation of effective regulations.

The Occupational Safety and Health Administration (OSHA), Department of Labor, published an announcement in the FEDERAL REGISTER on October 22, 1975 (40 FR 49123), that it would hold an informal fact-finding hearing on commercial diving operations. The Coast Guard participated in this informal hearing that was conducted in Washington, D.C. on November 11 through 14, 1975.

On June 15, 1976 OSHA published a 6-month Emergency Temporary Standard (ETS) for commercial diving in the FEDERAL REGISTER (41 FR 24272). A Memorandum of Understanding (MOU), covering the relationship between OSHA and the Coast Guard during the 6-month period of the ETS and also during the period of development of final Coast Guard regulations for commercial diving, was signed on June 9, 1976, by the Commandant of the Coast Guard and the Assistant Secretary of Labor for Occupational Safety and Health. The text of the MOU was published with the ETS (41 FR 24291) and contained a provision terminating the MOU "upon the effective date of the Coast Guard standards * * * pertaining to diving operations." The ETS was withdrawn by OSHA on November 5, 1976 (41 FR 48969).

On July 15, 1976, the Coast Guard published an ANPRM in the FEDERAL REGISTER (41 FR 29151) stating that it was considering new regulations prescribing occupational safety and health standards for commercial diving. The Coast Guard invited specific public advice and recommendations on nine enumerated areas, and any general comments to assist it in developing new occupational safety and health regulations for commercial diving in areas of Coast Guard jurisdiction.

During August 1976, the OSHA Advisory Committee on Construction Safety and Health met to discuss materials and information relating to the occupational safety and health aspects of commercial diving operations and to make recommendations to OSHA. The Coast Guard participated in this public proceeding.

On November 5, 1976 OSHA published a Notice of Proposed Rulemaking (NPRM) and Notice of Public Hearings in the FEDERAL REGISTER (41 FR 48950) covering commercial diving operations. Pursuant to the MOU between the Coast Guard and OSHA, the Coast Guard published a Notice in the FEDERAL REGISTER (41 FR 48969 and 41 FR 49208) joining OSHA in the public hearings, scheduled for December 16 through 17, 1976, in New Orleans, to receive public comments on the Coast Guard on the substance of the OSHA proposed standards. During the joint public hearings (December 16 through 21, 1976, and January 10 through 14, 1977) the Coast Guard gave the public an opportunity to comment on Coast Guard regulatory concepts that would be substantively similar to the OSHA proposed standards for commercial diving operations.

On July 22, 1977 OSHA published its final commercial diving standard in the FEDERAL REGISTER (42 FR 37650). Under section 4(b)1 of the Occupational Safety and Health Act of 1970, the OSHA standards do not apply to those diving operations over which the Coast Guard exercises its statutory authority to prescribe or enforce standards or regulations affecting occupational safety and health.

On November 10, 1977, the Coast Guard published a NPRM in the FEDERAL REGISTER (42 FR 58712), with corrections on November 21, 1977 (42 FR 59763), governing commercial diving

---

RULES AND REGULATIONS

operations from vessels and facilities subject to Coast Guard jurisdiction. In developing this proposal, the Coast Guard met at various times beginning in 1975 with members of the National Offshore Operations Industry Advisory Committee (NOOIAC). NOOIAC submitted its recommendations to the Coast Guard on June 15, 1977. These recommendations, along with the comments received as a result of the ANPRMs and joint OSHA/CG rulemaking activities, were taken into consideration for the purpose of the NPRM. Pursuant to the MOU the proposed regulation was considered to be substantively similar to the final OSHA commercial diving standard.

The public comment period for the NPRM remained open for written comments until December 27, 1977. A total of 29 written comments were received during the comment period. Commentors included private individuals; companies representing diving contractors, insurance consultants, manufacturers, a deepwater port, offshore exploration; industry and trade associations; five national recreational and sport diving training organizations; and a labor union.

As a result of these written comments, the regulations were revised in part. Many revisions have been made to the regulations to improve clarity without changing the substance of the regulations. Those changes that significantly alter the proposed regulations and those items that received considerable comment and have not been revised and discussed below.

This rule has been reviewed under the Department of Transportation's "Policies Procedures for Simplification, Analysis, and Review of Regulations" (43 FR 9582, March 8, 1978). An evaluation has been prepared, and has been included in the public docket.

DRAFTING INFORMATION

The principal persons involved in drafting this proposal are: Commander Peter T. Muth, Project Manager, Office of Merchant Marine Safety and Mr. Edward J. Gill, Jr., Project Attorney, Office of the Chief Counsel.

DISCUSSION OF MAJOR COMMENTS

PREAMBLE

Although the preamble to the proposed rule indicated that the proposal did not address the qualifications of individual dive team members, including the medical requirements, with the reasons therefor, two commentors made suggestions and recommendations in this area. One commentor commended the Coast Guard for its position on medical qualifications while suggesting that rulemaking for other personnel qualifications be initi-

ated. The other commentor suggested that, as a minimum, the Coast Guard incorporate into this final rule the diving medical guidelines including the psychological screening requirements of the U.S. Navy. The Coast Guard agrees that the qualification of individual dive team members, especially the medical requirements, are important, and has noted that the commercial diving industry, subject to the jurisdiction of the Coast Guard, has established a school to train commercial divers; has physicians trained and experienced in hyperbaric medicine either employed full time or on-call by individual companies and the commercial diving school; has developed and vigorously follows an on-the-job training program encompassing all facets of commercial diving activities; and has established safety and health programs within most individual companies. It is the intent of the Coast Guard to regulate commercial diving operations on vessels and facilities subject to the jurisdiction of the Coast Guard to the extent necessary to insure an acceptable level of personnel safety and health. After careful reconsideration, the Coast Guard has reaffirmed its prior determination that it will not regulate in these areas at this time; however, the Coast Guard intends to publish an Advance Notice of Proposed Rulemaking concerning the qualifications of dive team members including medical requirements.

GENERAL

Several commentors were unsure about the application of this regulation to one atmosphere observation bells, suits, or submersibles. By the definition of "diver," those applications are not covered. The definition of "PVHO" was rewritten to clarify any possible misunderstanding by specifically excluding one atmosphere devices and to preclude a potential erroneous interpretation that the exterior pressure criteria of the ASME Code and ASME PVHO-1 was not required. All the requirements of ASME PVHO-1 are mandatory for new PVHO's. The requirements of 46 CFR 54 or as an alternative, Section VIII, Division 1 of the ASME Code, are, and have been, mandatory for existing PVHO's and include external pressure criteria. The requirements of ASME PVHO-1 are not mandatory for existing PVHO's under § 197.328(b).

Two commentors expressed concern over the exemption from the regulations of diving operations for marine scientific research and development purposes being limited to those conducted by educational institutions. The commentors suggested the words "by educational institutions" be deleted. The Coast Guard does not agree and foresees considerable difficulty differentiating between commercial diving operations for profit under the guise of research and development,

and diving operations for purely marine scientific research and development purposes unless the limitation "by educational institutions" is retained.

The regulations allow the Coast Guard to accept substitutes for equipment, materials, apparatus, arrangements, procedures, or tests required by this subpart if the substitute provides an equivalent level of safety. Specific wording permitting equivalent substitutes has been removed from all sections of this rule except in the standard for helium, § 197.340(h). This permits the diving supervisor to determine equivalency to the required standards for helium when helium is obtained outside the United States without applying to the Commandant of the Coast Guard. This does not permit the diving supervisor to use helium meeting a lesser standard as a breathing gas, but only helium meeting the published standard.

Seventeen commentors offered 90 suggestions including numerous alternatives and alternative wording for § 197.208 on the designation of the person-in-charge and the other sections impacted by this section. These comments were accepted, in part, and the regulation has been completely rewritten to clearly define and assign responsibility where it belongs. This necessitated the addition of definitions for "diving supervisor" and "diving installation" and the addition § 197.210 and 197.404. The person-in-charge remains responsible for the vessel or facility, its operation and safety, and the records and reports required by statute or regulation. In addition, the person-in-charge must coordinate the activities on and of the vessel or facility with the diving supervisor so as not to endanger the dive team conducting diving operations. The diving supervisor is in charge of the planning and execution of the commercial diving operation and is responsible for the diving installation, the safety and health of the dive team, and the records and reports required. In addition, the diving supervisor must immediately notify the person-in-charge when a diving accident or casualty occurs, must keep the person-in-charge informed, and coordinate any changes to the planned diving operation with the person-in-charge.

EQUIPMENT

The equipment specifications and equipment requirements apply to each vessel or facility conducting commercial diving operations having a portable diving installation or having an installed diving installation. Nothing in this subpart amends or supercedes the requirements contained in other parts of titles 33 and 46 CFR for the design, plan approval, construction, certification, and inspection required of those vessels or facilities subject to this subpart conducting commercial diving op-

RULES AND REGULATIONS

erations and having installed diving systems. Therefore, permanently installed diving installations aboard certificated vessels must comply with 46 CFR 54 regarding pressure vessels, with 46 CFR 56 regarding pressure piping, and with 46 CFR 110 through 113 regarding electrical systems in addition to complying with this subchapter.

Three commentors recommended modification of the requirement that breathing supply hoses be made of kink-resistant material to allow use of synflex hose. The Coast Guard agrees that the wording of the proposal did not allow the use of synflex hose nor properly reflect what was intended. Section 197.312(a)(4) has been modified to clarify that breathing supply hoses are to resist kinking, and that the method of achieving this can be either by initial design and construction of the hose, or by supporting the hose in such a manner as to make it resistant to kinking.

Two comments were received on § 197.312(b)(2). The Coast Guard feels that the present wording clearly shows that markings are required only on diver and open bell umbilicals, not closed bell umbilicals, and that further clarification is unnecessary.

Paragraphs 197.314 (a)(1) and (c)(4) were modified to clarify intent and to specify the contents, dimensions, and packaging of the medical kit in response to several comments received.

In response to a commentor's question, the Coast Guard modified § 197.314(b) to clarify the two-way communications system requirement. This change permits substitution of the vessel or facility ship-to-shore, two-way communications system for the system required by this section if it is readily available to obtain emergency medical assistance.

Three commentors noted that the depth requirement as to when a decompression chamber was required differed between the Coast Guard and OSHA standards. Two commentors did not offer an opinion as to the depth when it should be required, but recommended that the two agencies agree to the same figure of either 130 fsw or 100 fsw. The other commentor proposed adoption of 66 fsw with the no-decompression limit, or adoption of 100 fsw with the no-decompression limit and an additional requirement of having a decompression chamber any time a diver is working in a "contained space" where there is a chance of becoming "hung-up." This commentor also noted that a secondary breathing gas supply was required when a decompression chamber is required.

The requirement to have a decompression chamber at the dive location also requires additional associated equipment for the chamber (i.e., handling gear to load, unload, and position the decompression chamber; hoses and piping; a secondary breathing gas supply; a larger primary breathing gas supply; and breathing gases for treatment of decompression sickness); additional personnel to load, unload, and operate the decompression chamber and associated equipment; a substantially larger dive location capable of providing the extra space needed and supporting the additional weight; and a method of transportation with at least a fivefold, increased weight-handling capability over a dive not requiring a decompression chamber. Additionally, the requirements for a standby diver, individual surface tending, and more detailed record keeping are based on the determination of where the increased risks to a diver exist.

The incidence rate of decompression sickness among all divers diving within the no-decompression limit at depths less than 130 fsw is very small. Gas embolism can occur at almost any depth, but occurs more frequently at depths less than 66 fsw. (This may be because most air dives take place at depths less than 66 fsw.) Also, the incidence rate occurs more frequently when using SCUBA equipment. However, among experienced divers the incidence rate of gas embolism is small.

It is the opinion of the Coast Guard, based on a review of the entire record as set forth in the preamble of the NPRM, the diver's work environment, and a review of the experience of hundreds of thousands of air dives by military, civilian, governmental, commercial, sport, and recreational, and scientific divers all using the U.S. Navy air tables, that the requirement for a decompression chamber need not be set at a depth less than 130 fsw to protect against potential decompression sickness. The Coast Guard feels a 20 fsw requirement in lieu of a 66 fsw or 100 fsw requirement is not an unreasonable depth to require equipment for treatment of gas embolism. However, a review of the record and comments cited in the NPRM and the experience of many dives does not support protecting commercial divers (professionals) for possible gas embolism by providing additional personnel and equipment for no-decompression dives at depths less than 130 fsw.

After careful reconsideration and reexamination of the comments and records mentioned above, the Coast Guard reaffirms the 130 fsw decompression chamber requirement. However, the Coast Guard agrees with the general philosophy of the commentors regarding a single Federal standard for the same marine activity and has been discussing this subject with OSHA to resolve this issue. Both the Coast Guard and OSHA have determined that additional public input on this subject is desirable and both agencies intend to request additional public comment in a future notice in the FEDERAL REGISTER.

In answer to a commentor, the requirement of § 197.314(c)(5) to have a "capability" could be discharged by having specialized equipment such as a Stoke's litter with the personnel needed to carry it available or by having sufficient personnel to assist an injured diver into the decompression chamber. The wording of this section allows future equipment development to occur that may replace the most common present system of having "sufficient personnel" as long as the objective of getting the injured diver inside the decompression chamber is met.

One commentor recommended that dives at depths less than 40 fsw, or those not involving decompression, be exempt from the requirements of § 197.318. The Coast Guard disagrees. Neither ascent nor descent rates nor bottom time can be determined without a timekeeping device. The diving supervisor may not be able to determine whether a diver has been at depths that require a decompression obligation without a gage available indicating diver depth (i.e., a diver working at 28 fsw for 6 hours vice at 32 fsw for 6 hours). Without the combined information of bottom time and depth available to the diving supervisor, the safety and health of the diver may be in jeopardy.

Many commentors objected to, and offered rewording for, "be made of corrosion-resistant material" where required for diving ladders, stages, and open bells (§§ 197.320 and 197.334). The Coast Guard agrees that the wording of the proposal was too restrictive and has rewritten those requirements. This wording allows either construction using corrosion-resistant material, or application of anti-corrosion coatings to protect the structural integrity of the device.

Two commentors suggested that the requirement of § 197.320(b)(3) be modified to allow the use of a diving ladder instead of a diving stage under certain conditions. The Coast Guard disagrees. Divers diving at depths deeper than 130 fsw, or outside the no-decompression limits, are more likely to be tired and need the additional assistance a diving stage affords over a diving ladder. A diving stage also provides a haven during in-water decompression stops. If because of conditions at the dive site, the use of a diving stage would likely cause an injury, § 197.202(b) allows a deviation from this requirement. If the use of the diving stage is unreasonable or impractical, § 197.206(b) provides that the Commandant of the Coast Guard may permit the use of alternative equipment or procedures that insure a degree of safety consistent with the minimum standard afforded by a diving stage.

One commentor suggested that § 197.326(b) be amended to allow ball

200 TRICKS OF THE TRADE FOR DIVERS

RULES AND REGULATIONS

valves to be used as PVHO pressure boundary shutoff valves in oxygen systems. The Coast Guard agrees and has amended the proposal accordingly.

Section 197.328(d)(3) has been changed in response to one commentor to clearly indicate that overpressurization of the PVHO is intended to be protected by this requirement and not the pressure piping. Pressure piping is protected by the pressure relief devices required by the ANSI Code.

The requirement that each PVHO must have a pressure sealing hatch (§ 197.328(c)(4) of the proposal) has been deleted. This requirement did not add anything that was not already required by the design Codes and was a point of confusion to two commentors.

Three commentors recommended modifications to the requirement for PVHO two-way voice communications systems. These comments were accepted, in part, and § 197.328(d) (6) and (7) and § 197.332(m) have been rewritten to clearly specify intent and set forth the requirements. The Coast Guard considers voice communications between the diving supervisor and occupants of a PVHO, between occupants in separately pressurized compartments of the same PVHO, and between the occupant of a closed bell and a diver in the water being supported from that closed bell as the minimum standards for the safety and health of the dive team members. Additionally, if two separate PVHO's are designed to mechanically couple and become in effect one PVHO, these two-way voice communications system requirements apply when the PVHO's are mechanically coupled. The Coast Guard did not intend to have redundant sound-powered communications systems in decompression chambers, and permits only one two-way voice communications system in a decompression chamber if the system is sound-powered. The configuration and operation of the required communications system is not specified, allowing any system that provides the required two-way voice contacts.

Four commentors pointed out that internal pressure gages were not required for PVHO's unless the PVHO atmosphere can be controlled internally. The Coast Guard agrees and has rewritten § 197.328(d)(7).

The Coast Guard has rewritten the viewport requirements of § 197.328(d) (8) and (9). As previously worded, it could have been interpreted to require that all occupants of dual- or multiple-lock PVHO's had to be seen from the exterior through one viewport, even if the PVHO has more than one viewport. In most situations, this would be impossible. The intent of the regulation is to require sufficient viewports to allow observation of all occupants from the exterior. If a PVHO is designed such that a single viewport would allow observation of all occu-

pants, that design would satisfy this requirement.

Three commentors made suggestions concerning the requirement for a fire extinguisher inside a PVHO. The Coast Guard reviewed the causes of several PVHO fires, and has amended the proposed regulations to require a means of extinguishing a fire in the interior. Past experience indicates that fire prevention is most important and can be enhanced by keeping combustible materials, sources of heat and sparks, and all nonessential or potentially hazardous equipment, including electrical systems, to an absolute minimum inside a PVHO. Known combustible materials or sources of ignition required inside a PVHO should be isolated from the PVHO atmosphere and purged with inert gas, where possible, or maintained in a area easily accessible by an occupant to facilitate extinguishing a fire. Localized fires that have been combatible in the past have been extinguished with water or sand.

Two commentors recommended that § 197.328(c)(19) of the NPRM be amended to exempt additional electrical equipment inside PVHO's such as communications speakers and medical measurement instrumentation. Electrical systems, besides being a potential shock hazard, can present a source of ignition as well as the fuel required for combustion. Additionally, electrical shock hazards and possible galvanic action of the PVHO need to be considered when designing and maintaining interior electrical systems. The Coast Guard has carefully reviewed the proposed requirements and the comments received in the context of present-day equipment available, and has rewritten § 197.328(d)(18).

One commentor requested clarification of § 197.330(a)(6). This requirement assists surface personnel in locating and retrieving a closed bell after the umbilical has been severed. The emergency locating device required is not limited to the following but could be, active (i.e., an acoustical pinger), passive (i.e., a sonar reflector or target), or some other device (i.e., a surface buoy with attaching line releasible by either the closed bell occupants and/or remotely from the surface).

Three commentors suggested alternative language and alternatives to the requirements for a 12-hour breathing gas supply independent of the surface. The Coast Guard agrees, in part, with the suggestions and has rewritten § 197.330(a)(8). This revision recognizes that scrubbing and recirculating of breathing gases is an alternative to an independent breathing gas supply of sufficient volume and pressure to last for 12 hours. Also, having a sufficient breathing gas supply does not by itself provide life support as other considerations must be taken into account (i.e., thermal protection). The revision also allows a reduced life support ca-

pability if there are two independent retrieval systems for the closed bell.

One commentor suggested that § 197.332(d) be reworded to account for shipping dogs. Shipping dogs are constructed to be operated from only one side of a man-way or hatch, are never used to obtain a pressure seal, and are only used during shipping to prevent damage to the decompression chamber. When the decompression chamber is occupied, shipping dogs are removed or disabled by securing them out of the way. The Coast Guard agrees and has revised this requirement.

The proposed illumination levels for the interior of a decompression chamber were addressed by five commentors. Two commentors suggested deletion of the requirement as illumination was already covered by "PVHO-General" requirements. Two commentors expressed concern regarding fire prevention. Comments also addressed the "convenience" aspects of bunk reading lights. The Coast Guard agrees, in part, with the philosophy expressed; however, the lighting requirements addressed within the decompression chamber requirements are in addition to "General" PVHO illumination requirements. The general PVHO illumination requirement addressed work and operating conditions. The decompression chamber interior illumination requirement is directed not toward "convenience items" but being able to visually observe, treat, medically diagnose, and medically assist, if necessary, occupants undergoing decompression or treatment for decompression sickness. Therefore, the Coast Guard has rewritten § 197.332(e) for clarity.

The requirement for compressed gas cylinders, § 197.338(e), has been modified to allow the use of cylinders designed and constructed under the requirements of Part 54 of this Chapter, which requires a greater design safety factor for pressure vessels aboard certificated vessels than the standard of 49 CFR 178 Subpart C.

Two commentors recommended that § 197.346(b) be modified to allow a diver to select equipment he will use for a particular dive. The Coast Guard agrees in part, and has modified this requirement by requiring that a helmet cushion and weighted shoes be provided to the diver, but has not required them to be worn by the diver. When using a heavy-weight diving outfit, the absence of weighted shoes could pose an unintended risk to a diver's safety under some conditions; however, this risk may be avoided by the use of leg or ankle weights.

One commentor observed that the requirements of § 197.346(d)(5) regarding a "life-line" and a "communications cable" can be met in some cases by a communications cable in the hose group that has a breaking strength equal to or exceeding that required of a life-line. The Coast Guard agrees,

RULES AND REGULATIONS

and under such a circumstance would not require a separate life-line.

One commentor suggested that § 197.346(f) be modified to also exclude from the diver-carried reserve breathing gas requirement, diving with a stage nearby having a sufficient supply of breathing gases or a closed or open bell. The Coast Guard disagrees. An inexhaustable supply of breathing gas just beyond the immediate reach of a diver in distress may never be used. A reserve breathing gas supply, when required, should always be within the immediate reach of a diver, except when it becomes a greater hazard to the diver's safety than the diver not having it. In such a case, alternatives, such as the commentor suggested, should be considered.

OPERATIONS

One commentor requested clarification of what was meant by the post dive requirement in the proposal to check the physical condition of the diver. This has been clarified in § 197.410(a)(7)(i).

Five commentors suggested the requirement proposed in § 197.420(a) to have an operations manual prepared for each vessel or facility from which diving operations are conducted be modified. The Coast Guard agrees, in part, and with the rewriting of responsibilities has revised this requirement so that the diving supervisor provides to the person-in-charge and the dive team an operations manual. The intent of the proposed requirement to have an operations manual tailored to a specific situation is retained by requiring certain modifications to be made in writing.

SPECIFIC DIVING MODE PROCEDURES

Two commentors proposed that the depth requirement for the use of a closed bell (§ 197.434(d) of this rule) be changed from 300 fsw to 350 fsw. The Coast Guard disagrees. The Coast Guard, however, realizes that there may be specific commercial diving operations at depths greater than 300 fsw where the use of a closed bell may not be indicated and feels that § 197.206(b) allows a viable alternative.

One commentor pointed out that the proposed requirement in § 197.434(f)(2), that a standby diver be available one hour before the return of a closed bell to the dive location during saturation diving is impractical. An operational emergency could arise at any time that could require returning the closed bell to the dive location. The Coast Guard agrees and has rewritten the proposed requirements as § 197.434(g). The standby diver requirement for closed bell retrieval during saturation diving has been removed. A requirement that a member of the topside crew be diver-qualified and available has been substituted.

One commentor requested clarification of the prohibition against live-boating at night. The intent was to prohibit liveboating operations when the direction that the umbilical tends in the water, or when the "bubbles" from the diver, are not visible to the dive team member at the dive location continuously tending the diver. Also, the vessel from which liveboating operations are being conducted should be visible to other vessels transiting the area for the safety of the diver. This clarification has been made by prohibiting liveboating from 1 hour after sunset to 1 hour before sunrise or during periods of restricted visibility as defined in a new § 197.436(b).

Two commentors proposed that the depth limitation for liveboating be changed from 200 fsw to 250 fsw. The figure of 200 fsw appearing in § 197.436(a) was an unnoticed, typographical error appearing in the NPRM. The Coast Guard intended that there be a limitation of 220 fsw which is compatible with the 220 fsw bell requirement. The Coast Guard disagrees with changing the limitation for liveboating from 220 to 250 fsw. However, § 197.206(b) provides an alternative when there is a specific commercial diving operation that requires liveboating at depths greater than 220 fsw.

One commentor felt the requirement for a diver pick-up boat during liveboating operations was unnecessary as the vessel from which liveboating is supported should be able to make the diver pick-up. The commentor felt a second vessel might exacerbate the hazard to the diver in the water. However, under the worst situation, the vessel is most likely to have its screws fouled with a severed umbilical and be dead-in-the-water. Further, liveboating by definition could be conducted from a barge. Diver pick-up, in either case, might be difficult without the required pick-up boat, if possible at all. The Coast Guard has retained the requirement for a boat for diver pick-up in § 197.436(a)(4) thereby allowing the person-in-charge the option to utilize his vessel or the boat for picking up the diver in distress, whichever under the specific circumstances would be more appropriate.

PERIODIC TESTS AND INSPECTIONS OF DIVING EQUIPMENT

One commentor recommended that the words "repair or modification" in § 197.450(a) be changed to "overhaul" because there are many repairs or modifications that may not affect the quality of the breathing gas output of an air compressor. The same argument could be used regarding the word "overhaul." The tests required are not only for quality but also for quantity. The tests required are to be performed after every repair or modification to the compressor (such as, the speed at which it is driven, pressure boundaries, intake and exhaust piping arrangements, etc.) which might affect the quantity and/or quality of the compressor output. Retightening a foundation mounting nut of the compressor or straightening a bent dip stick on the prime mover are not intended to be considered "repairs" under this section.

One commentor suggested that a Compressed Gas Association (CGA) pamphlet, G-4.1 entitled "Cleaning Equipment for Oxygen Service," be referenced in § 197.452 and other CGA pamphlets be referenced elsewhere in this regulation. The Coast Guard disagrees. The Coast Guard, in preparing the NPRM, considered all CGA standards through December 1976 and found that many of the standards had already made their way into regulations. Some of these regulations have been referenced in this subpart and thereby incorporated (i.e., 49 CFR 173.34 incorporated CGA pamphlet C-6, 1968 edition, and CGA pamphlet C-8, 1972 edition). The Coast Guard noted during its review of the CGA standards and publications that they were not developed with human life support under hyperbaric conditions as the main objective and therefore in some areas were neither complete nor acceptable.

One commentor recommended the exclusion of cylinders from the requirements of § 197.462 since they would be tested according to the appropriate DOT regulations. The Coast Guard disagrees. It is not the Coast Guard's intention to subject any pressure vessel to duplicate inspection and testing requirements. The "appropriate DOT regulations" apply to cylinders in interstate commerce and may not cover after purchase a significant percentage of cylinders used for diving. If a cylinder is inspected and tested annually with a hydrostatic test every fifth year in accordance with 49 CFR 173.34, it meets the requirements of this section.

One commentor expressed concern regarding the leak test requirement. In response, the Coast Guard has rewritten § 197.462(g) to set out the leak test procedures.

RECORDS

The revision of this regulation previously discussed regarding the person-in-charge and diving supervisor, required major revision to this portion of the regulations. The official logbook (Coast Guard form CG-706) required by statute is retained. Those vessels or facilities not required to have an official logbook by 46 U.S.C. 201 are required to have a logbook, as is the diving supervisor. The size, shape, and form of the logbook is left to the discretion of the person-in-charge or diving supervisor. The entries of the person-in-charge in either the official logbook or logbook have been reduced in quantity.

The entries required of the diving supervisor to be entered in the supervisor's logbook are much more detailed. They include entries similar to those required to be entered by the person-in-charge, specific information about the dive and divers, a record of the diving activity, equipment history including testing, etc. The Coast Guard recognizes that many of the records and entries required are not kept at the dive location. The Coast Guard does not require copying the information into the logbook or duplicating these existing records, as long as an entry is made in the diving supervisory's logbook at the dive location indicating where the records are physically available.

Several commentors suggested that form CG-2692 was not indicated for a diving casualty as required by § 197.486(b) but rather for a vessel casualty not involving diving. The Coast Guard agrees and has deleted this requirement. Section 197.486 was also rewritten to clarify that form CG-924E is required only when the dive location is a vessel, and that a written narrative report is required when the dive location is a facility.

In consideration of the foregoing, Chapter I of Title 46 of the Code of Federal Regulations is amended as follows:

PART 54—PRESSURE VESSELS

1. By adding a new § 54.01-17 to read as follows:

§ 54.01-17 Pressure vessel for human occupancy (PVHO).

Pressure vessels for human occupancy (PVHO's) must meet the requirements of subpart B (Commercial Diving Operations) of part 197 of this chapter.

PART 56—PIPING SYSTEMS AND APPURTENANCES

2. By adding a new § 56.50-110 to read as follows:

§ 56.50-110 Diving support systems.

(a) In addition to the requirements of this part, piping for diving installations which is permanently installed on the vessel must meet the requirements of subpart B (Commercial Diving Operations) of part 197 of this chapter.

(b) Piping for diving installations which is not permanently installed on the vessel need not meet the requirements of this part, but must meet the requirements of subpart B of part 197 of this chapter.

(c) Piping internal to a pressure vessel for human occupancy (PVHO) need not meet the requirements of this part, but must meet the requirements of subpart B of part 197 of this chapter.

RULES AND REGULATIONS

PART 110—GENERAL PROVISIONS

3. By adding a new § 110.05-8 to read as follows:

§ 110.05-8 Electrical systems internal to pressure vessels for human occupancy (PVHO).

Electrical systems internal to a pressure vessel for human occupancy (PVHO) need not meet the requirements of this subchapter, but must meet the requirements of subpart B (Commercial Diving Operations) of part 197 of this chapter.

4. And by adding a new subchapter V, consisting at this time of part 197, subpart B, to read as follows:

SUBCHAPTER V—MARINE OCCUPATIONAL SAFETY AND HEALTH STANDARDS

PART 197—GENERAL PROVISIONS

Subpart A—(Reserved)

Subpart B—Commercial Diving Operations

GENERAL

Sec.
197.200 Purpose of subpart.
197.202 Applicability.
197.204 Definitions.
197.205 Availability of standards.
197.206 Substitutes for required equipment, materials, apparatus, arrangements, procedures, or tests.
197.208 Designation of person-in-charge.
197.210 Designation of diving supervisor.

EQUIPMENT

197.300 Applicability.
197.310 Air compressor system.
197.312 Breathing supply hoses.
197.314 First aid and treatment equipment.
197.318 Gages and timekeeping devices.
197.320 Diving ladder and stage.
197.322 Surface-supplied helmets and masks.
197.324 Diver's safety harness.
197.326 Oxygen safety.
197.328 PVHO—General.
197.330 PVHO—Closed bells.
197.332 PVHO—Decompression chambers.
197.334 Open diving bells.
197.336 Pressure piping.
197.338 Compressed gas cylinders.
197.340 Breathing gas supply.
197.342 Buoyancy-changing devices.
197.344 Inflatable flotation devices.
197.346 Diver's equipment.

OPERATIONS

197.400 Applicability.
197.402 Responsibilities of the person-in-charge.
197.404 Responsibilities of the diving supervisor.
197.410 Dive procedures.
197.420 Operations manual.

SPECIFIC DIVING MODE PROCEDURES

197.430 SCUBA diving.
197.432 Surface-supplied air diving.
197.434 Surface-supplied mixed gas diving.
197.436 Liveboating.

PERIODIC TESTS AND INSPECTIONS OF DIVING EQUIPMENT

197.450 Breathing gas tests.

197.452 Oxygen cleaning.
197.454 First aid and treatment equipment.
197.456 Breathing supply hoses.
197.458 Gages and timekeeping devices.
197.460 Diving equipment.
197.462 Pressure vessels and pressure piping.

RECORDS

197.480 Logbooks.
197.482 Logbook entries.
197.484 Notice of casualty.
197.486 Written report of casualty.
197.488 Retention of records after casualty.

APPENDIX A: Air no-decompression limits.

AUTHORITY: (46 U.S.C. 239; 46 U.S.C. 390b; 46 U.S.C. 391a; 33 U.S.C. 1509(b); 43 U.S.C. 1333(d)(1); 43 U.S.C. 1331 et seq., as amended by Sec. 203 and 208 of Pub. L. 95-372; 46 U.S.C. 395; 46 U.S.C. 375; 46 U.S.C. 391; 46 U.S.C. 392; 46 U.S.C. 416; 49 U.S.C. 1655(b); 49 CFR 1.46 (b) and (s).)

Subpart A—[Reserved]

Subpart B—Commerical Diving Operations

GENERAL

§ 197.200 Purpose of subpart.

This subpart prescribes rules for the design, construction, and use of equipment, and inspection, operation, and safety and health standards for commercial diving operations taking place from vessels and facilities under Coast Guard jurisdiction.

§ 197.202 Applicability.

(a) This subpart applies to commercial diving operations taking place at any deepwater port or the safety zone thereof as defined in 33 CFR 150; from any artificial island, installation, or other device on the Outer Continental Shelf and the waters adjacent thereto as defined in 33 CFR 147 or otherwise related to activities on the Outer Continental Shelf; and from all vessels required to have a certificate of inspection issued by the Coast Guard including mobile offshore drilling units regardless of their geographic location, or from any vessel connected with a deepwater port or within the deepwater port safety zone, or from any vessel engaged in activities related to the Outer Continental Shelf; except that this subpart does not apply to any diving operation—

(1) Performed solely for marine scientific research and development purposes by educational institutions;

(2) Performed solely for research and development for the advancement of diving equipment and technology; or

(3) Performed solely for search and rescue or related public safety purposes by or under the control of a governmental agency.

(b) Diving operations may deviate from the requirements of this subpart to the extent necessary to prevent or minimize a situation which is likely to

RULES AND REGULATIONS

cause death, injury, or major environmental damage: The circumstances leading to the situation, the deviations made, and the corrective action taken, if appropriate, to reduce the possibility of recurrence shall be recorded by the diving supervisor in the logbook as required by § 197.482(c).

§ 197.204 Definitions.

As used in this subpart:

"ACFM" means actual cubic feet per minute.

"ANSI Code" means the B31.1 American National Standards Institute "Code for Pressure Piping, Power Piping."

"ASME Code" means the American Society of Mechanical Engineers "Boiler and Pressure Vessel Code."

"ASME PVHO-1" means the ANSI/ASME standard "Safety Standard for Pressure Vessels for Human Occupancy."

"ATA" means a measure of pressure expressed in terms of atmosphere absolute (includes barometric pressure).

"Bell" means a compartment either at ambient pressure (open bell) or pressurized (closed bell) that allows the diver to be transported to and from the underwater work site, allows the diver access to the surrounding environment, and is capable of being used as a refuge during diving operations.

"Bottom time" means the total elapsed time measured in minutes from the time the diver leaves the surface in descent to the time to the next whole minute that the diver begins ascent.

"Breathing gas/breathing mixture" means the mixed-gas, oxygen, or air as appropriate supplied to the diver for breathing.

"Bursting pressure" means the pressure at which a pressure containment device would fail structurally.

"Commercial diver" means a diver engaged in underwater work for hire excluding sport and recreational diving and the instruction thereof.

"Commercial diving operation" means all activities in support of a commercial diver.

"Cylinder" means a pressure vessel for the storage of gases under pressure.

"Decompression chamber" means a pressure vessel for human occupancy such as a surface decompression chamber, closed bell, or deep diving system especially equipped to recompress, decompress, and treat divers.

"Decompression sickness" means a condition caused by the formation of gas or gas bubbles in the blood or body tissue as a result of pressure reduction.

"Decompression table" means a profile or set of profiles of ascent rates and breathing mixtures designed to reduce the pressure on a diver safely to atmospheric pressure after the diver has been exposed to a specific depth and bottom time.

"Depth" means the maximum pressure expressed in feet of seawater attained by a diver and is used to express the depth of a dive.

"Dive location" means that portion of a vessel or facility from which a diving operation is conducted.

"Dive team" means the divers and diver support personnel involved in a diving operation, including the diving supervisor.

"Diver" means a person working beneath the surface, exposed to hyperbaric conditions, and using underwater breathing apparatus.

"Diver-carried reserve breathing gas" means a supply of air or mixed-gas, as appropriate, carried by the diver in addition to the primary or secondary breathing gas supplied to the diver.

"Diving installation" means all of the equipment used in support of a commercial diving operation.

"Diving mode" means a type of diving requiring SCUBA, surface-supplied air, or surface-supplied mixed-gas equipment, with related procedures and techniques.

"Diving stage" means a suspended platform constructed to carry one or more divers and used for putting divers into the water and bringing them to the surface when in-water decompression or a heavy-weight diving outfit is used.

"Diving supervisor" means the person having complete responsibility for the safety of a commercial diving operation including the responsibility for the safety and health of all diving personnel in accordance with this subpart.

"Facility" means a deepwater port, or an artificial island, installation, or other device on the Outer Continental Shelf subject to Coast Guard jurisdiction.

"Fsw" means feet of seawater (or equivalent static pressure head).

"Gas embolism" means a condition caused by expanding gases, which have been taken into and retained in the lungs while breathing under pressure, being forced into the bloodstream or other tissues during ascent or decompression.

"Heavy-weight diving outfit" means diver-worn surface-supplied deep-sea dress.

"Hyperbaric conditions" means pressure conditions in excess of surface atmospheric pressure.

"Injurious corrosion" means an advanced state of corrosion which may impair the structural integrity or safe operation of the equipment.

"Liveboating" means the support of a surfaced-supplied diver from a vessel underway.

"Maximum working pressure" means the maximum pressure to which a pressure containment device can be exposed under operating conditions (usually the pressure setting of the pressure relief device).

"No-decompression limits" means the air depth and bottom time limits of appendix A.

"Pressure vessel" means a container capable of withstanding an internal maximum working pressure over 15 psig.

"Psi(g)" means pounds per square inch (gage).

"PVHO" means pressure vessel for human occupancy but does not include pressure vessels for human occupancy that may be subjected to external pressures in excess of 15 psig but can only be subjected to maximum internal pressures of 15 psig or less (i.e., submersibles, or one atmosphere observation bells).

"Saturation diving" means saturating a diver's tissues with the inert gas in the breathing mixture to allow an extension of bottom time without additional decompression.

"SCUBA diving" means a diving mode in which the diver is supplied with a compressed breathing mixture from diver carried equipment.

"Standby diver" means a diver at the dive location available to assist a diver in the water.

"Surface-supplied air diving" means a diving mode in which the diver is supplied from the dive location or bell with compressed breathing air or oxygen or oxygen enriched air if supplied for treatment.

"Surface-supplied mixed-gas diving" means a diving mode in which the diver is supplied from the dive location or bell with a compressed breathing mixture other than air.

"Timekeeping device" means a device for measuring the time of a dive in minutes.

"Treatment table" means a depth, time, and breathing gas profile designed to treat a diver for decompression sickness.

"Umbilical" means the hose bundle between a dive location and a diver or bell, or between a diver and a bell, that supplies the diver or bell with a life-line, breathing gas, communications, power, and heat as appropriate to the diving mode or conditions.

"Vessel" means any waterborne craft including mobile offshore drilling units required to have a Certificate of Inspection issued by the Coast Guard or any waterborne craft connected with a deepwater port or within the deepwater port safety zone, or any waterborne craft engaged in activities related to the Outer Continental Shelf.

"Volume tank" means a pressure vessel connected to the outlet of a compressor and used as an air reservoir.

"Working pressure" means the pressure to which a pressure containment

RULES AND REGULATIONS

device is exposed at any particular instant during normal operating conditions.

§ 197.205 Availability of standards.

(a) Several standards have been incorporated by reference in this subchapter. The incorporation by reference has been approved by the Director of the FEDERAL REGISTER under the provisions of 1 CFR Part 51.

(b) The standards are available from the appropriate organizations whose addresses are listed below:

(1) American National Standards Institute, 1430 Broadway, New York, N.Y. 10018.

(2) American Society of Mechanical Engineers, United Engineering Center, 345 East 47th Street, New York, N.Y. 10017.

§ 197.206 Substitutes for required equipment, materials, apparatus, arrangements, procedures, or tests.

(a) The Coast Guard may accept substitutes for equipment, materials, apparatus, arrangements, procedures, or tests required in this subpart if the substitute provides an equivalent level of safety.

(b) In any case where it is shown to the satisfaction of the Commandant that the use of any particular equipment, material, apparatus, arrangement, procedure, or test is unreasonable or impracticable, the Commandant may permit the use of alternate equipment, material, apparatus, arrangement, procedure, or test to such an extent and upon such condition as will insure, to his satisfaction, a degree of safety consistent with the minimum standards set forth in this Subpart.

§ 197.208 Designation of person-in-charge.

(a) The owner or agent of a vessel or facility without a designated master shall designate, in writing, an individual to be the person-in-charge of the vessel or facility.

(b) Where a master is designated, the master is the person-in-charge.

§ 197.210 Designation of diving supervisor.

The name of the diving supervisor for each commercial diving operation shall be—

(a) Designated in writing; and

(b) Given to the person-in-charge prior to the commencement of any commercial diving operation.

EQUIPMENT

§ 197.300 Applicability.

(a) Each diving installation used on each vessel or facility subject to this subpart must meet the requirements of this subpart.

(b) In addition to the requirements of this subpart, equipment which is permanently installed on vessels and is part of the diving installation must meet subchapters F and J of this chapter.

(c) All repairs and modifications to pressure vessels used for commercial diving operations must be made in accordance with the requirements of section VIII, division 1 or division 2 of the ASME Code, ASME PVHO-1, part 54 of this chapter, or 49 CFR 173.34, as applicable.

(d) All repairs and modifications to pressure piping used for commercial diving operations must be made in accordance with the requirements of the ANSI Code or part 56 of this chapter, as applicable.

§ 197.310 Air compressor system.

A compressor used to supply breathing air to a diver must have—

(a) A volume tank that is—

(1) Built and stamped in accordance with section VIII, division 1 of the ASME Code with—

(i) A check valve on the inlet side;

(ii) A pressure gage;

(iii) A relief valve; and

(iv) A drain valve; and

(2) Tested after every repair, modification, or alteration to the pressure boundaries as required by § 197.462;

(b) Intakes that are located away from areas containing exhaust fumes of internal combustion engines or other hazardous contaminants;

(c) An efficient filtration system; and

(d) Slow-opening shut-off valves when the maximum allowable working pressure of the system exceeds 500 psig.

§ 197.312 Breathing supply hoses.

(a) Each breathing supply hose must—

(1) Have a maximum working pressure that is equal to or exceeds—

(i) The maximum working pressure of the section of the breathing supply system in which used; and

(ii) The pressure equivalent of the maximum depth of the dive relative to the supply source plus 100 psig;

(2) Have a bursting pressure of four times its maximum working pressure;

(3) Have connectors that—

(i) Are made of corrosion-resistant material;

(ii) Are resistant to accidental disengagement; and

(iii) Have a maximum working pressure that is at least equal to the maximum working pressure of the hose to which they are attached; and

(4) Resist kinking by—

(i) Being made of kink-resistant materials; or

(ii) Having exterior support.

(b) Each umbilical must—

(1) Meet the requirements of paragraph (a) of this section; and

(2) Be marked from the diver or open bell end in 10-foot intervals to 100 feet and in 50-foot intervals thereafter.

§ 197.314 First aid and treatment equipment.

(a) Each dive location must have—

(1) A medical kit approved by a physician that consists of—

(i) Basic first aid supplies; and

(ii) Any additional supplies necessary to treat minor trauma and illnesses resulting from hyperbaric exposure;

(2) A copy of an American Red Cross Standard First Aid handbook;

(3) A bag-type manual resuscitator with transparent mask and tubing; and

(4) A capability to remove an injured diver from the water.

(b) Each diving installation must have a two-way communications system to obtain emergency assistance except when the vessel or facility ship-to-shore, two-way communications system is readily available.

(c) Each dive location supporting mixed-gas dives, dives deeper than 130 fsw, or dives outside the no-decompression limits must meet the requirements of paragraph (a) of this section and have—

(1) A decompression chamber;

(2) Decompression and treatment tables;

(3) A supply of breathing gases sufficient to treat for decompression sickness;

(4) The medical kit required by paragraph (a)(1) of this section that is—

(i) Capable of being carried into the decompression chamber; and

(ii) Suitable for use under hyperbaric conditions; and

(5) A capability to assist an injured diver into the decompression chamber.

§ 197.318 Gages and timekeeping devices.

(a) A gage indicating diver depth must be at each dive location for surface-supplied dives.

(b) A timekeeping device must be at each dive location.

§ 197.320 Diving ladder and stage.

(a) Each diving ladder must—

(1) Be capable of supporting the weight of at least two divers;

(2) Extend 3 feet below the water surface;

(3) Be firmly in place;

(4) Be available at the dive location for a diver to enter or exit the water unless a diving stage or bell is provided; and

(5) Be—(i) Made of corrosion-resistant material; or

(ii) Protected against and maintained free from injurious corrosion.

(b) Each diving stage must—

(1) Be capable of supporting the weight of at least two divers;

(2) Have an open-grating platform;

(3) Be available for a diver to enter or exit the water from the dive location and for in-water decompression if the diver is—

(i) Wearing a heavy-weight diving outfit; or

RULES AND REGULATIONS

(ii) Diving outside the no-decompression limits, except when a bell is provided; and

(4) Be—(i) Made of corrosion-resistant material; or

(ii) Protected against and maintained free from injurious corrosion.

§ 197.322 Surface-supplied helmets and masks.

(a) Each surface-supplied helmet or mask must have—

(1) A nonreturn valve at the attachment point between helmet or mask and umbilical that closes readily and positively;

(2) An exhaust valve; and

(3) A two-way voice communication system between the diver and the dive location or bell.

(b) Each surface-supplied air helmet or mask must—

(1) Ventilate at least 4.5 ACFM at any depth at which it is operated; or

(2) Be able to maintain the diver's inspired carbon dioxide partial pressure below 0.02 ATA when the diver is producing carbon dioxide at the rate of 1.6 standard liters per minute.

§ 197.324 Diver's safety harness.

Each safety harness used in surface-supplied diving must have—

(a) A positive buckling device; and

(b) An attachment point for the umbilical life line that—

(1) Distributes the pulling force of the umbilical over the diver's body; and

(2) Prevents strain on the mask or helmet.

§ 197.326 Oxygen safety.

(a) Equipment used with oxygen or oxygen mixtures greater than 40 percent by volume must be designed for such use.

(b) Oxygen systems with pressures greater than 125 psig must have slow-opening shut-off valves except pressure boundary shut-off valves may be ball valves.

§ 197.328 PVHO—General.

(a) Each PVHO, contracted for or purchased after February 1, 1979, must be built and stamped in accordance with ASME PVHO-1.

(b) Each PVHO, contracted for or constructed before February 1, 1979, and not Coast Guard approved, must be submitted to the Coast Guard for approval prior to February 1, 1984.

(c) To be approved under paragraph (b), a PVHO must be—

(1) Constructed in accordance with Part 54 of this Chapter; or—

(2) Be built in accordance with section VIII, division 1 or division 2 of the ASME Code; and—

(i) Have the plans approved in accordance with § 54.01-18 of this chapter;

(ii) Pass the radiographic and other survey tests of welded joints required by section VIII, division 1 or division 2, as appropriate, of the ASME Code; and

(iii) Pass—(A) The hydrostatic test described in § 54.10-10 of this chapter; or

(B) The pneumatic test described in § 54.10-15 of this chapter and such additional tests as the Officer-in-Charge, Marine Inspection (OCMI) may require.

(d) Each PVHO must—

(1) Have a shut-off valve located within 1 foot of the pressure boundary on all piping penetrating the pressure boundary;

(2) Have a check valve located within 1 foot of the pressure boundary on all piping exclusively carrying fluids into the PVHO;

(3) Have the pressure relief device required by ASME PVHO-1;

(4) Have a built-in breathing system with at least one mask per occupant stored inside each separately pressurized compartment;

(5) Have a two-way voice communications system allowing communications between an occupant in one pressurized compartment of the PVHO and—

(i) The diving supervisor at the dive location;

(ii) Any divers being supported from the same PVHO; and

(iii) Occupants of other separately pressurized compartments of the same PVHO;

(6) If designed to mechanically couple to another PVHO, have a two-way communications system allowing communications between occupants of each PVHO when mechanically coupled;

(7) Have a pressure gage in the interior of each compartment that is—

(i) Designed for human occupancy; and

(ii) Capable of having the compartment pressure controlled from inside the PVHO;

(8) Have viewports that allow observation of occupants from the outside;

(9) Have viewports that meet the requirements of ASME PVHO-1 except those PVHO's approved under paragraph (b) of this section which have nonacrylic viewports;

(10) Have means of illumination sufficient to allow an occupant to—

(i) Read gages; and

(ii) Operate the installed systems within each compartment;

(11) Be designed and equipped to minimize sources of combustible materials and ignition;

(12) Have a protective device on the inlet side of PVHO exhaust lines;

(13) Have a means of extinguishing a fire in the interior;

(14) Have a means of maintaining the oxygen content of the interior atmosphere below 25 percent surface equivalent by volume when pressurized with air as the breathing mixture;

(15) Have a means of maintaining the interior atmosphere below 2 percent surface equivalent carbon dioxide by volume;

(16) Have a means of overriding and controlling from the exterior all interior breathing and pressure supply controls;

(17) Have a speech unscrambler when used with mixed-gas;

(18) Have interior electrical systems that are designed for the environment in which they will operate to minimize the risk of fire, electrical shock to personnel, and galvanic action of the PVHO; and

(19) Be tested after every repair, modification, or alteration to the pressure boundaries as required by § 197.462.

§ 197.330 PVHO—Closed bells.

(a) Except as provided in paragraph (b) of this section, each closed bell must meet the requirements of § 197.328 and—

(1) Have underwater breathing apparatus for each occupant stored inside each separately pressurized compartment;

(2) Have an umbilical;

(3) Have lifting equipment attached to the closed bell capable of returning the occupied closed bell when fully flooded to the dive location;

(4) Be capable of recompressing on the surface to the maximum design diving depth;

(5) Be constructed and equipped as required by § 197.332;

(6) Have an emergency locating device designed to assist personnel on the surface in acquiring and maintaining contact with the submerged PVHO if the umbilical to the surface is severed;

(7) Have a capability to remove an injured diver from the water; and

(8) Have a life support capability for the intact closed bell and its occupants for—

(i) Twelve hours after an accident severing the umbilical to the surface when the umbilical to the surface is the only installed means of retrieving the closed bell; or

(ii) A period of time, at least equal to 1 hour plus twice the time required to retrieve the bell from its designed operating depth and attach an auxiliary lifesupport system, after an accident severing the umbilical to the surface when the umbilical is one of the two independent installed means of retrieving the closed bell, each meeting the requirements of paragraph (a)(3) of this section.

RULES AND REGULATIONS

(b) A closed bell that does not meet the requirements of paragraphs (a)(3), (a)(4), and (a)(5) of this section, must be capable of attachment to another PVHO that—

(1) Allows the transfer of personnel and diver's equipment under pressure from the closed bell to the PVHO;

(2) Meets the requirements of paragraph (a)(3) of this section;

(3) Is capable of attachment to a decompression chamber meeting the requirements of paragraphs (a)(4) and (a)(5) of this section; and

(4) Allows the transfer of personnel and diver's equipment under pressure from the PVHO to the decompression chamber.

§ 197.332 PVHO—Decompression chambers.

Each decompression chamber must—

(a) Meet the requirements of § 197.328;

(b) Have internal dimensions sufficient to accommodate a diver lying in a horizontal position and another person tending the diver;

(c) Have a capability for ingress and egress of personnel and equipment while the occupants are under pressure;

(d) Have a means of operating all installed man-way locking devices, except disabled shipping dogs, from both sides of a closed hatch;

(e) Have interior illumination sufficient to allow visual observation, diagnosis, and medical treatment of an occupant.

(f) Have one bunk for each two occupants;

(g) Have a capability that allows bunks to be seen over their entire lengths from the exterior;

(h) Have a minimum pressure capability of—

(1) 6 ATA, when used for diving to 300 fsw; or

(2) The maximum depth of the dive, when used for diving operations deeper than 300 fsw, unless a closed bell meeting the requirements of § 197.330(a) (3), (4), and (5) is used;

(i) Have a minimum pressurization rate of 2 ATA per minute to 60 fsw and at least 1 ATA per minute thereafter;

(j) Have a decompression rate of 1 ATA per minute to 33 fsw;

(k) Have an external pressure gage for each pressurized compartment;

(l) Have a capability to supply breathing mixtures at the maximum rate required by each occupant doing heavy work; and

(m) Have a sound-powered headset or telephone as a backup to the communications system required by § 197.328(c) (5) and (6), except when that communications system is a sound-powered system.

§ 197.334 Open diving bells.

Each open diving bell must—

(a) Have an upper section that provides an envelope capable of maintaining a bubble of breathing mixture available to a diver standing on the lower section of the platform with his body through the open bottom and his head in the bubble;

(b) Have lifting equipment capable of returning the occupied open bell to the dive location;

(c) Have an umbilical; and

(d) Be—(1) Made of corrosion-resisting material; or

(2) Protected against and maintained free from injurious corrosion.

§ 197.336 Pressure piping.

Piping systems that are not an integral part of the vessel or facility, carrying fluids under pressures exceeding 15 psig must—

(a) Meet the ANSI Code;

(b) Have the point of connection to the integral piping system of the vessel or facility clearly marked; and

(c) Be tested after every repair, modification, or alteration to the pressure boundaries as set forth in § 197.462.

§ 197.338 Compressed gas cylinders.

Each compressed gas cylinder must—

(a) Be stored in a ventilated area;

(b) Be protected from excessive heat;

(c) Be prevented from falling;

(d) Be tested after any repair, modification, or alteration to the pressure boundries as set forth in § 197.462; and

(e) Meet the requirements of—

(1) Part 54 of this Chapter; or

(2) 49 CFR 173.34 and 49 CFR 178 Subpart C.

§ 197.340 Breathing gas supply.

(a) A primary breathing gas supply for surface-supplied diving must be sufficient to support the following for the duration of the planned dive:

(1) The diver.

(2) The standby diver.

(3) The decompression chamber, when required by § 197.432(e)(2) or by § 197.434(a) for the duration of the dive and for one hour after completion of the planned dive.

(4) A decompression chamber when provided but not required by this subpart.

(5) A closed bell when provided or required by § 197.434(d).

(6) An open bell when provided or required by § 197.432(e)(4) or by § 197.434(c).

(b) A secondary breathing gas supply for surface-supplied diving must be sufficient to support the following:

(1) The diver while returning to the surface.

(2) The diver during decompression.

(3) The standby diver.

(4) The decompression chamber when required by § 197.432(e)(2) or by § 197.434(a) for the duration of the dive and one hour after the completion of the planned dive.

(5) The closed bell while returning the diver to the surface.

(6) The open bell while returning the diver to the surface.

(c) A diver-carried reserve breathing gas supply for surface-supplied diving must be sufficient to allow the diver to—

(1) Reach the surface.

(2) Reach another source of breathing gas; or

(3) Be reached by a standby diver equipped with another source of breathing gas for the diver.

(d) A primary breathing gas supply for SCUBA diving must be sufficient to support the diver for the duration of the planned dive through his return to the dive location or planned pick-up point.

(e) A diver-carried reserve breathing gas supply for SCUBA diving must be sufficient to allow the diver to return to the dive location or planned pick-up point from the greatest depth of the planned dive.

(f) Oxygen used for breathing mixtures must—

(1) Meet the requirements of Federal Specification BB-0-925a; and

(2) Be type 1 (gaseous) grade A or B.

(g) Nitrogen used for breathing mixtures must—

(1) Meet the requirements of Federal Specification BB-N-411c;

(2) Be type 1 (gaseous);

(3) Be class 1 (oil free); and

(4) Be grade A, B, or C.

(h) Helium used for breathing mixtures must be grades A, B, or C produced by the Federal Government, or equivalent.

(i) Compressed air used for breathing mixtures must—

(1) Be 20 to 22 percent oxygen by volume;

(2) Have no objectionable odor; and

(3) Have no more than—

(i) 1,000 parts per million of carbon dioxide;

(ii) 20 parts per million carbon monoxide;

(iii) 5 milligrams per cubic meter of solid and liquid particulates including oil; and

(iv) 25 parts per million of hydrocarbons (includes methane and all other hydrocarbons expressed as methane).

§ 197.342 Buoyancy-changing devices.

(a) A dry suit or other buoyancy-changing device not directly connected to the exhaust valve of the helmet or mask must have an independent exhaust valve.

(b) When used for SCUBA diving, a buoyancy-changing device must have

RULES AND REGULATIONS

an inflation source separate from the breathing gas supply.

§ 197.341 Inflatable floatation devices.

An inflatable floatation device for SCUBA diving must—

(a) Be capable of maintaining the diver at the surface in a faceup position;

(b) Have a manually activated inflation device;

(c) Have an oral inflation device;

(d) Have an over-pressure relief device; and

(e) Have a manually operated exhaust valve.

§ 197.346 Diver's equipment.

(a) Each diver using SCUBA must have—

(1) Self-contained underwater breathing equipment including—

(i) A primary breathing gas supply with a cylinder pressure gage readable by the diver during the dive; and

(ii) A diver-carried reserve breathing gas supply provided by—

(A) A manual reserve (J valve); or

(B) An independent reserve cylinder connected and ready for use;

(2) A face mask;

(3) An inflatable floatation device;

(4) A weight belt capable of quick release;

(5) A knife;

(6) Swim fins or shoes;

(7) A diving wristwatch; and

(8) A depth gage.

(b) Each diver using a heavyweight diving outfit must—

(1) Have a helmet group consisting of helmet, breastplate, and associated valves and connections;

(2) Have a diving dress group consisting of a basic dress that encloses the body (except for head and hands) in a tough, waterproof cover, gloves, shoes, weight assembly; and knife;

(3) Have a hose group consisting of the breathing gas hose and fittings, the control valve, the lifeline, communications cable, and a pneumofathometer; and

(4) Be provided with a helmet cushion and weighted shoes.

(c) Each surface-supplied dive operation using a heavyweight diving outfit must have an extra breathing gas hose with attaching tools available to the standby diver.

(d) Each diver using a lightweight diving outfit must have—

(1) A safety harness;

(2) A weight assembly capable of quick release;

(3) A mask group consisting of a lightweight mask and associated valves and connections;

(4) A diving dress group consisting of wet or dry diving dress, gloves, shoes or fins, and knife; and

(5) A hose group consisting of the breathing gas hose and fittings, the

control valve, the lifeline, communications cable, and a pneumofathometer (if the breaking strength of the communications cable is at least equal to that required for the lifeline, the communications cable can serve as the lifeline).

(e) Each surface-supplied air dive operation within the no-decompression limits and to depths of 130 fsw or less must have a primary breathing gas supply at the dive location.

(f) Each surface-supplied dive operation outside the no-compression limits, deeper than 130 fsw, or using mixed-gas as a breathing mixture must have at the dive location—

(1) A primary breathing gas supply; and

(2) A secondary breathing gas supply.

(g) Each diver diving outside the no-decompression limits, deeper than 130 fsw, or using mixed-gas must have a diver-carried reserve breathing gas supply except when using a heavy-weight diving outfit or when diving in a physically confining area.

OPERATIONS

§ 197.400 Applicability.

Diving operations may only be conducted from a vessel or facility subject to the subpart if the regulations in this subpart are met.

§ 197.402 Responsibilities of the person-in-charge.

(a) The person-in-charge shall—

(1) Be fully cognizant of the provisions of this subpart;

(2) Prior to permitting any commercial diving operation to commence, have—

(i) The designation of the diving supervisor for each diving operation as required by § 197.210;

(ii) A report on—

(A) The nature and planned times of the planned diving operation; and

(B) The planned involvement of the vessel or facility, its equipment, and its personnel in the diving operation.

(b) Prior to permitting any commerical diving operation involving liveboating to commence, the person-in-charge shall insure that—

(1) A means of rapid communications with the diving supervisor while the diver is entering, in, or leaving the water is established; and

(2) A boat and crew for diver pickup in the event of an emergency is provided.

(c) The person-in-charge shall insure that a boat and crew for SCUBA diver pickup is provided when SCUBA divers are not line-tended from the dive location.

(d) The person-in-charge shall coordinate the activities on and of the

vessel or facility with the diving supervisor.

(e) The person-in-charge shall insure that the vessel or facility equipment and personnel are kept clear of the dive location except after coordinating with the diving supervisor.

§ 197.404 Responsibilities of the diving supervisor.

(a) The diving supervisor shall—

(1) Be fully cognizant of the provisions of this subpart;

(2) Be fully cognizant of the provisions of the operations manual required by § 197.420;

(3) Insure that diving operations conducted from a vessel or facility subject to this subpart meet the regulations in this subpart;

(4) Prior to the commencement of any commercial diving operation, provide the report required by § 197.402 to the person-in-charge;

(5) Coordinate with the person-in-charge any changes that are made to the report required by § 197.402; and

(6) Promptly notify the person-in-charge of any diving related casualty, accident, or injury.

(b) The diving supervisor is in charge of the planning and execution of the diving operation including the responsibility for the safety and health of the dive team.

§ 197.410 Dive procedures.

(a) The diving supervisor shall insure that—

(1) Before commencing diving operations, dive team members are briefed on—

(i) The tasks to be undertaken;

(ii) Any unusual hazards or environmental conditions likely to affect the safety of the diving operation; and

(iii) Any modifications to the operations manual or procedures including safety procedures necessitated by the specific diving operation;

(2) The breathing gas supply systems, masks, helmets, thermal protection, when provided, and bell lifting equipment, when a bell is provided or required, are inspected prior to each diving operation;

(3) Each diver is instructed to report any physical problems or physiological effects including aches, pains, current illnesses, or symptoms of decompression sickness prior to each dive;

(4) A depth, bottom time profile, including any breathing mixture changes, is maintained at the dive location for each diver during the dive, except that SCUBA divers shall maintain their own profiles;

(5) A two-way voice communication system is used between—

(i) Each surface-supplied diver and a dive team member at the dive location or bell (when provided); and

RULES AND REGULATIONS

(ii) The bell (when provided) and the dive location;

(6) A two-way communication system is available at the dive location to obtain emergency assistance;

(7) After the completion of each dive—

(i) The physical condition of the diver is checked by—

(A) Visual observation; and

(B) Questioning the diver about his physical well-being;

(ii) The diver is instructed to report any physical problems or adverse physiological effects including aches, pains, current illnesses, or symptoms of decompression sickness or gas embolism;

(iii) The diver is advised of the location of an operational decompression chamber; and

(iv) The diver is alerted to the potential hazards of flying after diving;

(8) For any dive outside the no-decompression limits, deeper than 130 fsw, or using mixed-gas as a breathing mixture—

(i) A depth, time, decompression profile including breathing mixture changes is maintained for each diver at the dive location;

(ii) The diver is instructed to remain awake and in the vicinity of the dive location decompression chamber for at least one hour after the completion of a dive, decompression, or treatment; and

(iii) A dive team member, other than the diver, is trained and available to operate the decompression chamber; and

(9) When decompression sickness or gas embolism is suspected or symptoms are evident, a report is completed containing—

(i) The investigation for each incident including—

(A) The dive and decompression profiles;

(B) The composition, depth, and time of breathing mixture changes;

(C) A description of the symptoms including depth and time of onset; and

(D) A description and results of the treatment;

(ii) The evaluation for each incident based on—

(A) The investigation;

(B) Consideration of the past performance of the decompression table used; and

(C) Individual susceptibility; and

(iii) The corrective action taken, if necessary, to reduce the probability of recurrence.

(b) The diving supervisor shall ensure that the working interval of a dive is terminated when he so directs or when—

(1) A diver requests termination;

(2) A diver fails to respond correctly to communications or signals from a dive team member;

(3) Communications are lost and can not be quickly reestablished between—

(i) The diver and a dive team member at the dive location; or

(ii) The person-in-charge and the diving supervisor during liveboating operations; or

(4) A diver begins to use his diver-carried reserve breathing gas supply.

§ 197.420 Operations manual.

(a) The diving supervisor shall—

(1) Provide an operations manual to the person-in-charge prior to commencement of any diving operation; and

(2) Make an operations manual available at the dive location to all members of the dive team.

(b) The operations manual must be modified in writing when adaptation is required because of—

(1) The configuration or operation of the vessel or facility; or

(2) The specific diving operation as planned.

(c) The operations manual must provide for the safety and health of the divers.

(d) The operations manual must contain the following:

(1) Safety procedures and checklists for each diving mode used.

(2) Assignments and responsibilities of each dive team member for each diving mode used.

(3) Equipment procedures and checklists for each diving mode used.

(4) Emergency procedures for—

(i) Fire;

(ii) Equipment failure;

(iii) Adverse environmental conditions including, but not limited to, weather and sea state;

(iv) Medical illness; and

(v) Treatment of injury.

(5) Procedures dealing with the use of—

(i) Hand-held power tools;

(ii) Welding and burning equipment; and

(iii) Explosives.

SPECIFIC DIVING MODE PROCEDURES

§ 197.430 SCUBA diving.

The diving supervisor shall insure that—

(a) SCUBA diving is not conducted—

(1) Outside the no-decompression limits;

(2) At depths greater than 130 fsw;

(3) Against currents greater than one (1) knot unless line-tended; and

(4) If a diver cannot directly ascend to the surface unless line-tended;

(b) The SCUBA diver has the equipment required by § 197.346(a);

(c) A standby diver is available while a diver is in the water;

(d) A diver is line-tended from the surface or accompanied by another

diver in the water in continuous visual contact during the diving operation;

(e) When a diver is in a physically confining space, another diver is stationed at the underwater point of entry and is line-tending the diver; and

(f) A boat is available for diver pickup when the divers are not line-tended from the dive location.

§ 197.432 Surface-supplied air diving.

The diving supervisor shall insure that—

(a) Surface-supplied air diving is conducted at depths less than 190 fsw, except that dives with bottom times of 30 minutes or less may be conducted to depths of 220 fsw;

(b) Each diving operation has a primary breathing gas supply;

(c) Each diver is continuously tended while in the water;

(d) When a diver is in a physically confining space, another diver is stationed at the underwater point of entry and is line-tending the diver;

(e) For dives deeper than 130 fsw or outside the no-decompression limits—

(1) Each diving operation has a secondary breathing gas supply;

(2) A decompression chamber is ready for use at the dive location;

(3) A diving stage is used except when a bell is provided;

(4) A bell is used for dives with an in-water decompression time greater than 120 minutes, except when the diver is using a heavy-weight diving outfit or is diving in a physically confining space;

(5) A separate dive team member tends each diver in the water;

(6) A standby diver is available while a diver is in the water; and

(7) Each diver has a diver-carried reserve breathing gas supply except when using a heavy-weight diving outfit or when diving in a physically confining space; and

(f) The surface-supplied air diver has the equipment required by § 197.346 (b) or (d).

§ 197.434 Surface-supplied mixed-gas diving.

The diving supervisor shall insure that—

(a) When mixed-gas diving is conducted, a decompression chamber or a closed bell meeting the requirements of § 197.332 is ready for use at the dive location;

(b) A diving stage is used except when a bell is provided;

(c) A bell is used for dives deeper than 220 fsw or when the dive involves in-water decompression times greater than 120 minutes, except when the diver is using a heavy-weight diving outfit or is diving in a physically confining space;

RULES AND REGULATIONS

(d) A closed bell is used for dives at depths greater than 300 fsw, except when diving is conducted in a physically confining space;

(e) A separate dive team member tends each diver in the water;

(f) A standby diver is available during all nonsaturation dives;

(g) When saturation diving is conducted—

(1) A standby diver is available when the closed bell leaves the dive location until the divers are in saturation; and

(2) A member of the dive team at the dive location is a diver able to assist in the recovery of the closed bell or its occupants, if required;

(h) When closed bell operations are conducted, a diver is available in the closed bell to assist a diver in the water;

(i) When a diver is in a physically confining space, another diver is stationed at the underwater point of entry and is line-tending the diver;

(j) Each diving operation has a primary and secondary breathing gas supply meeting the requirements of § 197.340; and

(k) The surface-supplied mixed-gas diver has the equipment required by § 197.346 (b) or (d).

§ 197.436 Liveboating.

(a) During liveboating operations, the person-in-charge shall insure that—

(1) Diving is not conducted in seas that impede station-keeping ability of the vessel;

(2) Liveboating operations are not conducted—

(i) From 1 hour after sunset to 1 hour before sunrise; or

(ii) During periods of restricted visibility;

(3) The propellers of the vessel are stopped before the diver enters or exits the water; and

(4) A boat is ready to be launched with crew in the event of an emergency.

(b) As used in paragraph (a)(2)(ii) of this section, "restricted visibility" means any condition in which vessel navigational visibility is restricted by fog, mist, falling snow, heavy rainstorms, sandstorms or any other similar causes.

(c) During liveboating operations, the diving supervisor shall insure that—

(1) Diving is not conducted at depths greater than 220 fsw;

(2) Diving is not conducted in seas that impede diver mobility or work function;

(3) A means is used to prevent the diver's hose from entangling in the propellers of the vessel; and

(4) Each diver carries a reserve breathing gas supply;

(5) A standby diver is available while a diver is in the water;

(6) Diving is not conducted with inwater decompression times greater than 120 minutes; and

(7) The person-in-charge is notified before a diver enters or exits the water.

PERIODIC TESTS AND INSPECTIONS OF DIVING EQUIPMENT

§ 197.450 Breathing gas tests.

The diving supervisor shall insure that—

(a) The output of each air compressor is tested and meets the requirements of § 197.340 for quality and quantity by means of samples taken at the connection point to the distribution system—

(1) Every 6 months; and

(2) After every repair or modification.

(b) Purchased supplies of breathing mixtures supplied to a diver are checked before being placed on line for—

(1) Certification that the supply meets the requirements of § 197.340; and

(2) Noxious or offensive odor and oxygen percentage;

(c) Each breathing supply system is checked, prior to commencement of diving operations, at the umbilical or underwater breathing apparatus connection point for the diver, for noxious or offensive odor and presence of oil mist; and

(d) Each breathing supply system, supplying mixed-gas to a diver, is checked, prior to commencement of diving operations, at the umbilical or underwater breathing apparatus connection point for the diver, for percentage of oxygen.

§ 197.452 Oxygen cleaning.

The diving supervisor shall ensure that equipment used with oxygen or oxygen mixtures greater than 40 percent by volume is cleaned of flammable materials—

(a) Before being placed into service; and

(b) After any repair, alteration, modification, or suspected contamination.

§ 197.454 First aid and treatment equipment.

The diving supervisor shall ensure that medical kits are checked monthly to insure that all required supplies are present.

§ 197.456 Breathing supply hoses.

(a) The diving supervisor shall insure that—

(1) Each breathing supply hose is pressure tested prior to being placed into initial service and every 24

months thereafter to 1.5 times its maximum working pressure;

(2) Each breathing supply hose assembly, prior to being placed into initial service and after any repair, modification, or alteration, is tensile tested by—

(i) Subjecting each hose-to-fitting connection to a 200 pound axial load; and

(ii) Passing a visual examination for evidence of separation, slippage, or other damage to the assembly;

(3) Each breathing supply hose is periodically checked for—

(i) Damage which is likely to affect pressure integrity; and

(ii) Contamination which is likely to affect the purity of the breathing mixture delivered to the diver; and

(4) The open ends of each breathing supply hose are taped, capped, or plugged when not in use.

(b) To meet the requirements of paragraph (a)(3) of this section, each breathing supply hose must be—

(1) Carefully inspected before being shipped to the dive location;

(2) Visually checked during daily operation; and

(3) Checked for noxious or offensive odor before each diving operation.

§ 197.458 Gages and timekeeping devices.

The diving supervisor shall insure that—

(a) Each depth gage and timekeeping device is tested or calibrated against a master reference gage or time-keeping device every 6 months;

(b) A depth gage is tested when a discrepancy exists in a depth gage reading greater than 2 percent of full scale between any two gages of similar range and calibration;

(c) A timekeeping device is tested when a discrepancy exists in a timekeeping device reading greater than one-quarter of a minute in a 4-hour period between any two timekeeping devices; and

(d) Each depth gage and timekeeping device is inspected before diving operations are begun.

§ 197.460 Diving equipment.

The diving supervisor shall insure that the diving equipment designated for use in a dive under § 197.346 is inspected before each dive.

§ 197.462 Pressure vessels and pressure piping.

(a) The diving supervisor shall insure that each volume tank, cylinder, PVHO, and pressure piping system has been examined and tested every 12 months and after any repair, modification, or alteration to the extent necessary to determine that they are in condition and fit for the service intended.

RULES AND REGULATIONS

(b) The following tests must be made to meet the annual requirements of paragraph (a) of this section:

(1) An internal and external visual examination for mechanical damage or deterioration. If a defect is found that may impair the safety of the pressure vessel, a hydrostatic test must be performed.

(2) A leak test.

(3) A pneumatic test.

(4) A hydrostatic test every fifth year instead of the pneumatic test.

(c) The following tests must be made after any repair, modification, or alteration to meet the requirements of paragraph (a) of this section:

(1) An internal and external visual examination for correctness and adequacy of repair, modification, or alteration.

(2) A leak test.

(3) A hydrostatic test when the repair, modification, or alteration affects the pressure boundary.

(d) When the pneumatic test on pressure vessels is conducted—

(1) The test pressure must be the maximum allowable working pressure stamped on the pressure vessel; and

(2) The test may be conducted only after suitable precautions are taken to protect personnel and equipment.

(e) When the pneumatic test on pressure piping is conducted

(1) The test pressure must be no less than 90 percent of the setting of the relief device; and

(2) The test may be conducted only after suitable precautions are taken to protect personnel and equipment.

(f) When a hydrostatic test on a pressure vessel is made, the test pressure must be—

(1) 1¼ times the pressure stamped on the pressure vessel built to division 2 of the ASME Code; and

(2) 1½ times the pressure stamped on the pressure vessel built to division 1 of the ASME Code.

(g) When a hydrostatic test on pressure piping is conducted, the test must be conducted in accordance with the ANSI Code.

(h) When the leak test on pressure vessels or pressure piping is conducted—

(1) The test must be conducted with the breathing mixture normally used in service;

(2) The test must be conducted at the maximum allowable working pressure; and

(3) The test pressure must be maintained for a minimum of 10 minutes to allow checking all joints, connections, and regions of high stress for leakage.

RECORDS

§ 197.480 Logbooks.

(a) The person-in-charge of a vessel or facility required by 46 U.S.C. 201 to have an official logbook shall maintain the logbook on form CG–706.

(b) The person-in-charge of a vessel or facility not required by 46 U.S.C. 201 to have an official logbook, shall maintain, on board, a logbook for making the entries required by this subpart.

(c) The diving supervisor conducting commercial diving operations from a vessel or facility subject to this subpart shall maintain a logbook for making the entries required by this subpart.

§ 197.482 Logbook entries.

(a) The person-in-charge shall insure that the following information is recorded in the logbook for each commercial diving operation:

(1) Date, time, and location at the start and completion of dive operations.

(2) Approximate underwater and surface conditions (weather, visibility, temperatures, and currents).

(3) Name of the diving supervisor.

(4) General nature of work performed.

(b) The diving supervisor shall insure that the following information is recorded in the logbook for each commercial diving operation:

(1) Date, time, and location at the start and completion of each dive operation.

(2) Approximate underwater and surface conditions (weather, visibility, temperatures, and currents).

(3) Names of dive team members including diving supervisor.

(4) General nature of work performed.

(5) Repetitive dive designation or elapsed time since last hyperbaric exposure if less than 24 hours for each diver.

(6) Diving modes used.

(7) Maximum depth and bottom time for each diver.

(8) Name of person-in-charge.

(9) For each dive outside the no-decompression limits, deeper than 130 fsw, or using mixed-gas, the breathing gases and decompression table designations used.

(10) When decompression sickness or gas embolism is suspected or symptoms are evident—

(i) The name of the diver; and

(ii) A description and results of treatment.

(11) For each fatality or any diving related injury or illness that results in incapacitation of more than 72 hours or requires any dive team member to be hospitalized for more than 24 hours—

(i) The date;

(ii) Time;

(iii) Circumstances; and

(iv) Extent of any injury or illness.

(c) The diving supervisor shall insure that the following is recorded in the logbook for each diving operation deviating from the requirements of this subpart:

(1) A description of the circumstances leading to the situation.

(2) The deviations made.

(3) The corrective action taken, if appropriate, to reduce the possibility of recurrence.

(d) The diving supervisor shall insure that a record of the following is maintained:

(1) The date and results of each check of the medical kits.

(2) The date and results of each test of the air compressor.

(3) The date and results of each check of breathing mixtures.

(4) The date and results of each check of each breathing supply system.

(5) The date, equipment cleaned, general cleaning procedure, and names of persons cleaning the diving equipment for oxygen service.

(6) The date and results of each test of the breathing supply hoses and system.

(7) The date and results of each inspection of the breathing gas supply system.

(8) The date and results of each test of depth gages and timekeeping devices.

(9) The date and results of each test and inspection of each PVHO.

(10) The date and results of each inspection of the diving equipment.

(11) The date and results of each test and inspection of pressure piping.

(12) The date and results of each test and inspection of volume tanks and cylinders.

(e) The diving supervisor shall insure that a notation concerning the location of the information required under paragraph (d) is made in the logbook.

NOTE.—R.S. 4290 (46 U.S.C. 201) requires that certain entries be made in an official logbook in addition to the entries required by this section; and R.S. 4291 (46 U.S.C. 202) prescribes the manner of making those entries.

§ 197.484 Notice of casualty.

(a) In addition to the requirements of subpart 4.05 of this chapter and 33 CFR 146.01-20, the person-in-charge shall notify the Officer-in-Charge, Marine Inspection, as soon as possible after a diving casualty occurs, if the casualty involves any of the following:

(1) Loss of life.

(2) Diving-related injury to any person causing incapacitation for more than 72 hours.

(3) Diving-related injury to any person requiring hospitalization for more than 24 hours.

RULES AND REGULATIONS

(b) The notice required by this section must contain the following:

(1) Name and official number (if applicable) of the vessel or facility.

(2) Name of the owner or agent of the vessel or facility.

(3) Name of the person-in-charge.

(4) Name of the diving supervisor.

(5) Description of the casualty including presumed cause.

(6) Nature and extent of the injury to persons.

(c) The notice required by this section is not required if the written report required by § 197.486 is submitted within 5 days of the casualty.

§ 197.486 Written report of casualty.

The person-in-charge of a vessel or facility for which a notice of casualty was made under § 197.484 shall submit a report to the Officer-in-Charge, Marine Inspection, as soon as possible after the casualty occurs, as follows:

(a) On form CG-924E, when the diving installation is on a vessel.

(b) Using a written report, in narrative form, when the diving installation is on a facility. The written report must contain the information required by § 197.484.

(c) The report required by this section must be accompanied by a copy of the report required by § 197.410(a)(9) when decompression sickness is involved.

§ 197.488 Retention of records after casualty.

(a) The owner, agent, or person-in-charge of a vessel or facility for which a report of casualty is made under § 197.484 shall retain all records onboard that are maintained on the vessel or facility and those records required by this subpart for 6 months after the report of a casualty is made or until advised by the Officer-in-Charge, Marine Inspection, that records need not be retained onboard.

(b) The records required by paragraph (a) of this section to be retained on board include, but are not limited to, the following:

(1) All logbooks required by § 197.480.

(2) All reports required by § 197.402(a)(2)(ii), § 197.404(a)(4), § 197.410(a)(9).

(c) The owner, agent, person-in-charge, or diving supervisor shall, upon request, make the records described in this section available for examination by any Coast Guard official authorized to investigate the casualty.

APPENDIX A .

The following table gives the depth versus bottom time limits for single, no-decompression, air dives made within any 12-hour period. The limit is the maximum bottom time in minutes that a diver can spend at that depth without requiring decompression beyond that provided by a normal ascent rate of 60 fsw per minute. (Although bottom time is concluded when ascent begins, a slower ascent rate would increase the bottom time thereby requiring decompression.) An amount of nitrogen remains in the tissues of a diver after any air dive, regardless of whether the dive was a decompression or no-decompression dive. Whenever another dive is made within a 12-hour period, the nitrogen remaining in the blood and body tissues of the diver must be considered when calculating his decompression.

AIR NO-DECOMPRESSION LIMITS

Depth (feet):	No-decompression limits (minutes)
35	310
40	200
50	100
60	60
70	50
80	40
90	30
100	25
110	20
120	15
130	10

(Source: U.S. Navy Diving Manual, 1 September 1973.)

(46 U.S.C. 239; 46 U.S.C. 390b; 46 U.S.C. 391a; 33 U.S.C. 1509(b); 43 U.S.C. 1333(d)(1); 43 U.S.C. 1331 et seq., as amended by Sec. 203 and 208 of Pub. L. 95-372; 46 U.S.C. 395; 46 U.S.C. 375; 46 U.S.C. 391; 46 U.S.C. 392; 46 U.S.C. 416; 49 U.S.C. 1655(b); 49 CFR 1.46 (b) and (s).)

Dated: November 9, 1978.

R. H. SCARBOROUGH,
Vice Admiral, U.S. Coast Guard,
Acting Commandant.

[FR Doc. 78-32282 Filed 11-15-78; 8:45 am]

2. Coast Guard Diving Regulations—Variance Procedures*

In the Federal Register, Volume 43, Number 222, of Thursday, November 16, 1978, the U. S. Coast Guard published their final rule on commercial diving operations which had an effective date of February 1, 1979.

This final rule created a new Part in Title 46 of the Code of Federal Regulations: Subchapter V - Marine Occupational Safety and Health Standards. The intent of these regulations was to regulate commercial diving operations on vessels and facilities subject to the jurisdiction of the Coast Guard to the extent necessary to insure an acceptable level of personnel safety and health.

Contained within the regulations is a variance provision which allows the Coast Guard to acccept substitute for equipment, procedures, materials, apparatus, arrangements, or tests required if the substitute provides an equivalent level of safety. Specifically:

Section 197.206: Substitutes for required equipment, materials, apparatus, arrangements, procedures or tests.
(a) The Coast Guard may accept substitutes for equipment, material, apparatus, arrangements, procedures or tests required in this subpart if the substitute provides an equivalent level of safety.
(b) In any case where it is shown to the satisfaction of the Commandant that the use of any particular equipment, material, apparatus, arrangement, procedure or test is unreasonable or impracticable, the Commandant may permit the use of alternative equipment, material, apparatus, arrangement, procedure, or test to such an extent and upon such condition as will insure to his satisfaction, a degree of safety consistent with the minimum set forth in this subpart.

A request for variance from the regulations should begin with the Officer-in-Charge, Marine Inspection at the local Marine Inspection Office or Marine Safety Office. At this level the request will be reviewed in accordance with the provisions of 46 CFR 197.206 and a decision on the merits of the request will be made. The person who requested the variance from the regulations will be notified in writing of the decision.

When preparing a request for variance from the regulations, the person should specifically address the following topics, as applicable:

(1) diving mode procedure;
(2) alternative decompression procedure;
(3) manning requirements:
(4) number of dives;
(5) number of divers;

* U. S. Coast Guard, District 1, Boston, Massachusetts.

(6) level of work required of divers;

(7) configuration of equipment to be used;

(8) anticipated water conditions;

(9) dive location; and

(10) remoteness from hyperbaric assistance.

These topics should be addressed as to how the requested variance would result in a more reasonable or practical diving operation, yet would preserve an equivalent level of safety as would be achieved by complying with the letter of regulations.

Should the person who requested the variance be aggrieved by the Officer-in-Charge, Marine Inspection, he may appeal the decision to the Chief, Marine Safety Division, at the District Office under whose control the local Marine Inspection Office or Marine Safety Office operates. The appeal must be made in writing within thirty days of the date of the decision being appealed. The appeal must contain a description of the decision being appealed and the reasons why the decision should be modified or set aside. Pending a ruling on the appeal, the decision of the Officer-in-Charge, Marine Inspection shall govern.

3. Marine Safety Manual*

COMMERCIAL DIVING EQUIPMENT/OPERATIONS CHECKLIST

PART A: GENERAL

Date/Time of Inspection _____

Vessel/Facility Name, Location, Address and Phone:

_____

_____

_____

Owner's Name, Address, Phone Number:

_____

_____

_____

Master's Name, Address, Phone Number:

_____

_____

_____

Operator's Name, Address, Phone Number:

_____

_____

_____

Person-in-Charge: _____

Designated in Writing? _____ Yes _____ No

Diving Supervisor: _____

Designated in Writing? _____ Yes _____ No

Date of Last Commercial Diving Inspection: _____

Responsible Vessel/Facility Personnel Accompanying
Coast Guard Inspector(s):

_____

_____

_____

Coast Guard Inspector(s):

_____

_____

* U. S. Coast Guard, District 1, Boston, Massachusetts.

PART B: EQUIPMENT   YES   NO

AIR COMPRESSOR SYSTEM (46 CFR 197.310):

1. Volume Tank Built and Stamped per ASME Code
2. Volume Tank has Check Valve, Pressure Gauge,
   Relief Valve, Drain Valve
3. Tested Every 12 Months or After Repair,
   Modification, etc.
4. Intakes Located Away from Fumes/Contaminants
5. Filtration System Efficient
6. Slow-Opening Shut-Off Valves if Working
   Pressure Exceeds 500 psig

BREATHING SUPPLY HOSES (46 CFR 197.312):

7. Maximum Working Pressure Meets Requirement
8. Bursting Pressure Four Times Maximum
   Working Pressure
9. Connectors Meet Required Standards
10. Kink Resistance Standards Met
11. Hose/Umbilical Length Marked As Required

FIRST AID AND TREATMENT EQUIPMENT AT EACH DIVE
LOCATION (46 CFR 197.312):

12. Required Medical Kit
13. American Red Cross Standard First Aid
    Handbook
14. Bag-Type Manual Resuscitator With Transparent
    Mask and Tubing
15. Capability to Remove and Injured Diver From
    Water
16. Two-Way Communications Standard Met (for Mixed-
    Gas Diving, Dives to 130 fsw, or Outside No
    Decompression Limits)
17. Decompression Chamber
18. Decompression and Treatment Tables
19. Breathing Gases Supply for Decompression
    Sickness
20. Medical Kit Can be Carried Into Chamber
    and Used for Hyperbaric Conditions
21. Capability to Assist Injured Diver Into
    Decompression Chamber

GAUGES AND TIMEKEEPING DEVICES (46 CFR 197.318):

22. Gauge Indicating Diver Depth at Surface-Supplied
    Dive Locations
23. Timekeeping Device at Each Dive Location

DIVING LADDERS AND STAGES (46 CFR 197.320):

24. Each Ladder Meets Structural, Material, and
    Installation Requirements
    (a) Available Where Required?
25. Each Diving Stage Meets Structural, Material, and
    Installation Requirements
    (a) Available Where Required?

SURFACE-SUPPLIED HELMETS AND MASKS (46 CFR 197.322):   YES   NO

26. Each Helmet/Mask Has Operating Non-return Valve,
    Exhaust Valve, and Two-Way Communication System
27. Each Helmet/Mask Meets Ventilation Requirements
28. Each Harness Has Position Buckling Device and
    Attachment Point for Umbilical That Meets Standards

OXYGEN SAFETY (46 CFR 197.326):

29. Oxygen Equipment Designed For Use and Has Slow-Opening
    Shut-off Valve If Required

PVHO's - GENERAL (46 CRF 197.328):

30. Contracted for or Purchased After 2/1/79,
    and Built and Stamped Per ASME Code
31. Contracted for or Constructed Before 2/1/79,
    not USCG- approved and Meets Requirements of
    46 CFR 197.328(b), (c), and (d)
32. Contracted for or Constructed Before 2/1/79,
    USCG- approved and Meets Standards of NVC 2-70
    and 46 CFR 61.10

PVHO's - CLOSED BELLS (46 CFR 197.330):

33. Meets Requirements of 46 CFR 197.330(a)
34. Meets Requirements of 46 CFR 197.330(b)
    in lieu of (a) (3), (a) (4), or (a) (5)

PVHO's - DECOMPRESSION CHAMBER (46 CFR 197.332):

35. Meets Requirements for Internal Dimensions,
    Ingress and Egress, Illumination, Visibility,
    and Habitability
36. Meets Requirements for Pressure Capability,
    Pressurization and Decompression, and Ventilation
37. Has Require External Pressure Gauge(s)

OPEN DIVING BELLS (46 CFR 197.334):

38. Meets Requirement for Breathing Mixture in Upper
    Section, and Has Umbilical
39. Lifting Equipment Meets Requirements
40. Meets Corrosion-Resistance Standards

PRESSURE PIPING (46 CFR 197.336):

41. Meets ANSI Code
42. Point of Connection to Vessel or Facility System
    Clearly Marked
43. Tested Every 12 Months or After Repairs, etc.

COMPRESSED GAS CYLINDERS (46 CFR 197.338):

44. Storage and Protection Standards Met
45. Tested Every 12 Months or After Repairs, etc.
46. Hydrostatically Tested Within 5 Years

BREATHING GAS SUPPLY (46 CFR 197.340):

47. Sufficient to Supply Diver and Standby Diver
48. Sufficient to Supply Decompression Chamber, Closed,
    or Open Bell When Provided or Required

49. Secondary Supply Adequate for Diver, Standby   YES   NO
    Diver, Decompression Chamber, Closed, or Open
    Bell as Required
50. Diver-Carried Reserve Supply Adequate
51. Primary and Diver-Carried Reserve Supply for SCUBA
    Diving Sufficient
52. Oxygen, Nitrogen, Helium, and Compressed Air
    Meet Standards

BUOYANCY-CHANGING DEVICES (46 CFR 197.342):

53. Connected to Helmet Exhaust Valve or Has
    Independent Exhaust Valve
54. Separate Inflation Source if Used for SCUBA
    Diving

INFLATABLE FLOTATION DEVICES (46 CFR 197.344):

55. Capable of Properly Supporting Diver; Has
    Manually-operated Inflation Device and
    Exhaust Valve, Oral Inflation Device, and
    Over-Pressure Relief Device

DIVER'S EQUIPMENT (46 CFR 197.346):

56. Each SCUBA Diver Has Required Equipment Available
57. Each Diver Using Heavyweight Diving Outfit Has
    Required Equipment Available
58. Each Diver Using a Lightweight Diving Outfit Has
    the Required Equipment Available
59. Primary, Secondary, and Diver-Carried Reserve
    Breathing Gas Supplies as Required by 46 CFR
    197.346(e), (f), and (g)

PART C: OPERATIONS

RESPONSIBILITIES OF PERSON-IN-CHARGE (46 CFR 197.402):

1. Cognizant of 46 CFR 197, subpart B
2. Receives Report on All Required Details of All
   Planned Dives
3. Insure Rapid Communications, Emergency Boat and
   Crew for Diver Pickup, and Coordination of
   Activities as Required

RESPONSIBILITIES OF DIVING SUPERVISOR (46 CFR 197.404):

4. Cognizant of 46 CFR 197, subpart B and Operations
   Manual
5. Provides Planning Report to Person-in-Charge for
   All Diving Operations
6. Provides Notification of Any Diving-Related Casualty,
   Accident, or Injury

DIVE PROCEDURES (46 CFR 197.410):

7. Dive Team Members Briefed Properly Before Each Dive
8. Depth, Bottom Time Profile Maintained At Dive
   Location For Each Diver During the Dive
9. Two-way Communications Systems as Required
10. Dive Debriefing Procedures Rigorously Observed

11. Special Required Procedures for Dives Outside　　YES　　NO
the No-decompression Limits, and For Decompression
Sickness, Are Observed
12. Diving Supervisor Terminates Dives in Accordance
With Requirements and Safe Practice

OPERATIONS MANUAL (46 CFR 197.420):

13. Provided to Person-in-Charge and Available at Dive
Location as Required
14. Provides for All Specific Diving Operations Conducted,
or Has Been Modified to Accomodate Adaptations
15. Provides for Safety and Health of Divers and Contains
Required Safety Procedures and Checklists, Dive Team
Member Assignments and Responsibilities, Equipment
Procedures/Checklists, and Emergency Procedures

PART D: SPECIFIC DIVING MODE PROCEDURES

1. SCUBA Diving Safety Procedures Observed (46 CFR 197.430)
2. Surface-Supplied Air Diving Procedures Properly
Observed (46 CFR 197.432)
3. Surface-Supplied Mixed-Gas Diving Procedures
Properly Observed (46 CFR 197.434)
4. Lifeboating Safety Procedures Properly Followed
(46 CFR 197.436)

PART E: PERIODIC TESTS AND INSPECTIONS OF DIVING EQUIPMENT

1. Required Samples and Tests are Performed of Breathing
Gases and Air Compressors Regarding Quality, Quantity,
Noxious or Offensive Odors, and Oxygen Percentage
2. Oxygen Equipment is Cleaned of Flammable Materials
as Required (46 CFR 197.452)
3. Medical Kits are Checked Monthly and All Required Supplies
Are Present (46 CFR 197.454)
4. Breathing Supply Boxes are Properly Tested, Inspected, and
Stored (46 CFR 197.456)
5. Depth Gauges and Timekeeping Devices are Properly Tested
and Inspected (46 CFR 197.458)
6. Diving Equipment Required is Inspected Before Each Dive
By the Diving Supervisor (46 CFR 197.460)
7. Tests and Examinations of Pressure Vessels and Pressure
Piping are Made Every 12 Months and After All Repairs or
Modifications, in Accordance With Requirements and ASME
and ANSI Codes.
8. All Required Log Entries Made and Log Maintained by
Diving Supervisor

Appendix B

1. Setup and Operation of Equipment*

This chapter will describe how to set up a typical oxy-acetylene welding or cutting outfit, and how to light the torch and adjust the flame. Precautions which must be observed during setup and lighting will be covered. The next chapter (7) will cover precautions which should be observed in the course of actual welding and cutting operations. Please do not attempt to set up and operate an outfit until you feel thoroughly familiar with the content of both chapters.

The make-up of a complete outfit was given in the opening paragraphs of Chapter 5. Please make sure that you have on hand everything needed before you start to set up.

Attaching Pressure-Reducing Regulators

Fasten the cylinders to be used in an upright position so that they cannot be knocked or pulled over. If cylinders are not on a suitable cylinder cart, they should be securely fastened, with chain or equivalent, to a workbench, wall, or post. As explained earlier in Chapter 3, acetylene cylinders should never be stored or used other than in a vertical position.

Remove the protective cap from the oxygen cylinder, and from the acetylene cylinder, if so equipped.

"Crack" the cylinder valves. Stand so that the gas leaving the cylinder outlet will not be directed onto your face or clothing. Open the valve quickly about one-quarter of a turn, then close it immediately. This will clear the valve outlet opening of accumulated dust or dirt which might, if not blown out, mar the seat of the regulator nipple or be carried into the regulator.

PRECAUTION: Never "crack" a fuel gas cylinder valve near
other welding or cutting work in progress, or near sparks, flame,
or other possible source of ignition.

Connect the oxygen regulator to the oxygen cylinder and the acetylene regulator to the acetylene cylinder. If the acetylene regulator and the acetylene cylinder have different threads, it will be necessary to use an adaptor between the regulator and the cylinder. As stated in Chapter 5, two quite different acetylene cylinder connections are widely used in the U.S.

* Chapter 6, *The Oxy-Acetylene Handbook,* courtesy of Union Carbide Corporation.

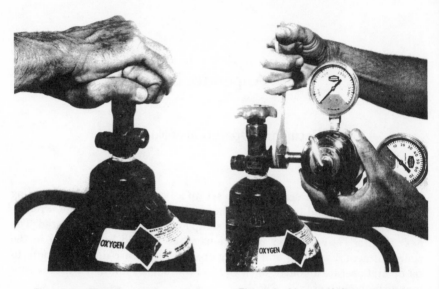

Fig. 6-1. Always crack cylinder valves, to blow out dust and dirt from the outlets.

Fig. 6-2. Always tighten regulator connection nuts with a wrench.

The CGA 510 connection has left-hand threads, internal on the cylinder outlet; the CGA 300 connection has right-hand threads, external on the cylinder outlet.

Tighten both regulator connection nuts firmly with a wrench. (Avoid use of adjustable wrenches. Wrenches with two or more fixed openings, designed specifically for use with gas welding and cutting apparatus, are available from all apparatus suppliers.)

> PRECAUTION: Should it ever be necessary to retighten the regulator union nut after the outfit has been set up and the cylinder valves opened, be sure to close the cylinder valve before tightening the nut.

Rotate the pressure-adjusting screw of each regulator to the left (counter-clockwise) until it turns freely. It is essential that the valve in the regulator be closed before cylinder pressure is admitted to the regulator. To achieve this, the pressure-adjusting screw must be backed off until it no longer is pushing against the pressure-adjusting spring in the regulator.

Open each cylinder valve SLOWLY. Stand in such a position that you can see the cylinder-pressure gauge hand on the regulator, but never stand directly in front of the regulator gauge faces. It is especially important that you open the oxygen cylinder valve only very slightly at first, and that you wait until the cylinder-pressure gauge hand has stopped moving before

Fig. 6-3. Always release regulator pressure-adjusing screw fully before opening the cylinder valve.

Fig. 6-4. Always open the oxygen cylinder valve as SLOWLY as possible.

opening the valve *fully*. Remember that acetylene cylinder valves should not be opened more than one and one-half turns.

Always leave the wrench in place on the acetylene cylinder valve while the valve is open. However, when two or more cylinders have been manifolded together, it is sufficient to leave a wrench on one of the cylinders. The point is this: you should not be forced to waste time looking around for a suitable wrench should an emergency make it necessary to close the cylinder valve or valves without delay.

Note: The cylinder-pressure gauge on each regulator shows you the *pressure* in each cylinder. In the case of both oxygen and acetylene, *pressure* is a rough measure of *contents*. If you are using a large cylinder of oxygen which when full contained 244 cf at 2200 psi and 70°F (6.5 m³ at 15200 kPa and 20°C), the cylinder is half-full when the cylinder-pressure gauge reads 1100 psi (517 kPa), so that you have 122 cf (3.2 m³) available. When the pressure in an acetylene cylinder is approximately 125 psi at 70°F (862 kPa at 20°C) it is also true that the cylinder is about one-half full. However, if you are using a liquefied fuel gas, such as propane, cylinder pressure remains constant until virtually all the liquid has been vaporized. For that reason, regulators designed for propane service are seldom supplied with cylinder-pressure gauges. Liquid oxygen cylinders are equipped with liquid-level gauges which will indicate the amount of liquid oxygen remaining in the cylinder.

Connecting Gas Supplies to the Torch

Always use hose and hose connections made specifically for gas welding and cutting purposes. Oxygen hose has a green cover; acetylene hose has a red cover. Never interchange oxygen and acetylene hose. Do not use acetylene hose with propane unless you know that is acceptable for use with propane. (Hose with natural rubber liner is satisfactory for acetylene service, but not for propane service.)

Make up all connections dry; do not use pipe-fitting compounds, thread lubricants, oil, or grease. All connections are designed with metal-to-metal seals. They do not require lubricants or sealants. However, they must always be made up wrench-tight, not merely hand-tight.

Never force connections which do not fit. If you cannot run the threads together by hand with ease, either the threads are damaged, or you are trying to put together parts that were not made to go together.

If the hose does not have connections on both ends, put these on next. Connection nuts for oxygen hose have right-hand threads, connection nuts for acetylene have left-hand threads. Instructions for installing hose connections are given in the Appendix.

Fig. 6-5. Always use wrench to open acetylene cylinder valve; leave wrench in place after opening valve.

Fig. 6-6. Always tighten all connection nuts firmly with a wrench.

Attach the oxygen hose to the oxygen regulator and to the oxygen connection on the torch. The torch connection is usually identified by a marking in the torch body or in the torch handle, opposite the oxygen valve. Cutting machine torches usually have two oxygen connections, one for the oxygen supplied to the cutting jet, one for the oxygen used on the preheat flames. Unless an adaptor is used on the torch to unite these connections, such a torch requires two oxygen hoses, two regulators, and two oxygen sources.

Attach the acetylene hose to the acetylene regulator, and to the acetylene connection on the torch. On some torches, the acetylene connection may not be specifically identified, even though the oxygen connection is labelled.

Tighten all hose connection nuts with a wrench.

Test all connections for leaks. First, close both torch valves. Then turn in the pressure-adjusting screw on the oxygen regulator until its delivery-pressure gauge reads about 25 psi (172 kPa). Turn in the pressure-adjusting screw on the acetylene regulator until its delivery-pressure gauge reads about 10 psi (69kPa). Using a suitable leak-test solution and a brush (you can buy such a solution ready-made, or make up your own by dissolving Ivory soap in water), check for leakage (which will be indicated by bubbling) at the cylinder valves, the cylinder-to-regulator connections, and at all hose connections, as indicated in Fig. 6-7. If leakage is detected at either cylinder valve stem, close the valve, release the pressure-adjusting screw on the regulator, remover the regulator from the cylinder, and return the cylinder to your supplier, as directed in Chapter 3. If a leak is detected at either cylinder-to-regulator connection, close the cylinder valve, tighten the regulator connection nut with a wrench once more, re-open the cylinder valve, and test again. If a leak is detected at any hose connection, retighten the connection nut with a wrench and retest. If any connection fails to pass the second test, release all pressure from that side of the system (oxygen or acetylene). To do this, close the cylinder valve, release the regulator pressure-adjusting screw, open the torch valve, and finally turn in the regulator pressure-adjusting screw until no pressure is indicated on either regulator gauge. Then break the leaky connection, inspect the mating seats carefully for nicks or foreign particles which may be the source of trouble. If none can be seen, wipe both seats carefully with a clean cloth, remake the connection, and retest after restoring pressure.

To check for leakage through the torch valves you should, after making sure that all other connections are leaktight, dip the torch tip or nozzle in water, or place leak-test solution across the tip or nozzle orifices. If bubbling occurs, open and close each torch valve rapidly to see if that will stop the leakage. If it does not, replacement of one or both torch valve stem assemblies, or reseating of the torch body, may be necessary. After lighting the torch (as directed hereafter) you should use leak-test solution to check for leakage around the torch valve stems, and tighten the valve packing nut or nuts as needed to stop the leaks.

Adjusting Operating Pressures

After making sure that the system is leak-tight, release the pressure-adjusting screws on both regulators, and open the torch valves. Then proceed as follows:

With torch oxygen valve open, turn in the pressure-adjusting screw on the oxygen regulator until the desired working pressure is indicated on the regulator delivery-pressure gauge. Then close the torch oxygen valve. If you are adjusting pressure for a cutting torch, open only the torch cutting oxygen valve. If you are adjusting pressure for a cutting attachment, open the oxygen valve on the torch handle and the cutting oxygen valve (but not the preheat oxygen valve) on the cutting attachment. Avoid setting pressures higher than those recommended by the equipment manufacturer for the welding head or cutting nozzle installed in your torch.

With the torch acetylene valve open not more than one full turn, turn in the pressure-adjusting screw on the acetylene regulator until the desired working pressure—NOT OVER 15 PSI (103 kPa)—is indicated on the regulator delivery-pressure gauge. Close the acetylene valve immediately.

> PRECAUTION: Never release acetylene, or any other fuel gas, near any possible source of ignition or into any space which is not adequately ventilated. If such conditions cannot be met, adjust pressure with the torch fuel gas valve closed. Readjust pressure, as necessary, after the torch has been lighted in accordance with the instructions which follow.

If acetylene or other fuel gas is being supplied to the torch from a piping system which is not equipped with regulators at each station outlet, merely open the service valve at the station outlet. Do not open the torch fuel gas valve until you are ready to light the flame.

Lighting the Flame

In lighting the torch and adjusting the flame, always follow the manufacturer's instruction for the specific torch being used. In general, the procedure to be followed in lighting an oxy-acetylene welding or heating torch is this:

1. Open the torch acetylene valve about one-half turn.
2. Immediately light the flame with a friction lighter. NEVER USE A MATCH.

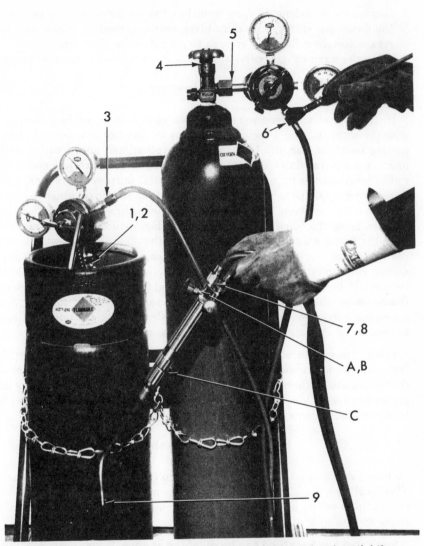

Fig. 6-7. After pressurizing both hose lines (with torch valves tightly closed) test for leakage at the following points, using an approved leak-test solution or a thick solution of Ivory soap and water: (1,2) Acetylene cylinder connection and acetylene cylinder valve spindle (3) Acetylene regulator-to-hose connection (4) Oxygen valve spindle (5) Oxygen cylinder connection (6) Oxygen regulator-to-hose connection (7,8) Hose connections at the torch (9) Torch tip (for leakage past the torch valves). Later, after lighting the torch, check for leakage at the throttle valve stems (A,B) and at the welding head-to-torch handle connection (C).

3. Reduce the acetylene flow, by throttling the torch acetylene valve, until the flame just starts to produce black smoke around its edges; then increase acetylene flow just enough to get rid of the black smoke.
4. Open the torch oxygen valve slowly until the desired flame is obtained

Flame Adjustment

If oxygen and acetylene working pressures have been set in accordance with the manufacturer's recommendations for the size of welding head or cutting nozzle in use, the lighting procedure outlined above will usually produce a neutral flame (as described in Chapter 4) which has about the right characteristics for most welding and cutting purposes. However, if the flame, when adjusted to neutral, burns away from the tip (in other words, if there is a gap between the tip and the flame) reduce the flow of oxygen slightly, using the torch oxygen valve, and then reduce the acetylene flow until the flame is again neutral. If you find that you must repeat this procedure two or more times to eliminate the gap between flame and tip or nozzle, your acetylene working pressure is probably too high, and should be reduced. If, however, you find that the neutral flame produced by following the recommended lighting procedure seems to be too "soft" for your purposes, you may open the acetylene valve a little, and then readjust the flame to neutral by opening the oxygen valve some more.

When using natural gas for cutting, do not attempt to secure truly "neutral" flames. Instead, adjust the oxygen flow until the inner cones of the flames are as short as possible. This is not hard to do, because any increase in oxygen flow beyond a certain level will cause the inner cones to lengthen, and become paler and more pointed.

Backfire and Flashback

During operation, the torch flame may go out with a loud pop or snap. This is called a "backfire", and is most frequently caused by accidental contact of tip or nozzle against the work, or by momentary interruption of the flame by a droplet of hot metal of slag.

A torch that has backfired can be relighted at once. It may even relight itself, if the flow of gas is directed against molten or hot metal. If a torch backfires repeatedly, however, without evident contact with the work, the cause should be investigated. Backfiring may be due to use of improper operating pressures, or to a loose tip or nozzle in the torch, or to dirt on the cutting nozzle seats.

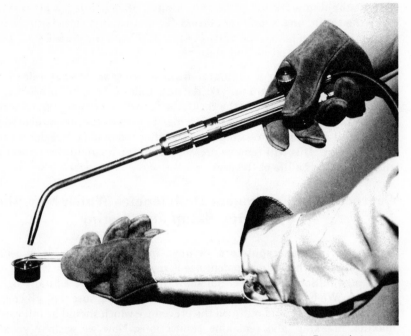

Fig 6-8. Always use a friction lighter when lighting a torch. Be ready to adjust the torch acetylene valve immediately after flame is lit.

If the flame goes out and burns back within the torch, which usually produces a pronounced hissing or squealing noise, immediately shut off the torch. This is termed a "flashback" and is always a sign that there is something wrong with the torch or with your operation of it.   After a flashback, *always* allow the torch to cool before attempting to relight it. *Always* check your operating pressures before attempting to relight it. Further, before relighting, allow oxygen (NOT acetylene) to flow through the torch for several seconds to help clear out soot which may have accumulated within the torch. Then relight, following the usual procedure. If what appears to be normal flame, or flames, is produced, proceed with your work, but be prepared to shut the torch off instantly if the flame goes out and that characteristic flashback sound is heard again. If there is a second flashback, remove the torch from service and return it to an approved repair station for check and necessary repair.

Stopping Work

To extinguish the flames, first close the torch fuel gas valve, then the oxygen valve. Closing the fuel gas (acetylene) valve first reduces the chance of allowing unburned fuel gas to escape and be ignited accidently.

When stopping work for an hour or longer, always release all pressure from the torch, hoses, and regulators. To do this, first close both cylinder valves, then open both torch valves. Finally, release the pressure-adjusting screws of both regulators and close both torch valves.

Before disconnecting a regulator from a cylinder, always release all pressure from the regulator. To do this, follow the same procedure set forth immediately above. If the regulator is likely to remain out of service for several weeks or more, it is a good idea to turn in the pressure-adjusting screw until some spring resistance is felt (after removing the regulator from the cylinder). This will remove pressure from the regulator valve seat and thus lengthen the life of the seat.

Correction of Equipment Deficiencies Which May Show Up During Setup and Testing

Never use torches, regulators, or hose in need of repair. It is usually difficult to tell whether equipment needs repair until you have hooked it up and tested it. Some flaws may not show up until you have actually lighted the torch. We have stressed the importance of making sure that all connections are leak-tight, and outlined the procedure which should be followed in making, breaking, and remaking connections. Now we wish to go a bit farther, and provide some general instructions covering what you should do when something is still obviously wrong.

Regulators: If the regulator-to-cylinder connection still leaks after you have broken it, cleaned the seating surfaces, re-made and re-tested it, the odds are that the regulator inlet nipple is marred or deformed so that it will not make up leaktight to any cylinder. In that case, the nipple must be replaced. You can't do that on the spot. The regulator must be turned over to a qualified repairman or repair station.

When you close a torch valve, after setting regulator pressure for leak-test or operation, the delivery-pressure gauge hand "jumps" a few psi. This is normal. If it "creeps", however,—that is, moves up slowly but steadily for more than a second or two after the torch valve has been closed—the regulator valve is leaking and should be repaired. While it is true that a slight amount of such creep will have no effect on operation of the torch after it is lighted, it is most unwise to continue to use a regulator that creeps. It should be removed from service and sent to a properly-equipped repair station for overhaul.

All regulators are equipped with screens or filters designed to prevent particles of dust from reaching the regulator valve. In many regulators, the filter is located in the inlet nipple itself and is clearly visible. When using such a regulator, make it a practice to look and see that the filter is in place before connecting the regulator to the cylinder. If the filter is missing or if it appears to be clogged with foreign material, replace it before proceeding further. This will take very little time if you will remember to keep a spare filter on hand. NEVER remove a filter until you are prepared to replace it.

Torches: If either throttle valve on a welding torch handle will not shut off completely (as revealed by bubbling when the torch tip is placed in water, with pressure in the hose and both valves closed as tightly as possible) you should release all pressure from the system and remove the valve stem assembly from the torch. Wipe clean both the seating surfaces in the torch and on the valve stem. Reassemble and retest. If the valve still will not shut off tightly, either reseating of the valve body or replacement of the valve stem assembly will be required. For reseating, the torch must be sent to a properly-equipped repair station.

If the cutting oxygen valve on a cutting torch or cutting attachment will not shut off tight, replacement of the valve seat or valve stem, following instructions supplied by the torch manufacturer, is usually required.

If you detect leakage around the valve stem of a torch throttle valve (test must be made after the torch has been lit) you can usually stop the leak by tightening the valve packing nut. Occasionally, it may be necessary to replace a valve packing washer, or replace the complete valve stem assembly. Always follow the instructions supplied by the torch manufacturer. Leakage around the stem of a cutting oxygen valve can usually be repaired on the spot by replacement of a packing washer or O-ring, following instructions of the manufacturer. Do not use substitute materials; use only parts supplied by the manufacturer or his distributor.

If a torch flame is misshaped or irregular, cleaning of the orifice in tip or nozzle is required. Use of stainless steel tip cleaners made especially for this purpose is recommended. A twist drill of the proper size can also be used, but it should be pushed straight in-and-out, not twisted. Do not attempt to use any tool which might enlarge or bell-mouth the orifice.

Hose: In addition to testing for leaks at all hose connections, you should always inspect your hose carefully for external evidence of damage before starting work. If such evidence is found, test that section of the hose by dipping it in a bucket of water while there is pressure in the hose. If that discloses leakage, it is imperative that the hose be discarded, or that the leaky section be cut out and replaced. (Instructions for splicing will be found in the Appendix.) **Never attempt to repair welding hose with tape.**

★ ★ ★ ★ ★ ★ ★ ★ ★

Nothing stated above should be considered as contradicting specific instructions furnished by the manufacturer of the equipment actually in use. Always follow his instructions. Never attempt repairs which are not covered by the manufacturer's instructions or by the general suggestions given above. Above all, and we repeat, DO NOT USE APPARATUS OR HOSE WHICH YOU KNOW IS IN NEED OF REPAIR.

QUESTIONS—CHAPTER 6

1. What are the steps to be followed in setting up a welding or cutting outfit?
2. What special precautions should be followed when connecting an oxygen regulator to an oxygen cylinder valve?
3. What are the steps to be followed in connecting an acetylene regulator to an acetylene cylinder valve?
4. What should be done to the pressure-adjusting screw of a regulator before opening the cylinder valve?
5. How are hose connections put in place?
6. How should the connections be tested for leaks?
7. What should be done in case of leakage?
8. What are the general rules for adjusting pressures?
9. What should be done upon stopping work?
10. What should be done if connections do not fit exactly?
11. What is a backfire?
12. What is a flashback?
13. What should be done when a flashback occurs?

2. Safe Practices in Welding and Cutting*

In Chapter 3, on "Oxygen and Acetylene", we discussed the precautions which should be observed in the handling and storage of oxygen and acetylene. In Chapter 5, on "Equipment for Oxy-Acetylene Welding and Cutting", we covered some of the safe practices which should be observed in the connection with the use and handling of equipment and accessories. In Chapter 6, the safe practices which should be observed in setting up the equipment and lighting the flame were highlighted. In this chapter, we'll devote most of the space to talking about the precautions and safe practices which should be observed during the actual practice of welding and cutting. First, however, we'd like to restate a few of the points already made. These precautions are so important that they warrant repetition. Keep them in mind at all times.

General Precautions

CAUTION! IMPORTANT! USE NO OIL! Oil, grease, coal dust, and some other organic materials are easily ignited and burn violently in the presence of high oxygen concentrations. Never allow such materials to come in contact with oxygen or oxygen-fuel gas equipment, including hose. Oxygen-fuel gas apparatus does not require lubrication.

Always call oxygen by its proper name. Do not call it "air". Never use it as a substitute for compressed air. A serious accident may easily result if oxygen is used as a substitute for compressed air. Oxygen must never be used in pneumatic tools, in oil preheating burners, to start internal combustion engines, to blow out pipelines, to "dust" clothing or work, for pressure testing or for ventilation.

Never use acetylene at pressures above 15 psi. Using acetylene at pressures in excess of 15 psi gauge pressure, or 30 psi absolute pressure, is a hazardous practice. The 30 psi absolute pressure limit (absolute pressure is gauge pressure plus atmospheric pressure) is intended to prevent unsafe use of acetylene in pressurized chambers such as caissons.

* Chapter 7, *The Oxy-Acetylene Handbook,* courtesy of Union Carbide Corporation.

Never use torches, regulators, or other equipment that is in need of repair. Treated with reasonable care, oxy-acetylene apparatus needs relatively little maintenance, but when a regulator "creeps" (indicating that its valve will not close completely), or a torch valve will not shut off tight, or you cannot make a leaktight hose connection to a regulator or a torch, get the apparatus to a qualified repair station.

Don't connect an oxygen regulator to a cylinder unless you are sure it is equipped with an inlet filter. Know where the filter is in your regulator. If it is mounted in the inlet nipple, always check visually to see that it is in place and intact before you attach the regulator to the cylinder.

Always use the operating pressures recommended by the manufacturer for the welding head or cutting nozzle in your torch. Using pressures higher than necessary not only makes flame adjustment more difficult, but can be a cause of flashback. In cutting, to use oxygen pressures higher than recommended can reduce cut quality as well as waste oxygen.

Always wear goggles when working with a lighted torch. Use only goggles supplied by reputable manufacturers for welding and cutting purposes. Use filter lenses of a shade dark enough to protect your eyes fully. Generally, shade 4 will serve for light cutting or sheet metal welding. For welding of plate or castings, or for heavy cutting, always use shades 5 or 6. (For more details, including recommendations for electric welding processes, refer to Sec. 7.2, ANSI Z49.1, "Safety in Welding and Cutting Operations", published by the American Welding Society.)

Do not use matches for lighting torches. Always use a friction lighter unless you have a stationary pilot flame, or some other reliable source of ignition that will keep your hand well away from the torch tip or nozzle.

Wear clothing suitable for the work to be done. Fire-resistant gauntlet gloves are recommended for all but the lightest type of welding. Wear woolen clothing if possible; wool is far more difficult to ignite than cotton or many of the synthetic materials. Try to keep the your outer clothing free from grease or oil. Don't have cuffs on your trousers to catch sparks. Avoid low-cut shoes when cutting; getting a drop of slag or hot metal in your shoes can be very painful.

Precautions During Work

Before you start to weld or cut, check the area to make certain that flame, sparks, hot slag or hot metal will not be likely to start a fire. Specific precautions which should be observed are given in the section on "Preventing Fires", which follows.

NEVER do welding or cutting without adequate ventilation. Standards for ventilation are set forth in Sec. 8 of ANSI Z49.1, "Safety in Welding and Cutting Operations", published by the American Welding Society. Standards covering allowable concentrations of toxic dust and gases are given in ANSI Z37, American National Standards Institute. The four paragraphs which follow are intended only to provide general guidelines for conditions frequently encountered. For complete information, it is imperative that ANSI Standards Z49.1 and Z37 be consulted.

When it is necessary to work in a confined space, make certain the space is adequately ventilated. If there are no overhead openings to provide natural ventilation, use an exhaust fan or blower. When screening an area, try to keep the bottom of the screens at least two feet above floor level. Do not take cylinders into a confined space. Test all equipment, including hose, for leaks before taking it into a confined space, and bring it out with you when your work is interrupted for any reason, even for a short time.

Never flow oxygen into a confined space in order to ventilate it, or to "clear the air". Remember that oxygen supports and accelerates combustion, and will cause oil, wood, and many fabrics to burn with great intensity. Clothing saturated with oxygen, or with oxygen-enriched air, may burst into flame when touched by a spark.

Do not weld brass, bronze, or galvanized steel except in a well-ventilated location. You must protect yourself against breathing the zinc oxide vapors usually generated when these materials are

ADEQUATE
FORCED
VENTILATION

Fig. 7-1. Adequate ventilation is essential when welding in confined places and when welding materials which give off fumes.

heated to welding temperatures. In open locations, it is usually sufficient to drive the vapors away by using a stream of air, or by suction, provided that does not send the vapors toward another person. In confined spaces which cannot be well ventilated, always use a mask which supplies clean air from an outside source.

When welding or cutting metals containing or coated with lead, cadmium, beryllium, or mercury, always wear a suitable air-line mask. No operator should be considered immune from the effects of these fumes. A straight filter-type mask is inadequate; nothing short of an air-supplied respirator is suitable. There must be sure protection against breathing fumes which occur when lead, mercury, beryllium, or their compounds are heated.

Use particular caution when welding or cutting in dusty or gassy locations. Dusty and gassy atmospheres in some mines and plants call for extra precautions to avoid explosions or fires from sparks, matches, or open flames of any type. Welding or cutting in any such "suspicious" location should be done only when proper precautions are taken, and only after a responsible official has inspected the situation and given approval for the work.

When welding or cutting is done underground, leak-testing of equipment set-ups should be performed carefully and frequently. Great care should be taken to protect hoses and cylinders from damage, and to protect timbers and other combustible materials from sparks and hot slag.

Never do any welding or cutting on containers that have held flammable or toxic substances until the containers have been thoroughly cleaned and safeguarded. Complete, detailed procedures are given in American Welding Society booklet A6.0-65 titled "Safe Practices for Welding and Cutting Containers That Have Held Combustibles". Here are some of the key points in that booklet:

1. Always start with the assumption that any used drum, barrel, or container may contain flammable (explosive) or toxic (poisonous) residue.
2. No work should be commenced until the container has been cleaned and tested sufficiently to assure that no flammable or toxic solids, liquids, or vapors are present.
3. Bear in mind that some non-poisonous substances can give off toxic (poisonous) vapors when heated.
4. Steam is usually an effective means of removing volatile or readily volatilizable materials from a container. Washing with a strong solution of caustic soda or other alkaline cleaner will remove heavier oils which steam may not volatilize.

5. Whenever possible, the container should be filled with water to within a few inches of the working area before attempting welding, cutting, or intense heating. Care should be taken to provide a vent opening for the release of heated air or steam.

6. When it is impractical to fill the container with water, an inert gas such as nitrogen or carbon dioxide may be used to purge the container of oxygen and flammable vapors. Maintain the inert gas during the entire welding or cutting operation by continuing to pass the gas into the container.

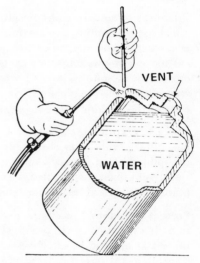

Fig. 7-2. Containers which have held flammable materials should be filled with water before welding or cutting. Be sure space above water level is vented.

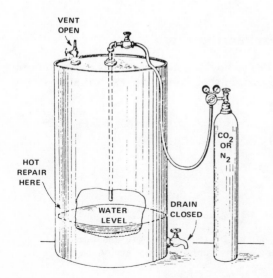

Fig. 7-3. Nitrogen or carbon dioxide may be used to purge closed vessels before welding or cutting. Maintain flow of gas until work is completed.

Other Safe Practices to Bear in Mind

Make sure that jacketed or hollow parts are sufficiently vented before heating, welding, or cutting. Air or any other gas or liquid confined inside a hollow part will expand greatly when heated. The pressure created may be enough to cause violent rupture of the part. A metal part which is suspiciously light is hollow inside, and should be drilled to vent it before heat is applied. After work is complete, the vent hole can be tapped and plugged if necessary.

Bushings in a casting should either be removed or securely fastened in place before heating the casting. Bronze bushings expand more than cast iron when heated to the same temperature. If a bushing is left in place, the casting may be damaged, or expansion may cause the bushing to fly out, creating a definite hazard. If a bushing cannot be removed, it should be securely fastened in place. Bolting large washers or pieces of plate over the ends of the bushing is the suggested method.

Don't drop stub ends of welding rods on the floor. Put them in a suitable container. Aside from the fire hazard that may be created by carelessly dropping a hot stub end, a serious fall may result from stepping on one. A small container partly filled with water and within easy reach is a good place to dispose of these short ends.

Protect cylinders, hose, legs, and feet when cutting. Do not cut material in such a position as will permit sparks, hot metal, or the severed section to fall on or against a gas cylinder, or the gas hoses, or your legs or feet. A suitable metal screen in front of your legs will provide protection against sparks and hot metal.

Preventing Fires

Where welding or cutting has to be done near materials that will burn, take special care to make certain that flame, sparks, hot slag, or hot

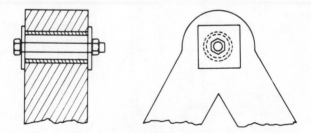

Fig. 7-4. If bushings cannot be removed before castings are heated, make sure they are restrained in some fashion, so that they cannot fly out.

metal do not reach combustible material and thus start a fire. This is particularly important in the case of cutting operations. Cutting produces more sparks and hot slag than welding, and locations where portable cutting equipment is used must, therefore, be thoroughly safeguarded against fire.

Refer to National Fire Protection Association Standard No. 51B, "Fire Protection in Use of Cutting and Welding Processes" for recommended practices.

Never use cutting or welding torches where sparks or open flame would be a hazard. Flames are a hazard in rooms containing flammable gas, vapors, liquids, dust, or any material that easily catches fire.

It is not safe to use cutting or welding equipment near rooms containing flammable materials unless there is absolutely no chance of sparks passing through cracks or holes in walls or floors, through open or broken windows, or open doorways. There is always the possibility that flammable vapors may escape from such rooms through doors or other openings, making it doubly necessary to keep sparks and flames away.

Before you cut or weld in a new location for the first time, always check with the nearest foreman or superintendent in authority. He may know of some serious fire hazard that might otherwise be overlooked.

If the work can be moved, take it to a location where there will be no possibility of setting fires. This must always be done when the metal to be welded or cut is in a place where open flames are barred. This practice may also be sensible in many other locations even if open flames are permitted.

If the work cannot be moved, materials that burn easily should, if possible, be taken a safe distance away. For cutting operations, this distance may be 30 to 40 ft. or more. Floors should be swept clean before the torch is lighted.

If flammable materials cannot be moved, use sheet metal guards, fire-resistant curtains, or similar protection to keep sparks close in to the work you are doing. Suitable protection to keep back sparks should always be used when it is not possible to move materials that will burn to a safe distance from the cutting or welding work. This also applies if sparks might lodge in wooden parts of the building, or drop through holes or cracks to the floor below.

Make sure that the guards are large enough and tight enough so that they do not permit sparks to roll underneath or slide through openings. Curtains should be weighed down against the floor or ground. For weights, use such things as angle iron, pipe, bricks or sand.

Use only fire-resisting guards. Do not use tarpaulins for shielding sparks since they may catch fire.

Fig. 7-5. When it is necessary to perform welding or cutting in the vicinity of combustible materials such as wood, set up screens to keep sparks from flying too far, and have water and sand available for use if needed.

Have someone stand by watch the sparks so that he can give warning if they begin to get beyond the protective guards. It is not reasonable to expect whoever is doing the welding or cutting to watch the sparks since his attention is on the work. In addition, the sparks cannot always be seen easily through goggles.

If welding or cutting over a wooden floor, sweep it clean and wet it down before starting work. Provide a bucket or pan containing water or sand to catch the dripping slag from any cutting that is done.

Before starting to cut off a piece of steel or iron, make sure it will not drop where there is any possibility of starting a fire. This is especially important when working in a high place where sparks or slag might be less apt to cause a fire down below than would a small piece of red hot steel. Pieces can be kept from falling by welding a rod or bar to the piece, and having a helper hold the rod or bar while the cut is made. Or the same thing might be accomplished by tying a chain or other suitable support to the piece.

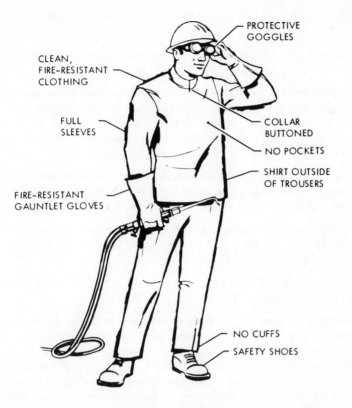

CLEAN,
FIRE-RESISTANT
CLOTHING

PROTECTIVE
GOGGLES

FULL
SLEEVES

COLLAR
BUTTONED

NO POCKETS

SHIRT OUTSIDE
OF TROUSERS

FIRE-RESISTANT
GAUNTLET GLOVES

NO CUFFS

SAFETY SHOES

Fig. 7-6. What the well-dressed welder will wear. Always select clothing materials which will provide maximum protection from sparks and hot metal.

When welding very close to wooden construction, protect it from direct heat. Wooden beams, partitions, flooring, or scaffolding should always be protected from the direct heat of the flame by sheet metal guards or asbestos. Protective guards should also be used to confine the sparks.

Use the correct oxygen pressure when cutting. An oxygen pressure greater than necessary will only cause extra sparks and increase the slag flow, to say nothing of increasing the oxygen expense.

Store extra cylinders away from important areas. Keep only enough cylinders near the work to insure an adequate supply of gases for the job at hand.

Be ready to put out any fire promptly with fire extinguishers, pails of water, water hose, or sand. When torches are to be used near wooden construction or materials that will burn, take every precaution to prevent fires, but always be prepared to put out fires that may start despite all precautions.

In hazardous locations, have a helper, or one or more extra men if necessary, on hand to watch for and be ready to extinguish a fire.

If there are sprinklers, maintain this protection without fail while cutting or welding is being done. It is of special importance to make sure that sprinklers are in working order during extensive repairs or building changes. If the sprinkler system must be shut down for a time, have this done when welding or cutting work is not in progress.

If there is a possibility that a smoldering fire may have been started, keep a man at the scene of the work for at least a half hour after the job is through. Have him look carefully for smoke or fire before leaving.

This is especially important when cutting torches have been used in locations where sparks may have started smoldering fires in wooden structures or in other slow burning materials.

Never forget that heavy cutting sparks sometimes fly 25 to 30 ft. or more and hold their heat for several seconds after landing.

When welding or cutting on bridges, structures, or at other outdoor sites, take care to avoid setting fire to grass or brush. Brush should be cleaned out or cautiously burned under or about structures before start of the work. Special care is necessary during a dry spell. A fire extinguisher and water or sand should be available to extinguish any fires started in the course of work. Before leaving the site, examine the premises thoroughly to be sure that sparks have not started smoldering fires.

QUESTIONS–CHAPTER 7

1. Why should oxygen never be used as a substitute for compressed air?
2. What should be done before starting to weld or cut?
3. What should be done when work must be performed in a confined space?
4. Should oxygen be fed into a confined space?
5. What should be done when working on materials that contain zinc?
6. What should be done if a sick feeling is experienced after working on material containing zinc?
7. What precautions should be taken when cutting iron or steel coated with lead or paint containing lead?
8. Is anyone immune from the effects of lead fumes?
9. What precautions should be taken before welding or cutting in dusty or gassy locations?
10. What precautions should be taken when welding or cutting is to be done on containers which have held a flammable material?
11. If a hollow part is to be welded or cut, what should be done first?
12. What kind of clothing should be worn for cutting work?
13. What are some of the ways in which possible fires from welding or cutting work can be prevented?

Useful References

Arcair Corporation. 1972. *Underwater Cutting and Welding Manual.* Lancaster, Ohio: Arcair Corporation.

Brady, Edward M. 1960. *Marine Salvage Operations.* Centreville, Maryland: Cornell Maritime Press.

Cayford, John E. 1966. *Underwater Work: A Manual of Scuba Commercial, Salvage and Construction Operations.* 2nd edition. Centreville, Maryland: Cornell Maritime Press.

Chapman, Charles. 1972. *Piloting Seamanship and Small Boat Handling.* New York: The Hearst Corporation.

Cichy, Francis, Schenck, Hilbert, and McAniff, John. 1978. *Corrosion of Steel Scuba Tanks.* Narragansett, Rhode Island: URI Marine Advisory Service.

E. I. DuPont De Nemours & Company. 1969. *Blaster's Handbook.* Wilmington, Delaware: E. I. DuPont Company.

Myers, John J., ed. 1969. *Handbook of Ocean and Underwater Engineering.* New York: McGraw-Hill Book Co.

Tucker, Wayne C. 1973. "Bubbles in the Blood." *Skin Diver Magazine* 22 (10): 20.

———. 1976. "Buoyancy and the Diver." *Skin Diver Magazine* 25 (6): 34.

———. 1980. *Diver's Handbook of Underwater Calculations.* Centreville, Maryland: Cornell Maritime Press.

Underwater System Design. (a journal published 6 times annually by Underwater Systems Design, 322 St. John St., London E. C. 1, England.)

U. S. Navy. 1979. *Diving Manual.* Washington D. C.: U. S. Government Printing Office.

———. 1976. *Salvor's Handbook.* Washington, D. C.: U. S. Government Printing Office.

Zinkowski, Nicholas B. 1971. *Commercial Oil-Field Diving.* 2nd Edition. Centreville, Maryland: Cornell Maritime Press.

Index

About the Authors

BETWEEN them the authors share a very wide range of experience in commercial diving. John Malatich began as a naval diver in 1934 and continued his long diving career four years later for Merritt Chapman & Scott, who were at that time the largest salvors in the United States. He headed up the team responsible for raising the sunken *Normandie,* the largest ship in the world at that time, and worked on a variety of underwater projects in Alaska and Greenland and in the eastern United States.

Wayne C. Tucker, who has a B. S. and M. S. in engineering, has taught diving courses at the University of Rhode Island and at the College of Oceaneering in Wilmington, California. In addition to operating his own consulting diving concern, he is currently a research associate with the U. S. Navy on deep submergence systems. He is the author of *Diver's Handbook of Underwater Calculations* and articles in *Skin Diver.*